AF477933

Has devolution worked?

Manchester University Press

DEVOLUTION series

series editor Charlie Jeffery

Devolution has established new political institutions in Scotland, Wales, Northern Ireland, London and the other English regions since 1997. These devolution reforms have far-reaching implications for the politics, policy and society of the UK. Radical institutional change, combined with a fuller capacity to express the UK's distinctive territorial identities, is reshaping the way the UK is governed and opening up new directions of public policy. These are the biggest changes to UK politics for at least 150 years.

The *Devolution* series brings together the best research in the UK on devolution and its implications. It draws together the best analysis from the Economic and Social Research Council's research programme on Devolution and Constitutional Change. The series has three central themes, all of which are vital components in understanding the changes devolution has set in train.

1 **Delivering public policy after devolution: diverging from Westminster**: Does devolution result in the provision of different standards of public service in health or education, or in widening economic disparities from one part of the UK to another? If so, does it matter?

2 **The political institutions of devolution**: How well do the new devolved institutions work? How effectively are devolved and UK-level matters coordinated? How have political organisations which have traditionally operated UK-wide – political parties, interest groups – responded to multi-level politics?

3 **Public attitudes, devolution and national identity**: How do people in different parts of the UK assess the performance of the new devolved institutions? Do people identify themselves differently as a result of devolution? Does a common sense of Britishness still unite people from different parts of the UK?

Has devolution worked?

The verdict from policy makers and the public

Edited by
John Curtice and Ben Seyd

Manchester University Press
Manchester and New York
distributed in the United States exclusively
by Palgrave Macmillan

Published by Manchester University Press
Oxford Road, Manchester M13 9NR, UK
and Room 400, 175 Fifth Avenue, New York, NY 10010, USA
www.manchesteruniversitypress.co.uk

Distributed in the United States exclusively by
Palgrave Macmillan, 175 Fifth Avenue, New York,
NY 10010, USA

Distributed in Canada exclusively by
UBC Press, University of British Columbia, 2029 West Mall,
Vancouver, BC, Canada V6T 1Z2

British Library Cataloguing-in-Publication Data
A catalogue record for this book is available from the British Library

Library of Congress Cataloging-in-Publication Data applied for

ISBN   978 07190 7559 9 hardback

First published 2009

18 17 16 15 14 13 12 11 10 09   10 9 8 7 6 5 4 3 2 1

Typeset
by Action Publishing Technology Ltd, Gloucester
Printed in Great Britain
by the MPG Books Group

Contents

List of figures and tables

List of contributors

John Curtice is Professor of Politics at Strathclyde University and a Research Consultant to the Scottish Centre for Social Research. He has written widely on public attitudes to devolution and is co-editor of *Has Devolution Delivered?* (Edinburgh University Press, 2006).

Michael Keating is Professor of Political and Social Sciences at the European University Institute, Florence, and Professor of Politics at the University of Aberdeen. His most recent books are *The Independence of Scotland* (Oxford University Press, 2009) and *Approaches and Methodologies in the Social Sciences* (edited with Donatella della Porta) (Cambridge University Press, 2008).

Iain McLean is Professor of Politics at Oxford University and a fellow of Nuffield College. He has published widely in UK political history and public policy. Current projects include 'Options for a New Britain' and 'What's Wrong with the British Constitution?'.

Alistair McMillan is Senior Lecturer in Politics at the University of Sheffield. His research interests include representation and electoral politics. He is author of *Standing at the Margins: Representation and Electoral Reservation in India* (2005). *State of the Union: Unionism and the Alternatives in the United Kingdom since 1707* (2005), co-authored with Iain McLean, won the W. J. M. Mackenzie Prize of the Political Studies Association of the UK for the best book in political science published during 2005.

Akash Paun is Senior Researcher at the Institute for Government, a non-partisan research centre focusing on the question of how to improve the performance of government. He was previously a researcher at the Constitution Unit at University College London, where he conducted research into constitutional change in Britain, in particular devolution and parliamentary reform.

Meg Russell is Reader in British and Comparative Politics at University College London, where she is also Deputy Director of the Constitution Unit. Her main research interest is parliaments (particularly the House of Lords and bicameralism), though she has also written on political parties and women's representation.

Ben Seyd is Lecturer in Politics at the University of Kent. His research focuses on public opinion and political behaviour. He has recently published analyses of public attitudes to constitutional change and patterns of political participation in Britain.

Acknowledgements

Inevitably a book like this based on an extensive programme of collaborative research incurs a large number of debts. The biggest is to the Leverhulme Trust, whose grant to the Constitution Unit under its 'Nations and Regions' research programme made the initial collaboration possible. The project as a whole was directed by Professor Robert Hazell, Director of the Constitution Unit at University College, London, and we are indebted to him and his colleagues for their support and encouragement. Considerable additional funding of the survey work on public attitudes came from the Economic and Social Research Council, largely through its 'Devolution and Constitutional Change' research programme directed by Professor Charlie Jeffery. We are grateful to our numerous collaborators in that work, including colleagues at the National Centre for Social Research (NatCen), who undertook all of the survey research. We would like to thank Manchester University Press for their patience while this book was completed. Finally, our respective universities, Strathclyde and Kent, provided the environment that made it possible to bring this book to a conclusion.

1

Introduction

John Curtice and Ben Seyd

Britain used to be considered a stable political system. Fifty years ago, while concerns were expressed about the constitutional stability of many western democracies, Britain's 'Westminster' system was seen to possess more secure foundations (Beer, 1982: 1–19; Wright, 1994: 15–21; King, 2001: 51–3). Yet over the last decade or so, Britain's political system has undergone a transformation. Elections are now conducted under new rules, judges have a more formal role in scrutinising government decisions, parliament has been reformed and, under a freedom of information regime, citizens have greater access to government records. But perhaps the most significant change in the way political power is exercised in the United Kingdom has been the decentralisation of power from central government to new bodies in Scotland, Wales, Northern Ireland and London. According to Anthony King (2007: 179), devolution marked the most radical shift in the British constitution since Lloyd George's reform of the House of Lords in 1911. For Vernon Bogdanor (2001: 1), devolution was the most significant change to the constitution since the franchise was extended in 1832. Yet, while constitutional experts might differ about past precedents, none denies the momentous nature of the devolution programme. The establishment of elected institutions in Edinburgh, Cardiff, Belfast and London represented a fundamental shift in the exercise of political authority in the United Kingdom. Instead of concentrating decision making on a single tier of government in London, policy making was now dispersed across a number of legislatures and executives.

We are now a decade on from the first elections to the devolved bodies. It is thus an opportune moment to ask how effective devolution has proved to be. There are many ways in which such evaluations could be conducted. Recent studies have examined the effectiveness of the devolved institutions' internal organisation and procedures (e.g. Cavanagh *et al.*, 2000; Arter, 2003; Rawlings, 2003; Lapsley, 2004; Winetrobe and Hazell, 2004), their ability to develop distinctive public policies (Greer, 2004; Keating, 2005;

Keating and McEwan, 2005) and their implications for economic performance (Cooke and Clifton, 2005; McGregor and Swales, 2005). In this book, our focus is less on such objective measures of performance than on the evaluations of those affected by devolution. In the following chapters, we consider the views and behaviour of elected party representatives, interest groups and citizens. We ask whether these groups have greeted devolution warmly or coolly. Is devolution perceived to have improved policy making and the quality of democracy? Are the existing devolution arrangements widely accepted, or is there pressure for further reform? The reactions of politicians, groups and citizens are a key element in judging whether or not devolution can be said to have succeeded. This book sets out what these reactions have been, and thus where devolution stands ten years on.

The focus of this book is on devolution in Scotland and Wales. We pay particular attention to the views of politicians and citizens in both those countries, and to the opinions and patterns of behaviour of interest groups in Scotland. But we also consider English reactions to the devolution programme by examining attitudes amongst people in England to the apparent 'anomalies' created by a devolution settlement in which their country did not share. Our coverage does not extend to Northern Ireland, which, exceptionally within the United Kingdom, had enjoyed significant legislative devolution before. The Belfast Agreement that led to its restoration in the province was both unique in its institutional design and intended to achieve objectives that were very different from those lying behind devolution to Scotland and Wales. In addition, the operation of the province's devolved institutions has subsequently had to be suspended on more than one occasion. Equally, we do not pay any attention to devolution to London, which was arguably as much a form of extended 'city' government as of 'regional' decision making (Travers, 2004: 8–9) and constitutes a much less radical change to the previously highly centralised governance structure in the United Kingdom.

The rationale for devolution

Britain is far from being the only country to have experienced a trend towards decentralisation during the last two or three decades. Some of the most radical changes have occurred in formerly centralised west European states such as Belgium, France, Italy and Spain, all of which have introduced 'regional' levels of government, in so doing often giving institutional recognition to distinctive 'national' identities and linguistic communities (Keating, 1998a; Ansell and Gingrich, 2003).

This development is often regarded as in large measure a consequence of globalisation (Ohmae, 1995; Keating and McGarry, 2001). One consequence of globalisation is that the role of international markets and institutions has been enhanced at the expense of existing state institutions, which have lost much of their ability to manage their country's economies and promote the economic interests of less advantaged regions. The role of government has become increasingly confined to 'supply side' measures, such as the development of an educated workforce and a pleasant living environment, qualities that will encourage international companies to locate in a particular area. Crucially, these supply side measures are often taken more effectively at a regional level. And if the role of regional government has become more important, then there seems to be a greater need to ensure that it is under effective democratic control.

At the same time, however, globalisation may – through the free movement of people between countries, for example – pose a threat to distinctive sub-state cultures. In response to such challenges, people then seek to protect established ways of life and national identities by securing greater political autonomy for themselves. Meanwhile, by reducing the role and autonomy of individual states, the internationalisation of both markets and rules of economic exchange has the paradoxical effect of making it easier for regions and stateless nations to contemplate becoming 'independent' themselves. Thus, across western Europe and beyond, we have witnessed greater demands for political autonomy on the part of distinctive regions and stateless nations that currently comprise part of a larger state.

These three catalysts – functional, democratic and nationalist – are evident in the hopes and expectations that accompanied the introduction of devolution in Britain. The first key functional argument was that the decentralisation of authority would avoid the imposition from London of policy decisions that were ill-suited to the particular economic and social needs of Scotland and Wales. It is noteworthy that the public appetite in Scotland and Wales for some devolution of political authority dates from the 1960s and 1970s, when tightening economic conditions forced many to question the benefits that centralised political authority supposedly provided for their countries (Paterson, 1998). It was argued that decentralising political – and fiscal – authority would permit the introduction of programmes that better met the needs and demands of citizens and groups, thus boosting economic and welfare performance. In this respect, the domestic British debate clearly echoes the wider arguments across Europe in favour of locating more decision making at the regional level. True, many proponents of devolution adopted a more sober view of the likelihood of the new institutions yielding significant changes in economic and social outcomes. This was particularly the case in Wales, where the limited policy and financial powers available to the Welsh Assembly restricted the ability of politicians to effect radical policy change. Nonetheless, and particularly in Scotland, there was a hope that devolution would trigger improvements in economic and policy performance. Thus, Donald Dewar, who became his country's initial First Minister, commended the Scottish Parliament for its potential to '... encourage vigorous sustainable growth in the Scottish economy. Policies on health, housing and education will respond more directly to Scotland's needs' (Scottish Office, 1997).

Alongside this functional argument for devolution in Britain was a second that focused on the democratic benefits offered by political decentralisation. This issue proved particularly acute during the long period of Conservative government between 1979 and 1997. The decline of the Conservative Party in Scotland, which began in the 1950s, meant that during this term in office, the party never had more than 22 of the 72 MPs in Scotland, while by 1987 it only had ten. The Conservatives never secured a majority of the parliamentary seats in Wales. It was thus possible to argue that the policies pursued by the UK Government in Scotland and Wales lacked popular support in those countries. Particular grievances included a reluctance in the 1980s to provide help to declining manufacturing industries, the introduction in Scotland of the deeply unpopular community charge or 'poll tax' in 1989, a year before the equivalent move was made in England, and more generally an undermining of established political and civic organisations such as local government, trade unions and professional bodies, that played a relatively important role outside England (Bradbury, 1998; Paterson, 1998).[1]

Devolution held out the promise that policy decisions in Scotland and Wales would be made by politicians elected by the publics in these two countries, rather than by an unrepresentative government in London. The creation of a tier of government more attuned to the distinctive views of a sub-state population would help to align elite attitudes and popular demands, a classic rationale for devolution (de Vries 2000; Bednar, 2005). In truth, despite their very different voting patterns, it is far from clear that the values and attitudes of people in Scotland and Wales are markedly

---

[1] In putting the case for devolution in the House of Commons, Donald Dewar highlighted Scottish concerns with the introduction of unpopular Conservative policies in the country, and argued that 'The essential cause of the bitterness and frustration to which I refer is the fact that we put the control of the legislative programme in the hands of a group of politicians who did not command significant support in Scotland; that was one of the problems, and it is at the heart of the devolution argument' (HC Debs, 12 January 1998, col. 22).

different from those of their counterparts in England. Most survey evidence suggests that, typically, the differences between them are modest rather than substantial (Miller *et al.*, 1996; Curtice, 1996; Brown *et al.*, 1996). But after nearly two decades of allegedly unrepresentative Conservative rule, the argument that devolution would produce more responsive and representative government became a key impetus behind devolution.

Alongside the desire to provide a more representative tier of government was a concern to subject decisions taken in Scotland and Wales to greater political scrutiny, and thus provide for greater accountability. While Britain was, prior to 1999, a centralised political system, not all important decisions were taken in London. Significant policy measures were devised and introduced in Edinburgh (through the Scottish Office) and, to a lesser degree, in Cardiff (through the Welsh Office). Yet many argued that scrutiny of these decisions was weak, hindered by the physical location of Scottish and Welsh MPs, for most of the time, at Westminster. In addition, many of these policy decisions were made by executive bodies headed by appointed, rather than elected, officials. Particular concern was expressed in Wales about the accountability of bodies such as the Welsh Development Agency, whose spending in the year before Labour took office in 1997 came to over £150 million of public funds (Cabinet Office, 1997). The establishment of directly elected bodies in Scotland and Wales would, it was hoped, allow for closer scrutiny of policy decisions taken in those countries, as well as providing electoral oversight of appointed 'quangos' (Mackintosh, 1998; Bradbury, 1998).[2]

For its supporters, therefore, devolution held out the promise of more representative and accountable decision making. However, these benefits derived not simply from the mere presence of a Scottish Parliament and Welsh Assembly, but also from the way these bodies would operate. In Scotland in particular, devolution was seen as a way of opening up decision making to greater direct engagement by citizens and groups. The final report of the Scottish Constitutional Convention, in 1995, argued that devolution represented '... a chance to effect fundamental improvements to the way Scotland is governed', going on to commend a parliament whose 'practices and procedures' would be deliberately different from those at Westminster, thereby providing for greater openness, transparency,

---

[2] It is debatable how far resentment at the activities of unelected 'quangos' permeated the views of ordinary people in Wales (Morgan, 1999: 210). But among campaigners, the role of a Welsh Assembly in ending the 'democratic deficit' was a significant part of their case for devolution, as Labour's White Paper, *A Voice for Wales*, made clear (Welsh Office, 1997: 7).

accessibility and accountability (Scottish Constitutional Convention, 1995; see also Crick and Millar, 1998; Brown 2000). The importance attached to these qualities can clearly be seen in the institutional design of the Scottish Parliament, with its provision for citizens' petitions, for committees to meet outside Edinburgh and for a Civic Forum to bring together elected representatives and interest and voluntary groups.

But apart from its anticipated functional and democratic benefits, there was also a nationalist rationale behind the demand for devolution. For political elites keen to maintain the Union, the significant levels of public support for nationalist parties (the Scottish National Party and Plaid Cymru) that first emerged in the 1960s represented the ominous beginnings of a potential move – in Scotland at least – towards the break-up of the United Kingdom. The United Kingdom has never been a unitary state, but rather a 'union state'[3] that provided for a separate legal system and religious settlement in Scotland, as well as separate territorial departments in the form of the Scottish and Welsh Offices (Elcock and Keating, 1998: 2–4; Keating 1998a: 35–8). But these arrangements no longer seemed sufficient to accommodate the nationalist sentiment that believed these two stateless nations deserved greater recognition in the form of distinctive political institutions. By establishing a national parliament in Edinburgh and a national assembly in Cardiff, devolution was intended to demonstrate that the distinctive sense of Scottish and Welsh identity could be given adequate institutional expression within the framework of a (multi-national) state (Mackintosh, 1998), and thereby eventually strengthen public support for the Union.

In sum, we suggest that the objectives and goals of devolution can be encapsulated in three principles: (1) improvements in economic and policy performance; (2) improvements in the quality of political representation, accountability and engagement; and (3) strengthening of the union between nations, in part by providing an outlet or expression for distinctive Scottish and Welsh identities. However, the claims that devolution would fulfil these three objectives were far from uncontested. The economic virtues of decentralisation are called into doubt by commentators who point to the economic 'externalities' and 'diseconomies of scale' that sub-national units may face (Brennan and Hamlin, 2000: chapter 11; Bednar, 2005). So far as the democratic benefits of decentralisation are concerned, commentators have pointed out that by adding an extra tier of

---

[3] The union was formed over three centuries, via the incorporation of Wales into England in 1536, the union of England and Wales with Scotland in 1707, and its extension to Ireland in 1800.

government, devolution would make it more difficult to ascertain who was responsible for policy outcomes (Brennan and Hamlin, 2000: 252–3). As a result, far from strengthening the accountability of policy makers, devolution might actually weaken it. Another objection was that decentralised tiers of authority are more easily accessed and 'captured' by interest groups. What, for decentralisation's proponents, is an open and participative form of government is, to its detractors, an opportunity for well-financed sectional groups to ensure their interests are acted upon (Bardhan and Mookherjee, 2006). Domestic critics also argued that, rather than strengthening the Union, devolution might further encourage separate Scottish and Welsh identities, thereby undermining support for, and identification with, the United Kingdom as a whole (Thatcher, 1998). And in granting privileges to Scotland and Wales denied to people in England, devolution risked a 'backlash' against the Union in its largest constituent part (Wright, 2000).

Moreover, even if devolution showed little sign of triggering the outright secession of any part of the United Kingdom, it could still induce instability within the Union. We have already noted that the United Kingdom is most accurately characterised as a 'union state', in which differing levels of power are delegated to its component parts, and on different terms. The devolution settlement continues this unequal set of relations. The powers and financial authority delegated to Scotland under the terms of the Scotland Act were considerably greater than those offered to Wales under the Government of Wales Act. The English regions – which account for almost 85 per cent of the United Kingdom's population – have not been granted any form of legislative devolution at all. Devolution in Britain is thus 'asymmetrical', with some units enjoying more powers of self-government than others. Such asymmetrical devolution is not unique; it is found in other 'plurinational' democracies such as Belgium, Canada and Spain (Keating, 2001: 110–33). But how stable are these asymmetrical constitutional arrangements? Some have suggested (for example, Dalyell, 1998) that delegating power to sub-state nations will not deliver constitutional stability, but precisely the opposite. Instead of being content with having their distinctiveness recognised, nationalist movements in such nations simply regard it as a signal to demand yet more powers. Some manifestations of this phenomenon can be seen in the asymmetrically devolved systems in Canada and Spain (Keating, 1998b; 2001: 109). The potential tensions of devolution in Britain are particularly strong, as the differences in autonomy between Scotland, Wales and England are even greater than in other asymmetrically devolved states (Keating, 2001: 115).

Research questions, methods and sources

Given these doubts, there is good reason to examine whether devolution really has worked. Our principal aim in this book is to assess how far devolution has succeeded in fulfilling the three main objectives set for the Scottish Parliament and Welsh Assembly at the time of their creation. We consider how far devolution has been seen in Scotland and Wales to deliver more effective policy decisions and more responsive and accountable government. We also examine whether devolution has satisfied or stimulated demands for political autonomy within Britain. The results – drawn from Scotland, Wales and England – will say a lot about the strength of the Union.

We explore these key questions with reference to the attitudes and behaviour of three groups: the public, interest groups and politicians. Previous analyses of devolution have typically focused on just one of these groups.[4] Yet the effectiveness and legitimacy of new political institutions can only be gauged by examining the views and behaviour of political elites, intermediary bodies, and the mass public together (for such an argument in the context of 'transitional' democracies, see Diamond, 1999: 64–70). After all, devolution to Scotland and Wales was intended to respond to the needs of, and provide benefits to, all of these groups. It would certainly be difficult to explore how successful devolution has been in providing for more representative decisions, more participative processes and more effective policies without taking into account the views of politicians (involved in policy making and its scrutiny), interest groups (involved in conveying sectional demands to the policy process) and citizens (involved in conveying demands to, and casting judgements on, policy makers).

In bringing together the perspectives of these three groups, we are alert to the possible similarities and differences in the way they have reacted to devolution. Do politicians, groups and the public concur on the successes and failures of devolution, or do their assessments diverge? Divergent evaluations may reflect different degrees of familiarity with the devolved institutions; elite actors closely involved in these bodies – such as elected representatives and interest groups – may reach different conclusions from those drawn by citizens, most of whom will have had little direct contact with the devolved institutions. Alternatively, divergent evaluations may arise because different groups apply different criteria in assessing the

---

[4] On the reaction to devolution of citizens, see Bromley *et al.* (2006) and Curtice (2006); of interest groups, see Keating (2005: chapter 3); of politicians, see Sinclair (2007).

performance of the devolved institutions. Thus, interest groups may judge the devolved bodies against one conception of representation (such as the access that groups enjoy to policy makers), while the public may adopt a rather different conception (the perceived responsiveness of policy making to popular preferences). Again, it is clear we can only adequately assess how successful devolution has been if we consider the views of politicians, interest groups and citizens in combination.

Devolution might also be judged differently in Scotland and Wales. Evaluations of performance might be expected to vary according to the extent of the powers devolved from the centre, the degree of financial autonomy wielded by the devolved institutions and the institutional design of those organisations. On all three counts, devolution in Scotland was very different from devolution in Wales (for a good summary of these differences, see Bogdanor, 2001: chapter 7). Thus, for example, to the extent that devolution was intended to deliver policies more attuned to the needs of citizens and groups in Scotland and Wales, we might anticipate rather more positive evaluations of devolution in Scotland, where the Scottish Parliament has primary legislative competence and an annual budget of just under £30 billion, than in Wales, where the Welsh Assembly has, until recently, only wielded secondary legislative powers and an annual budget of around £14 billion. Evaluations of the effectiveness of the policies pursued by the devolved administrations might similarly be anticipated to reflect the more extensive powers devolved to Scotland than to Wales. Comparison of the reactions to devolution in Scotland and Wales is a theme touched on throughout our analysis.

This book arises out of a 'Nations and Regions' research programme, co-ordinated by the Constitution Unit at University College London, which ran between 1999 and 2004.[5] The programme, which was generously funded by the Leverhulme Trust, was designed to provide a detailed evaluation of the initial impact of devolution in the United Kingdom. The programme comprised three broad strands, each of which contained several individual research projects. The first strand dealt with attitudes and identities, the second with the formal interactions between the various tiers of government in Britain, and the third with the role of England within the devolution settlement. Books summarising the findings from the second and third strands of the programme have already been published (Trench, 2006; Hazell, 2006); this volume represents the main outcome of the first research strand.

---

[5] Details of the programme and individual projects can be found at: www.ucl.ac.uk/constitution-unit/.

As a result of the wide focus of our research, the sources and methodologies utilised are extensive. They can be summarised as follows. The motivations of politicians during the debates on devolution from the 1960s onwards were ascertained via original documentary evidence, including confidential government papers that have since been placed in the public domain. The attitudes and behaviour of interest groups were gauged through an extensive programme of face to face interviews, conducted between 2000 and 2003. In all, over 130 interviews were conducted with senior members of interest groups in Scotland and North East England. Face to face interviews were also used to gauge the views of those elected to the devolved institutions in Scotland and Wales. At the same time, a more representative picture of the views of elected politicians was obtained via a postal survey sent to all members of the Scottish Parliament and Welsh Assembly in 2000, 2002 and 2004. Because this survey was undertaken on more than one occasion, we are able to track changes in attitudes among elected representatives. Repeated surveys also provided the backbone of our analysis of citizens' reactions to devolution. The 'Nations and Regions' programme itself funded dedicated modules of questions included in population surveys conducted in Scotland and England in 2000 and 2003. In addition, thanks to additional funding from other sources, notably the Economic and Social Research Council and the Scottish Government, not only were further surveys on attitudes to devolution conducted in Scotland (annually between 1999 and 2007) and Wales (in 1999, 2001, 2003 and 2007), but also in England (several occasions between 1999 and 2007).

Plan of the book

The book has two main parts. In the first half, we focus primarily on the actors closest to the devolved institutions: interest groups and elected politicians. We then turn in the second half to the reaction of citizens. Each part is now described in turn.

Our first substantive chapter, Chapter 2, conducts a historical review of the reactions among politicians to the rise in support for nationalist parties in Scotland and Wales from the 1960s. In so doing, Iain McLean and Alistair McMillan explain why devolution to Scotland and Wales occurred and why it eventually took the form that it did. They uncover the tensions and uncertainties in the minds of Labour and Conservative politicians in the wake of the nationalist 'threat'. By analysing how these pressures played out within, and between, the two parties, the chapter attempts to account for the limited nature, and ultimate failure, of the original devolution proposals in the 1970s, and why, by the time it came to power again in 1997, Labour was firmly committed to implementing devolution in the face of Conservative opposition. The chapter considers both the initial importance of the nationalist impetus towards devolution and then suggests why, thereafter, some of the functional and democratic arguments gained political resonance.

In Chapter 3, Michael Keating considers how interest groups have responded to the operation of devolution in practice. He compares the experience of Scotland, where powerful devolved bodies were established in 1999, with that of the North East of England, where only a weak form of administrative devolution existed. Comparing the two cases helps Keating to identify the impact legislative devolution in Scotland has had on the attitudes and behaviour of interest groups. The key question he addresses is the extent to which the *territorial* decentralisation of power has intersected with the *sectoral* arrangement of interest groups to create territorial policy communities. In other words, what has been the impact of redistributing the territorial division of political power on the way that sectoral groups – with their economic and social concerns – organise themselves and undertake lobbying? For evidence, Keating examines interest groups' organisational patterns (namely their physical distribution between different territorial levels within Britain), their orientations (which tier of policy making groups look to for the allocative, redistributory and regulatory decisions that affect them) and their frames of reference (the territorial level by which groups define policy issues and their own position within the policy process).

In Chapter 4, Meg Russell and Akash Paun consider how political parties – or at least their elected representatives in the devolved institutions – have reacted to the devolution project whose genesis they so closely shaped. Drawing on dedicated surveys conducted in three waves between 2000 and 2004, Russell and Paun focus on three key issues: how far do politicians believe the Scottish Parliament and Welsh Assembly have delivered improvements in policy performance, how far do elected representatives believe the devolved institutions have improved the policy process, and how adequate are the devolved institutions' powers now thought to be? Particular attention is paid to the perceived effectiveness of the procedures of the Scottish Parliament and Welsh Assembly.

Having considered how interest groups and party representatives have reacted to devolution in Scotland and Wales, we turn in Chapters 5 and 6 to the public's reaction. The focus of Ben Seyd's analysis in Chapter 5 is on the public's assessment of the performance of the devolved institutions. After considering the strength of the support for devolution in Scotland and

Wales before 1999, and identifying what the public hoped the devolved institutions would achieve, he examines how effective the devolved institutions have been seen to be in two respects: delivering better policy outcomes and improving the way in which decisions are taken. This enables him to assess how far devolution in Scotland and Wales has met initial public expectations.

Following this analysis of what the public believes are the functional and democratic achievements of devolution, in Chapter 6, John Curtice and Ben Seyd review the impact of devolution on the strength of the Union. They begin by considering whether devolution has weakened or strengthened the sense of Britishness among people in Scotland, Wales and England. They then turn to more direct indicators of support for the Union, by considering attitudes towards different constitutional options. Has devolution led to an increase in support for independence among people in Scotland, and for a more extensive form of devolution among people in Wales? How far are people in England content with the devolution 'settlement', or has the creation of law-making bodies in Edinburgh and Cardiff generated resentment towards Scotland and Wales? Curtice and Seyd's chapter provides important evidence on the potential stability of Britain's asymmetrical devolution programme.

In Chapter 7, John Curtice considers whether electoral behaviour in Scotland and Wales suggests that devolution has strengthened the accountability and responsiveness of political authority. For this to be the case, people's votes in devolved elections should reflect how well they think incumbent devolved administrations have performed and their views on the policies that should be implemented in future at the devolved level. Voters should not be using devolved elections to express their views on the performance of the UK Government or on issues that fall to Westminster to decide. Drawing on survey data, Curtice examines the relative importance of these two influences on how people vote, thereby providing a key test of how far devolution to Scotland and Wales has strengthened the quality of democracy in those parts of the United Kingdom.

In Chapter 8, we draw together the evidence of the book to consider how effective devolution has been in meeting its three main objectives: more effective policy making, more representative and accountable decision making, and a strengthening of the Union. Do both interest groups and ordinary citizens now feel they have more influence and involvement in the decisions that are taken in their name? Do politicians and the public feel that devolution has improved policy outcomes? Is the current devolution settlement sustainable in the long run or are there political pressures for further change that pose additional challenges to the Union? We identify a number of successes, but also some failures.

Devolving power away from the centre has been a common response
to a number of key pressures facing contemporary European states. Functionally, there has been pressure to take more decisions at a local level. This
in turn has fuelled demands for greater democratic control of regional
government. Politically, there has been pressure to recognise national identities and demands. Devolution to Scotland and Wales has been the United
Kingdom's particular response to these three challenges. Our aim in this
book is to provide some clues as to whether or not this response is likely to
succeed.

References

Ansell, C. and J. Gingrich (2003) 'Trends in decentralization', in B. Cain,
    R. Dalton and S. Scarrow, eds, *Democracy Transformed? Expanding
    Political Opportunities in Advanced Industrial Democracies*, New York:
    Oxford University Press

Arter, D. (2003) *The Scottish Parliament: A Scandinavian Style Assembly?*
    London: Frank Cass

Bardhan, P. and D. Mookherjee (2006) 'Decentralization, corruption and
    government accountability', in S. Rose Ackerman, ed., *International
    Handbook on the Economics of Corruption*, Cheltenham: Edward Elgar

Bednar, J. (2005) 'Federalism as a public good', *Constitutional Political
    Economy*, 16:2

Beer, S. (1982) *Britain Against Itself: The Political Contradictions of Collec-
    tivism*, New York: WW Norton

Bogdanor, V. (2001) *Devolution in the United Kingdom*, Oxford: Oxford
    University Press

Bradbury, J. (1998) 'The devolution debate in Wales during the Major
    governments: The politics of a developing union state?', in H. Elcock
    and M. Keating, eds, *Remaking the Union: Devolution and British Poli-
    tics in the 1990s*, London: Frank Cass

Brennan, G. and A. Hamlin (2000) *Democratic Desires and Devices*,
    Cambridge: Cambridge University Press

Bromley, C. *et al.*, eds (2006) *Has Devolution Delivered?* Edinburgh: Edin-
    burgh University Press

Brown, A. (2000) 'Designing the Scottish Parliament', *Parliamentary
    Affairs*, 53:3

Brown, A., D. McCrone and L. Paterson (1996) *Politics and Society in Scot-
    land*, Basingstoke: Macmillan

Cabinet Office (1997) *Executive Non-Departmental Public Bodies 1997*

Report, Cm 3712, London: Cabinet Office

Cavanagh, M., N. McGarvey and M. Shephard (2000) 'Closing the democratic deficit? The first year of the Public Petitions Committee of the Scottish Parliament', *Public Policy and Administration*, 15:2

Cooke, P. and N. Clifton (2005) 'Visionary, precautionary and constrained "Varieties of devolution" in the economic governance of the devolved UK territories', *Regional Studies*, 39:4

Crick, B. and D. Millar (1998) 'To make the Parliament of Scotland a model for democracy', in L. Paterson, ed., *A Diverse Assembly: The Debate on a Scottish Parliament*, Edinburgh: Edinburgh University Press

Curtice, J. (1996) 'One nation again?', in R. Jowell *et al.*, eds, *British Social Attitudes, the 13th Report*, Aldershot: Dartmouth

Curtice, J. (2006) 'A stronger or weaker union? Public reactions to asymmetric devolution in the United Kingdom', *Publius: The Journal of Federalism*, 36:1

Dalyell, T. (1998) 'The slide to independence', in L. Paterson, ed., *A Diverse Assembly: The Debate on a Scottish Parliament*, Edinburgh: Edinburgh University Press

de Vries, M. (2000) 'The rise and fall of decentralization: A comparative analysis of arguments and practices in European countries', *European Journal of Political Research*, 38:6

Diamond, L. (1999) *Developing Democracy: Beyond Consolidation*, Baltimore: Johns Hopkins University Press

Elcock, H. and M. Keating (1998) 'Introduction: Devolution and the UK state', in H. Elcock and M. Keating, eds, *Remaking the Union: Devolution and British Politics in the 1990s*, London: Frank Cass

Greer, S. (2004) *Territorial Politics and Health Policy: UK Health Policy in Comparative Perspective*, Manchester: Manchester University Press

Hazell, R., ed. (2006) *The English Question*, Manchester: Manchester University Press

Keating, M. (1998a) *The New Regionalism in Western Europe: Territorial Restructuring and Political Change*, Cheltenham: Edward Elgar

Keating, M. (1998b) 'What's wrong with asymmetrical government', in H. Elcock and M. Keating, eds, *Remaking the Union: Devolution and British Politics in the 1990s*, London: Frank Cass

Keating, M. (2001) *Plurinational Democracies: Stateless Nations and a Post-Sovereignty Age*, Oxford: Oxford University Press

Keating, M. (2005) *Government of Scotland: Public Policy Making After Devolution*, Edinburgh: Edinburgh University Press

Keating, M. and N. McEwan, eds (2005) 'Devolution and public policies', special edition of *Regional and Federal Studies*, 15:4

Keating, M. and J. McGarry (2001) 'Introduction', in M. Keating and J. McGarry, eds, *Minority Nationalism and the Changing International Order*, Oxford: Oxford University Press

King, A. (2001) *Does the United Kingdom Still Have a Constitution?* London: Sweet and Maxwell

King, A. (2007) *The British Constitution*, Oxford: Oxford University Press

Lapsley, I. *et al.* (2004) 'Has devolution increased democratic accountability?', *Public Money and Management*, 24:3

Mackintosh, J. (1998) 'A parliament for Scotland', in L. Paterson, ed., *A Diverse Assembly: The Debate on a Scottish Parliament*, Edinburgh: Edinburgh University Press

McGregor, P. and K. Swales (2005) 'Economics of devolution/decentralization in the UK: Some questions and answers', *Regional Studies*, 39:4

Miller, W., A. Timpson and M. Lessnoff (1996) *Political Culture in Contemporary Britain: People and Politicians, Principles and Practice*, Oxford: Oxford University Press

Morgan, K. (1999) 'Welsh devolution: The past and the future', in B. Taylor and K. Thomson, eds, *Scotland and Wales: Nations Again?* Cardiff: University of Wales Press

Ohmae, K. (1995) *The Decline of the Nation State: The Rise of Regional Economies*, New York: Free Press

Paterson, L. (1998) 'Scottish home rule: Radical break or pragmatic adjustment?', in H. Elcock and M. Keating, eds, *Remaking the Union: Devolution and British Politics in the 1990s*, London: Frank Cass

Rawlings, R. (2003) *Delineating Wales: Constitutional, Legal and Administrative Aspects of National Devolution*, Cardiff: University of Wales Press

Scottish Constitutional Convention (1995) *Scotland's Parliament, Scotland's Right*, Edinburgh: Scottish Constitutional Convention

Scottish Office (1997) *Scotland's Parliament*, Cm 3658, Edinburgh: Stationery Office

Sinclair, F. (2007) *Rethinking Representation 2: MSPs' Experiences of the Second Term of the Scottish Parliament*, Edinburgh: Scottish Council Foundation

Thatcher, M. (1998) 'Don't wreck the heritage we all share', in L. Paterson, ed., *A Diverse Assembly: The Debate on a Scottish Parliament*, Edinburgh: Edinburgh University Press

Travers, T. (2004) *The Politics of London: Governing An Ungovernable City*, Houndmills, Basingstoke: Palgrave Macmillan

Trench, A., ed. (2006) *Devolution and Power in the United Kingdom*, Manchester: Manchester University Press

Welsh Office (1997) *A Voice for Wales: The Government's Proposals for a Welsh Assembly*, Cm 3718, London: The Stationery Office

Winetrobe, B. and R. Hazell (2004) 'What has the Scottish Parliament achieved and what can it teach Westminster?', *Proceedings of the British Academy*, 128

Wright, T. (1994) *Citizens and Subjects: An Essay on British Politics*, London: Routledge

Wright, T. (2000) 'England, whose England?', in S. Chen and T. Wright, eds, *The English Question*, London: Fabian Society

2
How we got here

Iain McLean and Alistair McMillan

Men make their own history, but they do not make it just as they please; they do not make it under circumstances chosen by themselves, but under circumstances directly encountered, given and transmitted from the past.

K. Marx, *The 18th Brumaire of Louis Bonaparte*, second paragraph.

Devolution to Scotland and Wales reflects a fundamental change in the unionist settlement that has governed the nations of Scotland, Wales and England since 1707. In this chapter we examine the background to the revised constitutional status of Scotland and Wales, looking at the period from the 1960s, when the electoral success of the nationalist parties (the Scottish National Party and Plaid Cymru) first forced the dominant unionist parties (the Conservatives and Labour) to rethink their positions on devolution, to the 1990s, when devolution became a reality. In considering this historical background, we focus on two key questions. What was the impetus behind the decision to devolve power to Scotland and Wales? And why did the proposals for devolution take the shape they did?

The unionist settlement that emerged from 1707 provided for a common sovereignty under the monarch and the Westminster Parliament, with scope for religious autonomy (granted to the Scots alongside the Acts of Union through establishment of the Church of Scotland, contentiously to Ireland through the battle for Catholic emancipation, and eventually to Wales through disestablishment of the Anglican Church there). Union allowed the entrenchment of a shared representative and fiscal framework for the United Kingdom, and provided for a common basis for domestic and foreign policy, realised over time in the development of universal welfare provision and the expansion of the empire. By the late nineteenth century, party politics in Scotland and Wales was successfully absorbed into the encompassing Westminster system. Politicians from Scotland (Ramsay MacDonald) and Wales (Lloyd George) could find their place at the head of parties which appealed across Scotland, Wales and England. Scottish and Welsh nationalism did not disappear, but the distinctive political interests in these countries were encompassed by a British party system operating at Westminster. Plaid Cymru, formed in 1925, and the Scottish National Party, formed in 1934, did not effectively challenge the party system and so lacked direct political influence.

The initial spark for the devolution debate of the 1970s came with the victory of the Plaid Cymru candidate, Gwynfor Evans, in the Carmarthen by-election in June 1966. At the time, Labour was the dominant party in Wales, having won twenty-six out of thirty-two seats in the general election earlier that year, but Evans's victory was followed by a series of strong Plaid Cymru performances in by-elections in the Labour heartlands of the south Wales valleys (Madgwick, 1973; Philip, 1975). In Scotland, the Scottish National Party (SNP) had threatened Labour in by-elections in Glasgow Bridgeton in 1961 and, iconically, West Lothian in 1962, when Tam Dalyell won the seat. However, in the elections of 1964 and 1966, the SNP saw 'some modest progress, but no breakthrough' (Lynch, 2002: 115). In 1964, the SNP gained just 2 per cent of the Scottish vote, rising to 5 per cent in 1966 (Lynch, 2002: Tables 5.4 and 5.5). But in the Glasgow Pollok by-election in March 1967, the Labour vote fell by 21 per cent with the SNP taking 28 per cent of the vote. As Kellas (1971) notes, this by-election was significant because of the failure of the Conservatives to garner the Labour protest vote. The nationalist rise was consolidated by gains in burgh elections in 1967, and reached a peak with the Hamilton by-election in November 1967, when Winnie Ewing of the SNP won what had been the third safest Labour seat in Scotland. Then, in the 1968 burgh elections, the SNP vote increased to 18 per cent, up from 4 per cent in the equivalent elections in 1966.

Figure 2.1 shows the pattern of the nationalist party vote in Scotland and Wales in general elections between 1950 and 1997. It highlights the jump in support for Plaid Cymru and the SNP in the 1970 election, when both parties took just over 11 per cent of the vote in their countries. It shows the dramatic gains the SNP made in the 1974 elections, and the high point of October 1974 when, at just over 30 per cent of the Scottish vote, the party was on the threshold of taking advantage of the first past the post electoral system and gaining a windfall of seats at Westminster.

If Labour came to fear the challenge from the SNP to its electoral dominance in Scotland, the Conservatives were troubled by a more general decline in their electoral support in Scotland. At the 1955 general election, the Conservatives had won a shade over 50 per cent of the popular vote in Scotland; less than two decades later, by October 1974, that share had halved to 25 per cent. However, this decline of the Conservative vote in one part of the Union was not mirrored by a similar fall in another, Wales,

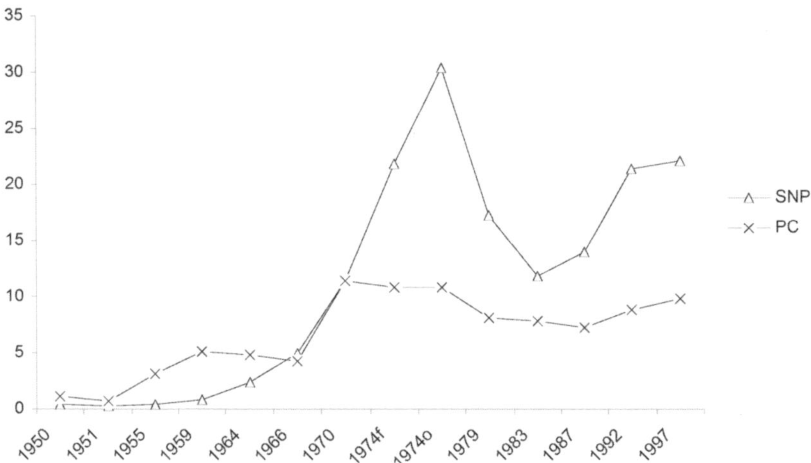

Figure 2.1 Nationalist vote in general elections in Scotland and Wales, 1950–97

Source: Yonwin, 2004.

for the simple reason that the Conservatives had never been electorally popular in the principality. As Wyn Jones *et al.* (2002: 235) note, Conservative weakness in Wales 'is longstanding and apparently deep-rooted'; since 1945, the party has never won more than one-third of the popular vote.

The rise of the SNP and, to a lesser degree, of Plaid Cymru, led to a drastic reassessment of ideology and policy making regarding British nationalism. The Labour and Conservative parties were traditionally wedded to unionism, but were forced to reconsider their positions in the light of what appeared to be a significant change in public attitudes and voting behaviour in Scotland and Wales. In the first part of this chapter, we consider how these two parties reacted to the growing nationalist challenge. For the Conservatives, the key switches in party stance took place in opposition, through Edward Heath's 'Declaration of Perth' in 1968 which reversed the party's traditional unionist position, and later Margaret Thatcher's more unionist decision to oppose the Scotland and Wales Bill's passage in 1976.[1] Labour's early response to the rise of Scottish

---

[1] The background to this change is covered comprehensively in Mitchell (1990). By examining the Conservative Party archives held in the Bodleian Library, Oxford, we have been able to embellish this account, and focus on the process by which the professional assessments of public opinion influenced policy

nationalism (and Heath's repositioning of the Conservative Party) came in the form of the establishment of a Royal Commission to consider devolution. By 1974, Labour's approach to devolution extended to a formal commitment to devolved bodies in Scotland and Wales, notwithstanding considerable internal divisions within the party.[2] These divisions were clearly manifested in the failure of the two devolution referendums in 1979. In the final part of our text, we trace the reasons why, in spite of this failure, the political commitment to devolution re-surfaced in the 1980s and 1990s, leading to the eventual devolution of political authority to Scotland and Wales by the Blair government.

No longer the unionist party: the Conservative switch

Apparently at Edward Heath's personal instigation, the Opinion Research Centre (ORC) carried out 'An investigation into the nature of the Liberal vote in the South-West and the Nationalist vote in Scotland and Wales' in November 1966. The findings of this were received with concern in Central Office: 'If anything, the picture as shown by the research is even more alarming than I had expected.'[3] This was probably an over-reaction – the samples in Wales and Scotland were obtained from the fifteen constituencies with the highest nationalist vote – but the interpretation of the findings was that the two main parties, and particularly the Conservatives, were out of touch with the people of Scotland and Wales. Support for

---

making within the party. These archives contain the Opinion Research Centre (ORC) polls and focus group reports, which were used by the leadership to support the switches on policy with regard to Scottish devolution. Details of the Conservative Party archive can be found at www.bodley.ox .ac.uk/dept/scwmss/cpa/index.html. The authors wish to thank Tracy-Jane Malthouse, who gave permission to access the papers in the Conservative Party archives.

2 We have tracked Labour's key policy changes from 1969 to 1974 via papers in the National Archive, which include reports of Cabinet, ministerial and civil service decision making, as well as internal Labour Party documents. On top of this, we also have access to data from the MORI polls which were undertaken for the Labour Party in 1974, when Harold Wilson was trying to drive the devolution policy through, against opposition within the Cabinet and a divided Scottish Labour Party.

3 The report on the survey is in the Conservative Party archive (henceforth CA) based in Conservative Central Office (CCO), London, 180/29/1/1. The comments on the nationalism survey are found in CA CCO 500/50/1, in a note from Tommy Thompson to the Chairman of the party, 27 March 1968.

Plaid Cymru and the Scottish National Party stood at just 7 per cent and 15 per cent of those who expressed a preference, but the ORC noted the 'enormous potential support for the Nationalists'.

The worry for the Conservatives was that they were not picking up the protest vote against the Labour government in either Scotland or Wales. Chris Patten, in a paper on 'Nationalism and regionalism' written after Gwynfor Evans's Carmarthen by-election success, argued that, 'There does not seem to be any level on which we can compete with the Nationalist Parties on their own terms unless we go the whole hog and come out in support of Home Rule for Scotland and Wales' (CCO 500/50/1, 26 July 1966). He noted that the Conservative Party was unlikely to benefit from any decline in the Labour core vote, although the Plaid Cymru challenge was likely to be localised and might even benefit the Conservatives by dividing the opposition in Cardigan and Montgomeryshire. The situation in Scotland was seen as more threatening. As a confidential note from the Conservative Research Department noted, 'The victory of Mrs Winifred Ewing in the Hamilton by-election brought about the same sort of change of climate as a bucket of ice cold water on a warm back.' The implications for the Conservatives were seen as dire:

> Any great upsurge of Nationalism in Scotland and Wales would result in humil-iation of the Conservatives since it would almost certainly involve transfer of our votes to the Nationalists and mean a string of lost deposits ... It is at least possible that the effect of a nationalist upsurge might ultimately eliminate the Conservative Party from Scotland, leaving the country virtually divided between the Socialists and the Nationalists – clearly an unacceptable situation.[4]

The problems for the Conservative Party in Scotland were set out in a withering focus group report on the 'Motivations behind Scottish Nation-alism', carried out by the ORC in March 1968:

> The Scottish Conservative Party has got an exceedingly bad image. It is thought to be out of touch, a bastion of 'Foreign' (English) privilege, West-minster orientated, associated with recalcitrant landowners. Most people are unfamiliar with the leading figures in the Scottish Conservative Party. The Scottish Conservative Party was the only Scottish Party which, on mention, often elicited mirthful or mirthless laughter. It was variously described as 'run by Lairds', 'Landowners' and 'the business community'. Among the insults heaped upon it were that 'conservatives are the dregs from England' and that Conservative MPs with Scots names 'are no true Scotsmen'. The Scottish Conservative Party was described as being comprised of 'misguided Scots'. (CA CCO 180/29/1/2, 4)

---

[4]   CA, Conservative Research Department (CRD), 3/28/6, 'An Analysis of Scot-tish Nationalism' and memo from Tommy Thompson to Anthony Barber, 'The Implications of the Nationalist win at Hamilton'.

The report concluded:

> What does emerge from the research is that the desire for a greater say by Scotland in her own affairs, greater autonomy of some sort, runs right through the nation. Even anti-nationalists who are still loyal to the Conservative Party share this feeling in a subdued form. It is, therefore, recommended that the Party should think through its attitude to the various possibilities that exist. Once this has been done, whether the final position is for some increased form of devolved power for Scotland or a rejection of any concession, it will be a much easier posture from which to fight ... In this situation it will be possible to mount a serious intellectual case that this known posture of the Conservative Party towards Scotland's aspirations is the best one for Scotland herself ... Anything would be better for the Conservative Party than the vague feeling that they are 'against Scotland' and representing 'English' interests. (CA CCO 180/29/1/2, 32–3)

The underlying worry was that the SNP was approaching the threshold of support where, under the first past the post system, it could seriously damage Conservative (and Labour) representation at Westminster. According to a Conservative Research Department paper from February 1968, at 30 per cent of the vote, the damage would be limited, but if the SNP garnered 40 per cent, it could take between thirteen and fifteen seats from the Conservatives, and nineteen to twenty-nine from Labour. For a party which had officially been called the Scottish Unionist Party until the 1964 election, any acceptance of devolution would be a major ideological change. However, the perception that the party was facing a crisis in Scotland drove the party towards radical measures. The need for change was pressed by the Thistle Group, formed in November 1967, and backed by a party committee under Sir William McEwen Younger (Mitchell, 1990: 53–5). This was the background to Heath's 'Declaration of Perth' at the Scottish Conservative conference in May 1968, at which he proposed the creation of a Scottish Assembly.

Although Heath, in his Perth speech, denied that the decision was driven by the desire to garner short-term popularity, party documents prepared for the Younger Committee reveal that this was certainly a consideration:

> For Conservatives to become advocates and later architects of home rule, thus spiking the guns of Socialists, Liberals and Nationalists alike, is the most dramatic step we could take to retrieve this strength. In the short run it would be calculated to win us additional seats in Scotland (and just conceivably in Wales) and put other seats out of danger. In the long run it could hardly fail to improve our position vis-à-vis the Socialists in the United Kingdom Parliament, provided that one makes the assumption that the present over-representation in that Parliament of Scotland and, more important, of

Wales ceased to be necessary once these nations had parliaments of their own.[5]

The Younger Committee was aware that an assembly could create tension with Westminster and have broader fiscal and representative implications; a Scottish Constitutional Committee (with Lord Kilbrandon identified as a potential member) was proposed to investigate such issues in more detail. The switch away from the traditional unionist position of the Conservative Party was bolstered by a paper on Scottish nationalism by the Tory historian Robert Blake. He drew a parallel between the situation of Scotland in the late 1960s and the treatment of Ireland in the late nineteenth century, arguing that the policy of trying to kill home rule with kindness had been delivered too late. Blake wrote:

> The point of the Perth speech is, I presume, to suggest a constitutional arrangement which may prevent it ever going beyond this stage. It is difficult to see what possible harm could come from such a proposal. It certainly will not make separatism any more likely than it already is [...] I conclude that there is nothing contrary to the spirit or tradition of Conservatism in taking a step which may well strengthen rather than weaken the Union. (CA CRD 3/28/6, 5 June 1968, pp. 4, 6)

There was, though, opposition to Heath's commitment to a Scottish Assembly, both in the Scottish party and in Westminster, where a third of Scottish Conservative MPs were against the measure and other Conservative MPs felt the decision had been taken without adequate consultation (Mitchell, 1990: 57). However, the only public repudiation came from Enoch Powell, who made a speech in September 1968 in Prestatyn in which he declared that unless Scotland or Wales wanted to be separate nations Great Britain must be governed and administered as one nation (Smith, 1977: 10). In any event, the assessment from the party organisation was that the effect of the 'Declaration of Perth' had been positive:

> The Scottish Conference as a whole had been a great success, and press reaction to the policy announcement had been most satisfactory. It had not been damned by either side; we had seized the initiative; the proposal had been recognised in responsible quarters as a contribution to thought and without the pretence that we had an instant solution; and it gave the Party in Scotland something real on which to work. (CA Leader's Consultative Committee (LCC) 68/239, 20 May 1968)

---

5   CA CRD 3/28/7, the Government of Scotland Policy Group, 'The Government of Scotland (Secret)', 1 May 1968.

Labour's response: 'bashing the nationalists'

The reaction of Harold Wilson's Labour government to the success of Plaid Cymru and the SNP was to establish a Ministerial Committee on Devolution in 1967, overseen by the Prime Minister, the Secretary of State for Wales (first Cledwyn Hughes, then, from 1968, George Thomas), the Secretary of State for Scotland (Willie Ross), and the Lord President of the Council (Dick Crossman). The Committee considered a Welsh Council (promoted by Cledwyn Hughes), which had been endorsed by the Labour Party in Wales at its annual conference in May 1966. The policy was also given popular support in a poll in the *Western Mail* (25 September 1968), which was headlined 'We want our own parliament, say 60 p.c. in Wales'.[6] However, any such proposal was squashed through opposition from Willie Ross, who was worried by the implications for Scotland. Willie Ross and George Thomas were both unionists, and favoured a short-term policy of 'bashing the nationalists' and strengthening the powers of the Secretaries of State for Scotland and Wales. The Ministry of Public Buildings and Works was singled out as a possibility for relocation to Scotland. Crossman, whose inclination was to take the issue of devolution (or federalism) more seriously, was forced to conclude:

> It was argued that a Scottish Parliament on the lines of that in Northern Ireland would not attract support from any body of opinion in Scotland, and that if the demand for a separate Parliament was not to be conceded it would be better to make no concession to the nationalists and not even suggest that further devolution was under consideration, but to concentrate during the next few months on hammering home to the public the financial benefits accruing to Scotland from the unitary system and the economic disadvantages of separatism.[7]

There was concern that the Ministerial Committee on Devolution had not reacted to the changing situation in Wales and Scotland:

> THE SECRETARY OF STATE FOR ECONOMIC AFFAIRS [Peter Shore] said that since the Committee had started its work the Scottish Nationalists had enjoyed considerable success in the recent local elections. In his view the proposals set out in the draft report were too modest to be effective in meeting this changed political situation. The first step should be to find out by survey what form of Government the majority of the Scots and Welsh people wanted

---

6   Based on an ORC poll (a quota sample of 760 people), spread evenly across Conservative, Labour and Liberal voters.

7   National Archives (henceforth NA), T 330/185, Lord President [Crossman] reporting on Ministerial Committee on Devolution for Scotland and Wales, 'Devolution for Scotland and Wales', 24 June 1968.

and then to decide the most appropriate course to take; if necessary, a Home Rule solution should be considered.[8]

But resistance to any substantive policy of devolution came from the Treasury, which briefed Roy Jenkins as follows:

> If the Chancellor feels that the political circumstances permit it, we would prefer the 'No change' approach … The changes canvassed … are likely to lead to less efficiency in administration and in the use of resources, to staff increases and to increased demands for public expenditure … There is anyway not much evidence in Wales of a widely supported demand for more devolution […] We would certainly recommend the Chancellor to support the conclusions against home rule Parliaments and also against the proposed Council for Wales […] *Administrative Devolution.* The division of programmes between England and Wales or between both of them and Scotland always makes it more difficult to control public expenditure. There is a marked tendency for Scotland to get either its due proportion on any service, or more if special arguments can be found, but never less.[9]

The Treasury attempted to counter any push for devolution with a research paper outlining the administrative costs of any such change, backed up with the publication of a 'Scottish Budget' in October 1969 which sought to show how much Scotland was being subsidised by England (and would suffer if independent) (Kellas 1971: 456).

Harold Wilson was not happy with the conclusions of the Devolution Committee, and suggested that Crossman, Ross and Thomas could develop a 'more warm hearted' paper on devolution. Crossman records in his diary (22 June 1968; Crossman, 1977: 106) that 'I thought this was too silly and told him so.' Neither Ross nor Thomas was likely to suddenly shift towards a pro-devolution position. Crossman reiterated his view that a long-term solution would be on federalist lines: 'They [Scotland and Wales] have no economic and social problems which need special peculiar treatment.'[10]

Wilson was not to be discouraged, and it was on his initiative that a Royal Commission on the Constitution was established to look into the issue of the government of Scotland and Wales. Privately, it was trumpeted as a means of countering Edward Heath's 'Declaration of Perth', and also of postponing any real decision. The minutes of the meeting between Crossman (then the Secretary of State for Social Services) and the Prime Minister that agreed to establish the Royal Commission in October 1968

[8]   NA T 330/185, minutes of the revised draft conclusions of the Ministerial Committee on Devolution for Scotland and Wales, 27 May 1968.

[9]   NA T 330/185, conclusions of the Ministerial Committee on Devolution for Scotland and Wales, K. E. Couzens, 'Report to Chancellor', 19 June 1968.

[10]   NA PREM 13/2151, Privy Council Office to Prime Minister, 25 June 1968.

state: 'It was argued that it would be inadvisable to seek further administrative devolution at the present time simply as a means of appeasing
nationalist opinion in Scotland and Wales, the wide support for which
would evaporate once the Government's economic policies succeeded.'[11]
The Royal Commission was a classic piece of Wilsonian statecraft, designed
to make it appear that the government was doing something about the
government of Scotland and Wales, without undermining the unionist
tendencies of his Cabinet colleagues. It sought to counter the Conservatives' new approach to Scottish administration, whilst delaying any real
policy decision until after the general election.

The 1974 elections: 'riding the back of the tiger'

The Royal Commission on the Constitution, known as the Kilbrandon
Commission after its second chairman, reported in October 1973. The
report included a survey of attitudes towards self-government across Great
Britain carried out in 1970, which showed Scotland as having the highest
level of support for self-determination, although not much higher than
other English regions, with respondents in Wales notably unenthusiastic
(McLean and McMillan, 2005: 181–3). This was not reflected in the
recommendations of the report, which supported elected assemblies for
Scotland and Wales.

In the same month as the Kilbrandon report was published, the
Arab–Israeli war saw oil prices increase massively. The SNP linked the issue
of constitutional change and North Sea oil through an 'It's Scotland's Oil'
campaign. Within a week of Kilbrandon reporting, the SNP won a by-election in the 'safe' Labour seat of Glasgow Govan with 42 per cent of the
vote, thereby returning Margo MacDonald to Westminster.

As the February 1974 election approached, there was a renewed
concern that the Labour vote in Scotland was vulnerable to the SNP challenge. MORI, the polling organisation set up by Bob Worcester, was
commissioned to undertake a series of surveys of Scottish opinion. Twelve
days before the election, Bernard Donoughue, the Prime Minister's political adviser, wrote in his diary, '[W]orried by the party's Scottish poll
showing us doing badly, and worse than last time, with a strong trend to
nationalist policies and a large majority wanting a Scottish Parliament.
Scotland could be the wild card which kills us' (16 February 1974;
Donoughue, 2005: 23).

[11]   NA CAB 130/390, 23 October 1968.

The next day he wrote:

> Ron Hayward [General Secretary of the Labour Party] approached me to press on Wilson the importance of Scotland. Unless we can get our Scottish politicians to move towards devolution, we shall lose a lot of seats. Our special Scottish poll is very depressing – Labour is behind the Tories and everybody is demanding a Scottish Parliament. The problem apparently is Willie Ross, the party spokesman on Scotland, who is adamantly against all Scottish Nationalist arguments. (Donoughue 2005: 25)

The Labour Party manifesto for the February 1974 election avoided any mention of devolution. However, Willie Ross was not against spending more money in Scotland, and the manifesto stated that: 'Revenues from North Sea oil will be used wherever possible to improve employment conditions in Scotland and the regions elsewhere in need of development.'

While Labour was able to form a government after the February 1974 election, the position was finely balanced. In Scotland the SNP won 22 per cent of the vote, but just seven seats. The politicians knew, however, that a small increase in the vote for the nationalists could lead to a substantially different result. The Prime Minister was pressed to address the SNP challenge. Alex Neil, the Scottish Labour Party's Research Officer, argued that the SNP was not just a flash-in-the-pan, and was gaining strength from strategic voting as the possibility that Labour could be defeated became more evident. He cited recent polling research:

> The Labour Party's confidential study of public opinion in Scotland carried out [by MORI] during the 1974 General Election Campaign as well as a number of other studies of this nature have shown that the Scottish National Party now has the same Constituency as the Labour Party in Scotland. In other words the SNP depend for their votes on men rather than women, young people rather than older people, and working people rather than middle or upper class people. This of course represents a direct challenge to the Labour Party in Scotland much more than it is a challenge to any other major Party [...] if the SNP success continues at its present rate then we may find that after a General Election in September or October there would be between 20 and 30 members of Parliament from the Scottish National Party. The implications of such a high representation of SNP Members of Parliament should be obvious enough. Really we would be in a situation where Scotland would be negotiating independence [...] Finally I should like to point out that this Paper is not presented in any state of panic but rather an attempt at a logical and rational appraisal of the political realities facing the Labour Party in Scotland today ... [O]ur failure to realise and to effectively challenge the threat from the Scottish National Party may mean the loss of power for the Labour Party in Britain as a whole.[12]

[12] NA PREM 16/127, Labour Party Paper (SR5/74) by Alex Neil, 'The political situation in Scotland to-day: The rise of the Scottish National Party', June 1974.

The divisions in the Scottish Labour Party were exposed in the summer of 1974, when the party's Scottish Executive first of all (at a sparsely attended meeting which coincided with a World Cup match between Scotland and Yugoslavia) affirmed the policy that a Scottish Assembly was 'irrelevant to the real needs of Scotland' and derided 'constitutional tinkering', and then (at a special Scottish conference at the Dalintober Street Co-operative Halls in Glasgow – the so-called 'battle of Dalintober Street') was forced by the national leadership to reverse the policy (Marr, 1995: 138–41; McLean and McMillan, 2005: 162).

The precariousness of the position was set out by the Cabinet Secretary, John Hunt, in a note to the Prime Minister on the Kilbrandon Report in July 1974:

> (i) The crucial step is the establishment of elected assemblies. This could be the beginning of a slippery slope towards separatism.
> (ii) The establishment of assemblies, and of the regional governments associated with them, would be irreversible.
> (iii) No form of devolution would satisfy Scottish aspirations unless acceptable arrangements were made over North Sea oil. Decisions on the two subjects must keep in step.
> (iv) Any system of devolution is likely to cause friction and to be potentially unstable; but legislative devolution . . . seems to involve least risks. (NA PREM 16/126)

Hunt concluded that it was a question of how willing ministers were to take a risk on devolution. Bernard Donoughue urged Wilson to take on the challenge of the SNP:

> Whatever we do now in devolutionary terms we are riding the back of the tiger. Therefore we should strive to meet the challenge of the covert message of the SNP and set out radical proposals for improving Scotland's self-image with the money from oil as well as nationalising land and salmon. The landlords are a perfect target for us. Many SNP members ought to be in the Labour Party and say openly that what they want is a Scottish Socialist Party – not the present Scottish Labour Party'.[13]

Within the Treasury, every effort was made to combat the political demands for decentralisation, hypothecation, and special treatment for Scotland. However, civil servants were forced to admit that North Sea oil had transformed the notional finances of Scotland, so an exercise like the 1969 Scottish Budget, which had sought to highlight Scottish fiscal

---

[13] NA PREM 16/127, marked from BD to PM, 19 July 1974. The date coincides with Donoughue's diary entry of 16 July 1974: 'I worked on Kilbrandon Scottish devolution papers, which are very boring and show Whitehall retreating terrified from devolution' (Donoughue, 2005: 164).

dependence within the United Kingdom, was impossible. A note from February 1974 suggests: 'the essential argument is that the rest of the United Kingdom has effectively subsidised Scotland for as long as anyone can remember, and it is now unreasonable that the Scots should expect to get the benefit of the continuing subsidy and hog the oil revenues for themselves'.[14] However, the Treasury accepted that some presentational concessions might be necessary:

> The question of North Sea oil revenues may raise a serious threat to the fiscal unity of the UK unless it is carefully handled; and … since we all believe it is important to maintain that unity in the interests of the country as a whole, what the Government says on this subject publicly will have to be carefully considered [...] I think we shall have to dress the thing up in such a way that Scotland will appear to be getting a large extra benefit, although in practice we should want to keep it small.[15]

Wilson decided that the Labour Party must make some commitment to devolution. He did not have the full backing of his Cabinet, with Roy Jenkins arguing that 'it would be insanity to break up the United Kingdom for the sake of a few extra seats at a general election' (Ziegler, 1993: 452). Having already played his Royal Commission card, in June 1974 Wilson produced a Green Paper, 'Devolution within the UK: Some alternatives for discussion'. As the title suggests, it was not a firm commitment to introduce reform, but it did its political job. Cabinet objections could be met with the promise that the important issues would be addressed at a later stage, and the party could go into the October 1974 election with its first ever Scottish manifesto. 'Powerhouse Scotland' was delivered to every home in Scotland, promising a directly elected Scottish Assembly, a Scottish Development Agency, the establishment of a Centre for Oil Drilling Technology and a British National Oil Corporation to be sited in Scotland (Lynch, 2002: 129).

The Prime Minister protected the devolution plan from Cabinet objections throughout 1974–75, using a strategy of restricting key decision making to a small group based on the Lord President of the Council, Ted Short, and the Secretaries of State for Scotland and Wales, and allowing the programme to become entrenched while delaying any final decision by Cabinet on the principle of devolution. The Cabinet minutes from the summer of 1974 note that the Ministerial Group on Devolution had

---

[14] NA T 319/2928, note by A. J. Wiggins, 'Kilbrandon and North Sea Oil', 14 February 1974.

[15] NA T 319/2928, note by W. S. Ryrie, 'Kilbrandon: North Sea Oil', 20 May 1974.

proposed elected assemblies in Scotland and Wales, but reflect that the general discussion was not uniformly supportive:

> In discussion it was argued that the Government should have more time to weigh a decision of such historical importance and that it was regrettable that their hand had to some extent been forced by external political pressure. In the circumstances they had to be alive to political realities: but it would be important for the proposed White Paper to assert the positive argument for the integrity of the United Kingdom and to relate the case for elected assemblies in Scotland and Wales to the problems which would be involved. (NA T 328/1032)

Any firm commitment was postponed to a Cabinet meeting on 5 September, the minutes of which suggest a similar atmosphere:

> The Prime Minister, summing up the discussion, said that the Cabinet were concerned at the far-reaching and perhaps destructive nature of the proposals on devolution which were current and were reluctant to commit the Government to detailed and specific proposals before the full implications had been worked out. However, a movement towards devolution had been started by the setting up of the Kilbrandon Commission itself, and the present government was committed to making proposals in a White Paper. (NA T 328/1032)

The main opponents were the Chancellor, Denis Healey, the Home Secretary, Roy Jenkins, and Tony Crosland, the Secretary of State for the Environment, who wanted a minimal commitment for the impending general election, and then a serious rethink (Donoughue, 2005: 169–70, 415).

In the October 1974 election, the Labour Party's vote share in Scotland held steady, while it secured one additional seat. The SNP continued to gain support, winning 30 per cent of the vote and eleven seats, its gains coming at the expense of the Conservatives. The Green Paper and 'Powerhouse Scotland' had done their job of protecting the Labour Party's position in Scotland, and with a small overall majority in Westminster, Wilson was in a slightly more comfortable position. However, he now had to deliver on the devolution commitment.

In an attempt to change the tone of the Cabinet discussion, Wilson tried a change of scene, and in January, June and September 1975 Cabinet think-ins on devolution were held at Chequers. At the January meeting Wilson emphasised the electoral importance of devolution, and sought to 'get devolution rolling forward' (Donoughue 2005: 285). But Bernard Donoughue's diary records that speakers were split 2:1 against rapid devolution, and the Prime Minister was up against serious opposition, with the Foreign Secretary, Jim Callaghan, joining the 'go-slow' movement.[16]

---

[16] 'Short pointed out that much earlier on Callaghan had supported devolution. "Ah," said Jim, "that was before we won the election"' (Donoughue, 2005: 294).

In June, Harold Lever, the Chancellor of the Duchy of Lancaster, wrote to Wilson, putting the 'go-slow' position. As well as emphasising the administrative problems and economic incoherence likely to accompany devolution, he argued that there would be an English backlash, and wondered if the threat of nationalist pressure had been overstated:

> It is only Nationalist pressure which has caused us seriously to consider executive and legislative devolution to Scotland and Wales. As I see it, our present strategy is to introduce such devolution on a scale sufficiently substantial to satisfy all but the more extreme nationalised opinion in these two countries, so as to avoid the break up of the United Kingdom and the electorally disadvantageous loss of the Scottish and Welsh seats in the Westminster Parliament [...] In my view there is now a very strong case also for moving slowly in Scotland and Wales. Since the devolution now envisaged seems certain to give the Nationalists what they want in the not very distant future, we ought to allow some time to see whether we have not overrated their strength [...] The referendum results suggest that public opinion in both Wales and Scotland may not be nearly as sympathetic to nationalism as had been supposed. (NA BD 108/198)

The evidence on public support for devolution (Chapter 5, Table 5.2) suggests that, in Wales at least, Harold Lever's concerns were justified. Labour was hardly electorally threatened in Wales by the nationalist party, Plaid Cymru, which never won more than 12 per cent of the vote – or 10 per cent of the seats – in general elections. Labour's proposals on devolution to Wales were adopted more for their consistency with the – more electorally salient – proposals for devolution to Scotland than for a belief in their intrinsic importance. Nonetheless, in the Welsh Office there was a determined effort to support Ted Short against the Treasury attack on the devolution programme. This involved a reiteration of the manifesto commitment to take action, and the electoral cost of backing down, combined with a scepticism about the ability of centralised economic policy to address nationalist concerns: 'The argument that macro-economic measures and central regional aid can solve the problems of Scotland and Wales will meet with little assent in view of past experience of such measures.'[17]

At the September Cabinet think-in, Wilson's strategy of continuing with the devolution programme whilst prevaricating in the light of Cabinet objections was challenged by Healey, who was supported by Jenkins. As Donoughue noted, 'possibly a majority of Cabinet opposes devolution', and he reflected that: 'H[arold] W[ilson] does not support it either really. His position is that we are committed to it: we proposed it, we put it in our

---

[17]   NA BD 108/198, brief for Secretary of State on Lord President's reply to Chancellor of Exchequer's memo (DS(75)24), June 1974.

manifesto, and we produced a White Paper – therefore we cannot go back on it. But he does not believe in it' (Donoughue, 2005: 494).

As the reluctant convert to devolution, Willie Ross, the Secretary of State for Scotland, ruefully reminded the Cabinet: '[I]t was too late. He had warned them years ago and they would not listen or support him. Now they must live with it' (Donoughue, 2005: 493). The Cabinet agreed to live with it. In October 1975, Wilson eventually gained the support of Healey and the Cabinet. Wilson was buoyed by the argument that the Scottish Assembly would expose divisions in the SNP, but the Cabinet support was won through attrition rather than argument.

Thereafter, as Jones and Jones (2000: 256) note, 'devolution was to dog the government until its downfall in 1979'. Wilson's statecraft worked in Scotland, but it failed in Wales, and most importantly it failed in England. By pressing on with devolution, the Labour government was able to hold together a fragile coalition in the House of Commons, and withstand the Scottish challenge from the SNP. But this was achieved at great cost, including disruption of the parliamentary timetable, and a growing discontent amongst a range of Labour MPs, including those from the North East who were unhappy about the Labour government rewarding people in Scotland for voting SNP (McLean and McMillan, 2005: 164). An initial Scotland and Wales Bill was defeated on a guillotine motion in February 1977, brought down by rebels from the North of England together with Scottish and Welsh Labour MPs, including Neil Kinnock, hostile to devolution.[18] The proposals were reintroduced as separate Scotland and Wales Bills, and these did secure their passage through the Commons following the creation of the Lib-Lab pact in March 1977. However, the new legislation was hobbled by the 'Cunningham amendment', which stated that any 'Yes' vote in the referendums that were to be held in Scotland and Wales before the legislation was implemented would not be binding unless it represented more than 40 per cent of the territory's electorate. More generally the legislation was cumbersome and badly drafted: 'a classic example of bad legislation emerging from legislators with an eye on electoral advantage' (Mitchell, 1999: 651). Lord Crowther-Hunt described the Wales Act as 'a dog's breakfast' which was so badly written that 'it must amount to sabotage by the drafters in London' (quoted in Bogdanor, 1999: 192).

[18]   Marr (1995: 142) quotes a speech by Neil Kinnock in February 1975, in which he states: 'I believe that the emancipation of the class which I came to this House to represent, unapologetically, can best be achieved in a single nation and in a single economic unit, by which I mean a unit where we can have a brotherhood of all nations and have the combined strength of working class people throughout the United Kingdom.'

Did Wilson's statecraft really work in Scotland? It is impossible to test the counterfactual; what would have happened if the anti-devolution sentiment within the Cabinet had overcome Wilson's push towards a devolution settlement after the October 1974 election? It would have pleased many in the unionist wing of the Labour Party in Scotland, but there would certainly have been much greater momentum behind a schismatic Scottish Labour Party, rather than the squib of a party that broke away with Jim Sillars in 1976.[19] The SNP might have emerged as the dominant political party in Scotland, or it might have been exposed as a single-issue party with limited appeal when it was forced to run on its own agenda. However, a testament to Wilson's statecraft is shown by the time-series of System 3 polls on Westminster voting intentions, shown in Figure 2.2. It indicates that the tortuous passage of the devolution bill in parliament was rewarded with a leap in support for Labour in Scotland, and a steady decline in support for the SNP. By aligning itself with the pro-Scottish devolution cause, the Labour Party re-established itself as the dominant party in Scotland.

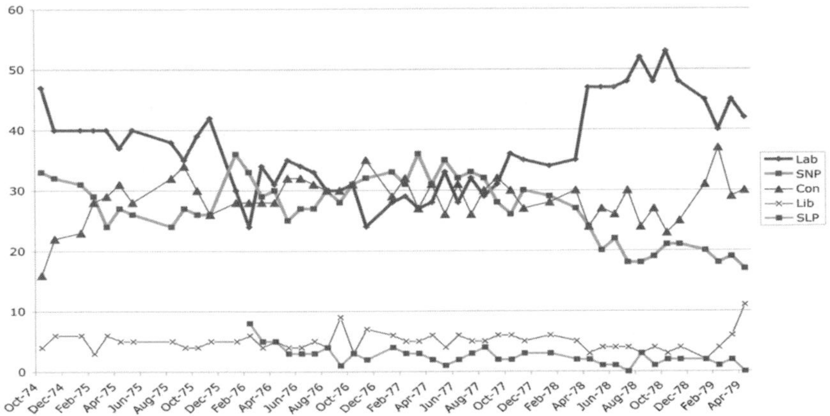

Figure 2.2   System 3 opinion polls for Westminster,
October 1974–May 1979

Source: Lynch, 2002: Table 6.6.

Thatcher and the restitution of unionism

The Conservative commitment to devolution was sustained beyond the October 1974 election and the subsequent leadership battle which resulted

---

[19]   Labour MP Jim Sillars created a breakaway party, the Scottish Labour Party (SLP), in 1976 in protest at Labour's failure to create a Scottish Assembly. The SLP was disbanded after a poor showing in the 1979 general election, with Sillars joining the Scottish National Party.

in Margaret Thatcher's victory. Thatcher inherited a Scottish party that had a number of prominent supporters of devolution, notably Alick Buchanan-Smith and Malcolm Rifkind. Thatcher continued to support some measure of Scottish devolution whilst in opposition, and, indeed, Mitchell (1990: 74) notes that 'One of the most remarkable features of Mrs Thatcher's early years as Tory leader was her apparent ambivalence regarding devolution.' In her autobiography, Thatcher describes the party devolution commitment she inherited as 'an extremely painful hook from which it would be my unenviable task to set it free' (Thatcher, 1995: 322). The unhooking had to be done carefully.

Margaret Thatcher's approach was to gradually change the emphasis in Conservative policy. She did this in a number of ways, including through her rhetoric and organisation of the party. Most importantly, she resisted any move to support the Labour government's devolution policy, and instead focused her party on attacking the details of the government's proposals. A party document on how to respond to the White Paper on devolution outlines this strategy:

> (a) We were interested in devolution as a means of dispersing Government power, not as a mechanism for making the break up of the UK a real possibility.
> (b) We should attack the clumsy and apparently unworkable aspects of the White Paper, drawing attention to the clear dangers of increasing bureaucracy, increasing burdens on taxpayers, and more tardy and inefficient administration.
> (c) We should especially attack any weakening of central Government control over public expenditure which would result from the Government's proposals.
> (d) We should try to avoid making a number of firm, long term, detailed commitments on the subject, as it was thought that the Government proposals were unlikely in their present form to survive a prolonged period of debate, during which public opinion might change considerably.[20]

The aggressive line on the legislative programme of the Labour government allowed the Conservatives to gloss over their own divisions about what measures to implement. Mrs Thatcher used her speech to the Conservative conference in May 1976 to indicate her qualified support for devolution and her abiding unionism:

> [I]t remains our policy, which this Conference supported yesterday, that there should be a directly elected Scottish Assembly. But let me make this crystal clear. I could not support an Assembly – none of us could support an Assembly – if we thought it was likely to jeopardise the Union. We believe that the Union is more likely to be harmed by doing nothing, than by responding to the wish of the Scottish people for less Government from Westminster. (Thatcher, 1976)

[20] CA LCC/75/85, 'Devolution policy', 1 December 1975.

The shift in emphasis in Conservative policy away from devolution was reinforced by changes in personnel. Willie Whitelaw was replaced as devolution spokesman by the more sceptical Francis Pym. After the key decision to impose a three-line whip on Conservative MPs in 1976, Alick Buchanan-Smith and Malcolm Rifkind resigned from the Shadow Cabinet in order to support the Scotland and Wales Bill. Anti-devolutionists, such as Teddy Taylor, became more prominent in party discussions of devolution.

Thatcher (1995: 322) puts the shift in Conservative policy down to her 'instinctive Unionist' beliefs, which were bolstered by opposition to the devolution commitment amongst members of the Scottish party. She also suggests that her beliefs were reinforced by a private opinion poll carried out by the ORC in November 1976, which she felt showed a lack of support for constitutional change (Thatcher, 1995: 324). [21] The Conservative withdrawal from actively supporting Scottish devolution under Mrs Thatcher was not made explicit. She records that she did not take part in the 'No' campaign on the referendums in Scotland and Wales, although 'that was the result I wanted'; of the aftermath of the referendums she writes 'devolution was dead: I did not mourn it' (Thatcher, 1995: 430).

From referendum to referendum

While a narrow majority of Scottish voters supported the devolution proposals in the referendum in March 1979, the measure was brought down by the requirement that it be supported by 40 per cent of the electorate. In Wales, the rejection of devolution in the 1979 referendum was comprehensive, with a resounding 80 per cent voting against the measure. The Labour government fell in a vote of no-confidence later that month, as the SNP showed its disillusionment and voted with the Conservatives. The Labour Party, while bruised by the Welsh response to the devolution referendum and the bitter divisions that this revealed in the Welsh party, maintained its commitment to Scottish devolution. Within the nationalist parties, the failure of the devolution programme led to a period of retrenchment. In the SNP this was particularly bitter, with their poor showing in the 1979 general election followed by a period characterised by 'internal conflicts, electoral irrelevance and organisational decline' (Lynch, 2002: 161). The Glasgow Hillhead by-election in 1982 saw a

---

[21] Although whether Thatcher was right about this is debatable. Other data on public attitudes collected around the same time suggest unionist sentiment was far from overwhelming (see Chapter 5, Table 5.1 and McLean and McMillan, 2005: Table 8.11).

victory for the newly formed Social Democratic Party, whilst the SNP lost its deposit.

While the movement for devolution had taken a blow, it remained active, most notably through the Campaign for a Scottish Assembly. This helped ensure that, by 1989, it was possible to establish in Scotland a broad-ranging Scottish Constitutional Convention, including representation from both the Labour and Liberal parties together with religious, civil and trade union organisations. The significance of the Convention lay in the consensus it forged between these groups on the principle of devolution to Scotland (McCrone and Lewis, 1999: 21). Although a Campaign for a Welsh Assembly was established in 1987 (changing its name to the Parliament for Wales Campaign in 1993), it operated without the support of the political parties (McAllister, 1999: 638). Indeed, McCrone and Lewis (1999: 28) report that 'Wales had no Constitutional Convention and the Welsh public were largely ignorant of the issue of devolution and displayed little enthusiasm for it.'

According to James Mitchell (1999: 653), 'The overriding explanation for Scottish Labour's eventual enthusiasm for devolution was Margaret Thatcher.' Although successive Welsh and Scottish Conservative Secretaries of State were given un-Thatcherite freedom to maintain public spending and accommodate regional interests, one issue came to symbolise the alleged mistreatment of Scotland under the Thatcher government: the poll tax. The introduction of this tax in Scotland a year before its roll-out in England and Wales provided a highly visible symbol of the Thatcherite treatment of Scotland, and one on which the SNP could out-protest the Labour Party. At the Glasgow Govan by-election in November 1988 the SNP overturned a Labour majority of 19,509. This loss, according to Taylor, Curtice and Thompson (1999: xl) was possibly the biggest accident on the road to devolution:

> Labour made the fatal mistake of putting up a lacklustre candidate against a charismatic former Labour MP, Jim Sillars, who was standing in the by-election in the SNP's colours and whose wife had captured the very same seat for the SNP in a by-election 15 years earlier. Shocked at the apparent threat to its bastion, defeat propelled Labour into participation in the Scottish Constitutional Convention which ... developed the plans on which Labour's devolution plans were largely based.

The Govan victory showed that the SNP could still outflank the Labour Party on both its proposals for Scottish autonomy and in the vociferousness of its attack on the Thatcher government. It forced Labour to take more concrete steps to consolidate its position. Since the 1980s the Scottish Labour Party had repeatedly affirmed its support for devolution

(Mitchell, 1999: 653), and the Govan defeat led them to take a much more active role in promoting the policy through the Constitutional Convention. This destabilised the SNP, which withdrew participation, realising that Labour would dominate the convention, thereby allowing Labour to portray the SNP as narrow and sectarian (Brand and Mitchell, 1997: 45).

The final report of the Constitutional Convention in 1995 recommended a Scottish Parliament endowed with primary legislative authority and limited tax varying powers, with 129 members elected via the Additional Member System variant of proportional representation (ostensibly limiting Labour dominance of the legislature, but also minimising the chances of the SNP gaining an overall majority of seats in the new body). These proposals were adopted wholesale by Labour, and formed the basis of its legislative programme for a Scottish Parliament once in office after 1997. In many ways, this programme bore similarities to that proposed by the Wilson government twenty years before. Then, however, devolution to Scotland was a tactic to deal with the SNP's electoral threat. In the 1990s, while a Scottish Parliament still presented a means for Labour to fend off the nationalist threat, the experience of Thatcherism meant many within the party – particularly those in Scotland – wanted to go further. The net result was a stronger form of devolution: in addition to granting the Scottish Parliament limited tax raising authority, Labour also proposed demarcating the boundaries between Edinburgh and London by listing the areas that would be reserved to Westminster rather than, as in the late 1970s, circumscribing the powers that would come under the competence of the Scottish Executive.

Strategic considerations also dictated a difference from the experience of devolution in the 1970s. The Labour Party's presentation of devolution in 1997 suggested that the government and civil service had learnt some key lessons from the protracted legislative struggle of 1976–78. At the insistence of the Labour leader, Tony Blair, parliamentary passage of the Scotland Bill and the Government of Wales Bill was preceded by popular referendums, including a separate question on the tax raising competence of the proposed Scottish Parliament. A referendum had not been part of the recommendations of the Constitutional Convention, and came as a surprise to some of the major players in the devolution campaigns in Scotland and Wales.[22]

[22] 'Just days before the announcement of a pre-legislative referendum in June 1996, Shadow Secretary of State for Wales, Ron Davies, had categorically denied the likelihood of a referendum. The decision was a unilateral one by Blair designed to outflank opposition from within his own party and from his opponents' (McAllister, 1999: 639). In Scotland, the decision to hold a

For Wales, devolution was proposed – much as it was by Wilson in the late 1970s – as much to provide some consistency with Scotland as because of either elite or mass-level demands within the principality. While popular support for devolution had grown since 1979 (see Chapter 5, Table 5.2), the Labour Party was internally divided on the merits of a Welsh Assembly, and the public was felt to be lukewarm. For this reason, the Welsh referendum was scheduled for the week after the corresponding Scottish vote, in an attempt to bolster public support for devolution (Butler and McLean, 1999: 13). Fierce debates among Labour politicians in Wales about the merits of devolution had resulted in the 1970s in a compromise proposal for a directly elected Welsh Assembly with secondary legislative powers only. Little had occurred in the interim to shift this position. Unlike in Scotland, the nationalist party – Plaid Cymru – was not a serious electoral threat to Labour. And, while Wales never voted for a Conservative government (the Tories' share of the vote in Wales peaked at 32 per cent in 1979), the irritation, among elite actors at least, was as much with Conservative appointees to executive posts in Wales as with the lack of policy representation (Paterson and Wyn Jones, 1999: 175–6). Labour's thinking on devolution to Wales had thus progressed little from the debates of the 1970s. In Jonathan Bradbury's assessment, 'As hard as "A Voice for Wales" tries to make the less obvious form of executive devolution intelligible, attractive and innovative, it moves only incrementally on from the 1970s proposals. Welsh readers of this densely argued White Paper could be forgiven for thinking whether what was on the table in 1997 was really all that different from that which they rejected in 1979' (Bradbury, 1997: 130).

What was different, in both Wales and Scotland, was the political context surrounding the referendums in 1997. The change was particularly noticeable in Wales, as Kenneth Morgan notes:

> In 1979 devolution was reluctantly pushed on to a divided party and an apathetic public by a declining minority government, manifestly at the end of its tether. In 1997, by contrast, devolution was enthusiastically promoted as a legislative priority by a fresh government with an overall majority of 179 seats and the further backing of the Liberal Democrats and the Nationalists. (Morgan, 1999: 210)

Devolution gained popular approval in Scotland and Wales (in the latter case, admittedly, by a very narrow majority) because the Labour Party

---

referendum on the tax-raising powers of a Scottish Parliament was taken without the knowledge of John McAllion, Labour's shadow minister nominally in charge of devolution (McCrone and Lewis, 1999: 19).

was less internally divided over devolution than in the 1970s and, more importantly, was popular among voters. This different political context can most clearly be seen in the changing pattern of Labour voters' support for devolution. In 1979, 44 per cent of Labour voters in Scotland reported supporting devolution in the referendum, while just 17 per cent in Wales did likewise. In 1997, the equivalent proportions increased markedly, to 66 per cent in Scotland and 34 per cent in Wales (Surridge and McCrone, 1999: Table 3.1; Evans and Trystan, 1999: Table 5.7).[23]

Conclusion

This chapter has traced the main contours of the devolution debate in Scotland and Wales, from the first serious proposals to decentralise political authority in the late 1960s and 1970s, to the eventual realisation of these proposals after 1997. What answers does our account suggest to the two key questions we posed at the beginning: why did devolution occur, and why did it take the shape it did?

Devolution was a response to the rise in support of the nationalist parties in both Scotland and Wales, but the strategic considerations of the Conservative and Labour parties meant that the Scottish situation was taken more seriously. The ability of the SNP to reach beyond the relatively small proportion of voters who supported independence, and mobilise a broader coalition of voters discontented with the main unionist parties, made it a real threat. For the Conservatives, the loss of Scottish seats threatened their unionist identity, while for Labour, it threatened their majority at Westminster. Devolution offered the Conservatives a chance to rebrand themselves in Scotland, addressing both the nationalist threat and their longer-term decline in the country. For Labour, devolution enabled them to deflect the accusation that an oil-rich Scotland would be neglected at Westminster.

A commitment to devolution did not come without a cost. It was an issue which cut across established lines of partisan support – both Labour and the Conservatives were internally divided on the policy – and it emphasised the territorial segmentation of UK politics. The painful passage of devolution legislation through the 1974–79 parliament brought these

[23] The shift among Labour supporters is part of the reason for the devolution referendum's success in 1997. The other key factor is the increase in the proportion of Labour supporters; in 1979, 42 per cent of survey respondents identified themselves as Labour supporters, while in 1997, the figure had risen to 53 per cent (Surridge and McCrone, 1999: Table 3.1).

difficulties to the fore. The government struggled to provide coherent answers to major practical issues, such as the extension of devolution to Wales, the situation of England in a post-devolution settlement, the fiscal position of the devolved governments and the requirement for referendums. Yet despite the shaky foundations, the Callaghan government persevered with the devolution project, until finally crumbling in the aftermath of the 1979 referendums.

The devolution debate of the 1990s faced many of the same difficulties as in the 1970s, and was again largely driven by Labour's strategic interest in stymieing the SNP. However, rather than cutting across partisan lines, by the 1990s devolution, particularly in Scotland, was very clearly aligned on party lines, and was almost a polarising issue. Mrs Thatcher's instinctive unionism had been bolstered by her experience of the devolution debate in the 1970s, and her initial conciliatory line on extra power for Scottish government was dropped. Allied with Scottish voters' unwillingness to embrace the Thatcherite project and the disaster that was the Scottish poll tax, the Conservatives' unionist stance left them isolated. Labour, which had maintained its devolution commitment, was able to combine a concern at being electorally outflanked by the SNP with a more principled frustration at the iniquities of political representation in a centralised state. Again, Wales largely followed Scotland's lead. The nationalist threat to Labour in Wales was minor and, while frustration at the imposition of Conservative policies undoubtedly existed in Wales, it was less keenly felt than north of the border.

Devolution to Scotland and Wales can be seen as part of a unionist strategy of maintaining the territorial integrity of the United Kingdom – and thus, for the Labour Party, preserving an important electoral base – while at the same time recognising the iniquities that can arise from centralised governments characteristic of unitary political systems. These iniquities were always latent, but were exacerbated by a Conservative government after 1979 pursuing radical policies among populations few of whom voted for it. Labour's unionist strategy was lopsided. In Scotland, the serious threat to its electoral base from the SNP was felt to require a moderately powerful devolved body. This requirement increased over time, as that body came to be seen not only to provide a means of dampening nationalist support, but also to insulate Scotland from the imposition of unwelcome policies from London. While much of the Blair government's proposed Scottish Parliament was foreshadowed by the party's commitments two decades earlier, it was a more robust form of devolution that arose from the Scottish Constitutional Convention than from the compromises of the Wilson and Callaghan governments. In Wales, Labour was less exposed to electoral threats and concerns over political representation; as a result, devolution served fewer functions and the devolved institutions needed to be equipped with fewer formal powers and responsibilities.

As our opening quotation suggests, historical factors are often seen to circumscribe contemporary actions. However, while an older social science might have stressed the structural constraints under which political actors make decisions, more recent social science theories suggest that changing the nature of political institutions creates new incentives and stimuli for action. As a result, new institutions can trigger very different decisions and actions from those intended by their designers. We have set the scene for the introduction of devolution to Scotland and Wales. How the public, politicians and groups would respond to these new rules was hardly predictable. The following chapters examine what this response has been.

References

Bogdanor, V. (1999) *Devolution in the United Kingdom*, Oxford: Oxford University Press

Bradbury, J. (1997) 'The Blair government's white papers on British devolution: A review of Scotland's Parliament and A Voice for Wales', *Regional and Federal Studies*, 7:3

Brand, J. and J. Mitchell (1997) 'Home Rule in Scotland: The politics and bases of a movement', in J. Bradbury and J. Mawson, eds, *British Regionalism and Devolution: The Challenges of State Reform and European Integration*, London: Jessica Kingsley

Butler, D. and I. McLean (1999) 'Referendums', in B. Taylor and K. Thomson, eds, *Scotland and Wales: Nations Again?* Cardiff: University of Wales Press

Crossman, R. (1977) *The Diaries of a Cabinet Minister: Volume Three, Secretary of State for Social Services 1968–70*, London: Hamish Hamilton and Jonathan Cape

Donoughue, B. (2005) *Downing Street Diary: With Harold Wilson in No. 10*, London: Jonathan Cape.

Evans, G. and D. Trystan (1999) 'Why was 1997 different?', in B. Taylor and K. Thomson, eds, *Scotland and Wales: Nations Again?* Cardiff: University of Wales Press

Jones, R. and I. Jones (2000) 'Labour and the nation', in D. Tanner, C. Williams and D. Hopkin, eds, *The Labour Party in Wales 1900–2000*, Cardiff: University of Wales Press

Kellas, J. (1971) 'Scottish nationalism', in D. Butler and M. Pinto-Duschinsky, eds, *The British General Election of 1970*, London: Macmillan/St Martins Press

Lynch, P. (2002) *SNP: The History of the Scottish National Party*, Cardiff: Welsh Academic Press

Madgwick, P. with N. Griffiths and V. Walker (1973) *The Politics of Rural Wales: A Study of Cardiganshire*, London: Hutchinson

Marr, A. (1995) *The Battle for Scotland* (revised edn), London: Penguin

McAllister, L. (1999) 'The road to Cardiff Bay: The process of establishing the National Assembly for Wales', *Parliamentary Affairs*, 52:4

McCrone, D. and B. Lewis (1999) 'The Scottish and Welsh referendum campaigns', in B. Taylor and K. Thomson, eds, *Scotland and Wales: Nations Again?* Cardiff: University of Wales Press

McLean, I. and A. McMillan (2005) *State of the Union: Unionism and the Alternatives in the United Kingdom since 1707*, Oxford: Oxford University Press

Mitchell, J. (1990) *Conservatives and the Union: A Study of Conservative Party Attitudes to Scotland*, Edinburgh: Edinburgh University Press

Mitchell, J. (1999) 'The creation of the Scottish Parliament: Journey without end', *Parliamentary Affairs*, 52:4

Morgan, K. (1999) 'Welsh devolution: The past and the future', in B. Taylor and K. Thomson, eds, *Scotland and Wales: Nations Again?* Cardiff: University of Wales Press

Paterson, L. and R. Wyn Jones (1999) 'Does civil society drive constitutional change?', in B. Taylor and K. Thomson, eds, *Scotland and Wales: Nations Again?* Cardiff: University of Wales Press

Philip, A. (1975) *The Welsh Question: Nationalism in Welsh Politics 1945–1970*, Cardiff: University of Wales Press

Smith, G. (1977) 'The Conservative commitment to devolution', *Spectator*, 19 February

Surridge, P. and D. McCrone (1999) 'The 1997 Scottish referendum vote', in B. Taylor and K. Thomson, eds, *Scotland and Wales: Nations Again?* Cardiff: University of Wales Press

Taylor, B., J. Curtice and K. Thomson (1999) 'Introduction and conclusions', in B. Taylor and K. Thomson, eds, *Scotland and Wales: Nations Again?* Cardiff: University of Wales Press

Thatcher, M. (1976) Speech to the Scottish Conservative Conference, 15 May, available at www.margaretthatcher.org/speeches/displaydocument.asp?docid=103028 (15 March 2007)

Thatcher, M. (1995) *The Path to Power*, London: HarperCollins

Wyn Jones, R., R. Scully and D. Trystan (2002) 'Why the Conservatives do (even) worse in Wales', in L. Bennie, C. Rallings, J. Tonge and P. Webb, eds, *British Parties and Elections Review*, 12

Yonwin, J. (2004) *UK Election Statistics: 1918–2004*, House of Commons Research Paper 04/61, London: House of Commons

Ziegler, P. (1993) *Wilson: The Authorised Life of Lord Wilson of Rievaulx*, London: Weidenfeld & Nicolson

3

The territorialisation of interest representation: the response of groups to devolution

Michael Keating

Functional and territorial differentiation have traditionally been presented as competing principles of social and political organisation (Durkheim, 1964). For much of the nineteenth and twentieth centuries, modernisation was assumed to lead to the attenuation of the territorial principle in favour of the functional one. Markets were established across national territories, breaking down pre-modern differences. Class politics assumed the same form everywhere. Interest groups articulated sectoral or class demands, which were the same throughout the national territory. Thus the unitary state, with a single set of political and administrative institutions, faced a unitary set of demands from societal groups. Both the electoral politics of the age of mass democracy, and the corporatist forms of intermediation that arose after the Second World War, were conducted in a unitary territorial framework.

However, there is now a growing recognition of the importance of territory. The 'new regionalism' describes the rise of territorial systems of production, new and rediscovered forms of identity and political mobilisation, localised patterns of economic exchange and new forms of policy making at various spatial levels (Keating, 1998; Scott, 1998). Government has altered scale as meso or regional governments have been established in all the large countries of Europe, and some smaller ones as well (Loughlin, 2001). Historic nations or cultural regions have gained institutional recognition. Above the state, a new political and administrative system has been created in the European Union. This has altered the relationship between function and territory as bases for interest representation. To some extent, territory has displaced function as the basis for common interests, under the pressure of inter-regional competition for advantage in the European single market.

Yet while it may be the basis for common interests, the emerging meso level of government (Sharpe, 1993) also represents a new arena for political competition among sectoral interests as they seek to shape the policy agenda of devolved governments. The resulting relationships may be conflictual, contractual or negotiated. Interests may be locked in confrontation, or the meso level may become the site of new forms of concertation or neo-corporatism as groups and governments come together to forge a common programme of economic and social development. This may give rise to territorial policy communities. This is a rather new concept. The literature on policy communities and networks (Richardson and Jordan, 1979; Rhodes, 1981; Wright and Wilks, 1987; Rhodes and Marsh, 1992) usually sees these as functionally defined. The notion of territorial policy communities, however, introduces a territorial element that can operate in two ways. Functional policy communities may become territorially differentiated, and cross-functional communities may emerge at new territorial levels.

The degree to which territorial communities that share a common territorial identity and set of core values have emerged in the wake of devolution is approached in this chapter through a study of the changing orientations and attitudes of interest groups. The working hypothesis is that the degree and scope of the territorialisation of interest groups will depend partly on the competences devolved to the new territorial governments. The wider the latter, the more groups will be drawn in to the devolved level of government and the more pluralist the competition between them will be. The stronger and more exclusive the powers of the devolved governments, the more difficult it will be for groups to bypass the regional tier in favour of the centre. Britain's current system of – asymmetrical – political devolution makes it possible to compare the effects of different kinds of institutional change in the different territories. Specifically, Scotland, with a strong form of devolution, is compared with the North East of England, with a much weaker set of institutions.

Devolution in Great Britain

Pre-devolution Britain was a unitary state but one within which territorial interest representation was encouraged through administrative devolution and regional development machinery. Policy autonomy at the sub-state level was confined to a few areas like Scottish education, and the main role of the Secretary of State for Scotland was to adapt central policy and to defend the country's material interests (Midwinter *et al.*, 1991). In

England, the Regional Economic Planning Councils that existed between 1965 and 1979 assembled the regional, social and economic partners and stimulated them to frame regional demands, which then fed into a centralised economic strategy. So politics was conducted at sub-state level, but, in the absence of authoritative decision-making power, it would not be accurate to talk of a Scottish (Kellas, 1989) political system let alone regional English ones. Social compromises were not struck at the territorial level and there was, *pace* Moore and Booth (1989), no Scottish corporatism. The orientations of actors, interest groups and politicians varied, some being focused on the UK level while others confined themselves to networks around the Scottish Office, although these were more channels for lobbying the centre than loci of decision-making (Keating, 1975). Most recognised a trade-off between access and autonomy, fearing that greater autonomy for the Scottish level of government would prejudice access to the centre. So there were some distinct groups in Scotland, corresponding to the broader responsibilities of the Scottish Office and other agencies. On the other hand, in the regions of England, regional planning initiatives and administrative devolution were ended after 1979 and not revived until the 1990s.

In this regime, it was not necessary to choose between territorial, sectoral and class interest articulation, as these could be played out at different levels of administration or at different times. So Scotland could mount a territorial lobby to defend its economic interests, uniting the Scottish Office, various industrial sectors, business and trade unions, while at the same time these groups competed over general policy matters within the British political space. Thus, most groups operated at both the British and the sub-state level depending on strategic considerations and the needs of the moment.

These arrangements came under strain from the 1970s onwards. Pressures from nationalists and home rulers in Scotland increased greatly over the Conservative years from 1979 to 1997, when Scotland consistently voted against the governing party. English regionalism was relatively weak and focused on issues of economic development rather than political autonomy. These differences are reflected in the current highly asymmetrical institutional arrangements. Scotland has a national parliament, with primary legislative and administrative powers over all matters not expressly reserved to Westminster, and a ministerial executive. Wales was initially granted a national assembly with administrative and secondary legislative powers over a list of specified matters, and an executive not distinguished from the assembly itself. There is no assembly for England, which remains directly under the aegis of the Westminster Parliament and British Government, though Regional Development Agencies were established for the English regions, dominated by business leaders, together with regional assemblies nominated from local government and the social partners.

For all the differences between them, however, all of these arrangements represent a strengthening of the territorial dimension of government. They provide, in their various ways, an opportunity for local actors to mobilise around distinct policy agendas and priorities. On the other hand, the vertical or sectoral dimension of policy making remains strong, as key powers are retained by the centre, notably on the big economic and welfare state issues. British political parties remain quite centralised, although there are centrifugal pressures arising from the electoral challenge of nationalism in Scotland. European integration, while providing some opportunity for the devolved administrations to operate on their own, also serves to draw politics back to the centre (since European Union relations are largely reserved to the UK Government). Experience in other European countries shows that formal political or administrative decentralisation can be undermined by continuing centralist practices both in government and civil society (Keating, 1998; Loughlin, 2001). Given these countervailing centralist pressures, it remains an open question how interest groups will adapt to the decentralisation of political authority.

Research questions and sources

Our main aim in this chapter is to explore the adaptation of interest groups to devolution, at the organisational, attitudinal and behavioural levels, and assess the degree to which territorial communities of interests have emerged or strengthened. In each case, we first of all examine patterns of organisational change at the formal level. We then look at dominant orientations – whether a group directs its interests and lobbying primarily to the regional, UK, European or other levels – and at relationships and alliances among sectoral and territorial interests. Thereafter, we explore territorial frames of reference, that is the degree to which policy issues are seen through a regional/Scottish, UK or European frame, and core values, that is shared assumptions among policy actors about social values. Devolution alters the opportunity structure for groups, providing new channels of access and potentially resulting in the inclusion of groups that previously were marginalised. Other groups that were well integrated into the old system may be less happy. Our broad hypothesis is that groups will adapt to changes in the spatial scale of government. More specifically, this gives rise to five hypotheses:

- First, interest groups will adapt organisationally to devolution, on the basis of whether their concerns belong in the devolved or reserved spheres, but that historic patterns will condition the response. Uncertainties about precise competences and influence will lead groups to experiment at an early stage, before settling down to a new division of responsibilities.
- Second, devolution will bring more actors into the policy process as it provides more points of access. Some will gain and some will lose.
- Third, devolution will strengthen an existing tendency to adopt a territorial frame of reference for defining and appreciating policy issues. So instead of judging the impact of policy on a sector defined across the United Kingdom, interest groups will think of their sector within their part of the United Kingdom as a distinct interest, and will appreciate broader issues for their impact on that territory rather than on the United Kingdom as a whole.
- Fourth, devolution will alter relationships among policy actors and sectors, bringing them into greater contact with each other within a common framework. This will strengthen the sense of territorial political community and force actors to address each others' concerns as sectoral and class compromises and trade-offs need to be reached within the territory rather than displaced to the centre. This will broaden the political agenda and might even force actors to adopt development strategies that are more inclusive, as predicted by some new regionalist writing (Cooke and Morgan, 1998).
- Fifth, these effects will depend on the extent of political devolution. Mere administrative devolution or the creation of specialised agencies will not oblige actors to engage in dialogue. Actors dissatisfied with outcomes will be able to defect from the sub-state policy process at will, especially if they retain good links with central government. Strong political devolution, as in Scotland, will create a stronger institutional boundary and oblige all actors to play within the local political arena. We therefore hypothesise that government, in the form of elected and locally accountable assemblies and executives, is different from mere 'governance' in which social co-operation is more discretionary.

The evidence for these hypotheses in Scotland and North East England is examined under three headings. 'Pre-devolution networks' maps the policy communities prior to devolution. The key issues here are the extent to which policy communities contained a territorial element, and the dominant attitudes of groups to devolution before its introduction. This provides a baseline from which we can examine the effects of devolution in Scotland and the North East of England. 'Attitudes, institutional changes and orientations' considers how groups have reacted to devolution, both in terms of attitudes towards devolved government and in terms of organisational changes. Under the heading, 'Frames of reference, values and priorities', we focus on what devolution has meant for the way that groups perceive policy issues in sectoral and territorial frames and for the interactions among groups.

The analysis is based on interviews conducted with a range of interest groups in Scotland and the North East of England. Interviewees comprised representatives of business organisations, trade unions and social interest groups. We conducted ninety-one interviews in Scotland; fifty-nine of these were initial interviews conducted in 2000–2, with thirty-two being follow-up interviews undertaken in 2003.[1] In North East England we conducted forty initial interviews in 2000–1, and twenty-one follow-ups in 2003. Groups were asked about their organisation and how it had changed since devolution, and about their links with the devolved, UK and European levels of government, with their sectoral counterparts at other levels, and with other sectoral groups within the territory. In order to identify what frames of reference they spontaneously used, our interviewees were then asked their views about a series of policy issues including economic policy, the European single currency, social inclusion and devolution, without any prompting from us about the territorial frame of reference.

Scotland

Pre-devolution networks

Before 1999, Scotland had its own interest groups and policy communities (Kellas, 1989; Midwinter *et al.*, 1991; Paterson, 1994; Brown *et al.*, 1996). Data produced for the Consultative Steering Group during a pre-devolution consultation exercise suggested that some groups were purely Scottish (20 per cent), others were affiliated with, or were regional branches of, UK groups (50 per cent), while some groups were organised on a regional basis within Scotland but not at a national level.[2] In a few cases, there was no

---

[1] The interviews were conducted by Michael Keating with the assistance, successively, of Linda Stevenson and Paul Cairney.

[2] In Scotland, the term regional is used to denote regions within Scotland. The term national is notoriously ambiguous as it is used to refer to the United Kingdom, to the British, and to the Scottish level. For clarity, we will use the

Scottish level at all, only a UK one (5 per cent). There was no consistent rationale for these distinctions. Some groups operated on a Scottish basis for purely historical reasons: for example the Scottish Trades Union Congress (STUC) has its origins in a decision of the (British) Trades Union Congress (TUC) in the late nineteenth century to exclude trade councils. Teachers were organised separately because of the historic distinctiveness of Scottish education. Other groups operated on a Scottish basis because of the need to lobby the Scottish Office. In contrast, the Scottish business community had declined as firms were taken over by British or multi-national corporations and the main business groups were organised at a UK level. Equally, during the twentieth century most Scottish trade unions were absorbed into their UK counterparts and tended to support centralised economic and welfare policies, conscious of Scotland's dependence on UK resources. Yet alongside this system of sectoral interest representation was an elaborate set of arrangements for articulating Scottish territorial interests, and Scotland could mobilise a territorial lobby on shared economic interests cutting across sectoral, class and party divisions while not attenuating them. Politicians, civil servants and groups were conscious of the rules of the game, in which they could stand up for Scotland on key economic issues, while disagreeing on many policy questions.

While this system of administrative devolution had general support, opinion among interest groups about moving to political devolution was divided. Big business groups tended to be hostile, fearing that devolved government would be more interventionist and under leftist control. They also feared the division of the United Kingdom's single market and consequent obstacles to business mobility. Party politics was a factor too, since groups traditionally close to the Conservative Party, such as large business or landowners, enjoyed a status and access that they feared they might lose under a devolved government controlled by other parties. In the 1970s and 1980s this opposition had often been vocal and organised, but by the mid-1990s, realising that devolution was likely to come about, big business groups retreated to a sceptical neutrality (Lynch, 1998). Meanwhile, the trade unions, like the Labour Party, had historically embraced both pro- and anti-devolution wings, but since the late 1960s had tended to favour devolution, albeit with guarantees for the unity of the British welfare state, labour market and economic management (Keating and Bleiman, 1979). During the 1980s and 1990s, the STUC provided organisational support

---

terms UK, British and Scottish to refer to the various levels. The United Kingdom includes England, Scotland, Wales and Northern Ireland. British refers to England, Scotland and Wales.

for the devolution movement and argued for strong economic development powers for the Scottish Parliament, albeit within a UK-wide
economic framework. Finally, the voluntary sector, new social movements
and groups that did not have a niche in the old system tended to favour
devolution, seeing a Scottish Parliament as a means of increasing their
access to government.

Attitudes, institutional changes and orientations

Our research shows that virtually all groups in Scotland have come to
accept devolution as the new 'rules of the game'. Given the battles over
devolution during the last thirty years, it is notable that, since 1999, all
groups accept the devolution of political authority and the need to accommodate themselves to the new institutions in Scotland. Among our
interviewees, we found no hankering for a return to centralised government, and no sympathy whatever for the campaign of destabilisation waged
by sections of the Scottish press against the Scottish Parliament in its first
years of existence.

But how have groups responded organisationally to devolution? Some
UK organisations that previously operated Scottish divisions or 'arms' have
devolved power internally, allowing these divisions more influence over
issues relating to devolved matters. There is also evidence that UK organisations that only had a minimal presence in Scotland prior to devolution
have strengthened their operations in Scotland. Some groups, which operated at the regional or local level within Scotland, have also strengthened
their representation at the Scottish level. However, these responses often
depend on level of resources at the individual group's disposal; less well
endowed bodies, like individual trade unions and social groups, have had
more difficulty than richer groups in adapting their organisation to the new
system.

Meanwhile, the orientation of groups is likely to be affected not only
by which tier of government makes those decisions in which they have an
interest, but also by their territorial scope. In the case of businesses, territorial scope might refer to the location of their ownership and the location
of their production facilities; in the case of trade unions or social organisations, it would refer to the location of their members. Another
consideration is the field of operation of the group or, in the case of companies, their market. A final factor is the level at which the activity is
regulated. All these factors help determine the territorial orientation of the
groups we are exploring in this chapter, as the following discussion of how
particular sectors have adapted to devolution illustrates.

The business community has adapted in various ways. Large firms are mostly externally owned, are regulated mainly at the UK and European levels and trade in UK and global markets. The main focus of attention for their representative groups are UK Government departments and they were initially little engaged with the new institutions. They do, however, have to pay attention to the Scottish level, because some matters affecting them, such as transport or planning policy, are devolved. They also play in the Scottish arena to sustain legitimacy in the face of increased political exposure and this has led to some gestures to social responsibility. During the second legislative session of the Scottish Parliament between 2003 and 2007, business was drawn more into Scottish networks as the Executive has stressed economic development matters and sought consensus around its economic strategy. This, for a sector that has traditionally been rather fragmented, has presented something of a challenge (Raco, 2003). The Confederation of British Industry (CBI) has introduced an internal devolution, so that its Scottish branch has authority to decide on matters within the remit of the Scottish Parliament. There has been some enhancement of the policy making capacity of its Scottish office and it maintains good links into the relevant departments of the Scottish Government.[3] Over time it has become closer and more influential, as the Scottish Government has emphasised economic growth as its priority. Most of the members of CBI Scotland, however, are British and multinational enterprises and its main policy lines are British. The Institute of Directors represents individuals rather than firms and has traditionally taken a more strictly free-market approach than the CBI. It, too, has introduced internal devolution, but the policy lead comes from London. The Scottish Chambers of Commerce (SCC) is a federation of local chambers and most of the policy leadership comes from the British level, with an input from local chambers, but the SCC does maintain links into the Scottish Government and the parliamentary committees.

Small businesses tend to be Scottish owned and to operate in the Scottish market. They are generally regulated at the UK or European levels but are also dependent on locally produced public goods including grants, infrastructure and the services of Scotland's network of business support agencies. Small business has consequently been rather more favourable to devolution than big business, and its federation enjoyed observer status at the Scottish Constitutional Convention in the 1990s. However, small business has not enjoyed the 'insider' status of larger business organisations such as the CBI; as a result, representative bodies for small businesses have

---

[3] As the Scottish Executive became known in 2007.

had to work harder to engage with the Scottish Parliament. Other groups representing sections of the business community have been forced to engage with devolved government in Scotland as a result of the new policy issues being dealt with.

In agriculture and fisheries, businesses are locally owned and operated, but regulated at Scottish and European levels. The National Farmers Union of Scotland is separate from its English counterpart and presses for the distinct interests of Scottish agriculture. Devolution has reinforced its dual territorial and sectoral concerns, but there are common interests with English farmers, with whom they share an office in Brussels to keep abreast of European matters. In the Highlands and Islands, farmers are organised by the Crofting Foundation, formerly the Crofters' Union. As agriculture is a devolved matter, both unions are closely linked to decision makers in the Scottish Government although less strongly to the Parliament, with its urban bias. At the same time, agricultural policy is highly Europeanised, so farming interests have been very concerned with Scottish representation in the European Union. The Scottish Rural Property and Business Association (SRPBA) (formerly the Scottish Landowners' Federation), which represents large estates, is the equivalent of the Country Land and Business Association (formerly Country Landowners' Association) in England, although they are a separate body, dealing with issues under Scottish law. At one time, they might have been seen as the defenders of the aristocracy and the lairds, and of the old rural order, but in recent years many estates have passed into the hands of capitalist enterprises and are part of big business; the SRPBA now favours foreign ownership of estates as a way to bring in investment. Landowners long enjoyed a rather protected status in Scotland, especially under Conservative governments, but the parties of the centre-left have historically favoured land reform and it was inevitable that this would become a priority issue for the Scottish Parliament. The SRPBA have therefore had to adapt rather quickly to devolution and get into the Scottish political game, by changing their name, broadening their scope and becoming more active at the political level.

Scotland has its own representative organisations in the fisheries sector, although these have traditionally been rather fragmented, by locality and sector. Indeed, for many years, it was the Scottish Office that sought a united lobby to defend Scottish fishing interests in the United Kingdom and in Europe. Now the dominant body is the Scottish Fishermen's Federation, which accounts for about 90 per cent of Scottish fishermen and is the main fishing body in the United Kingdom. The Fishermen's Association Limited, founded in 1995, is formally a UK body with membership extending to Northern Ireland, but is based in Aberdeen. Repeated crises in the fishing industry, and the need to present a united front in Europe, have forced these two groups to co-operate more, despite the legacy of past divisions.

Ironically, the joint effects of devolution and Europeanisation in agriculture and fisheries serve to strengthen the UK level, since the Department of Environment and Rural Affairs (DEFRA) is the nexus of all the networks, supranational, UK and devolved as well as sectoral networks. Scottish agricultural groups often use Scottish Government institutions as allies and as channels of influence to UK and European levels, in much the way that they used the old Scottish Office. Indeed this tendency might have increased, since direct access to Whitehall departments by Scottish farming interests seems to have decreased since devolution.

Trade unions have also been drawn into engaging with the devolved bodies. This partly reflects union support for devolution since the 1960s, and partly reflects a more instrumental concern with policy influence. Most unions are organised on a UK basis, although the STUC is completely separate from the British TUC, with unions affiliating to both. Labour regulation is largely a reserved matter and Scottish unions tend to leave policy making on this issue to the British TUC and the UK level of the unions. However, training policy, local economic development, public sector employment and social issues are devolved, so unions have been drawn into Scottish policy networks. This engagement has also been helped by the attitude of Scottish Labour towards trade unions, which has generally been more positive than that of New Labour in London. A manifestation of this was the signing, in 2002, of a concordat between the STUC and the Scottish Government (then known as the Scottish Executive), providing for regular consultation, including meetings with civil servants.

Individual unions have adapted according to whether they are primarily concerned with reserved or devolved matters. In primary and secondary education, the main union is the Educational Institute of Scotland (EIS) which was established as a professional body by Royal Charter in 1847. Its presence has both enhanced the role of the profession in Scottish policy making and maintained a distinct policy community from the rest of the United Kingdom. Other public sector trade unions need to concern themselves with the Scottish level, which directly affects their members' pay and conditions, but the fact that most wages are still negotiated at a British or UK level means that there is also a strong focus on London. Normally this takes the form of joint negotiating machinery involving Whitehall and the devolved administrations, although there is no obligation on them to agree with each other. If the UK Government were to be successful in decentralising wage bargaining in future, this would no doubt change. However, even before devolution, school teachers' pay and conditions were negotiated separately, and this has remained the case, further maintaining the distinctive independence of the Scottish teaching unions. In contrast, for example, university pay is negotiated on a UK basis and in 2004 this was even extended to take in the old Scottish colleges which became universities in the 1990s.

Other groups have developed UK or Scottish orientations depending on the tier of government responsible for shaping their interests. In many cases, groups have had to adopt, or strengthen, their Scottish orientation as the devolved institutions have gained powers that enable them materially to shape a group's interests. Thus, while Scottish universities see their market in UK terms, and are concerned that educational standards should be equivalent throughout the United Kingdom, they have also been drawn into closer engagement with the devolved institutions, particularly since higher education policy in Scotland has diverged from that in England (Keating, 2005a). The medical profession, too, has supplemented a UK orientation – the regulation of the profession, along with qualifications and training standards, are 'reserved' matters – with a stronger focus on Scottish decision makers. This has largely been due to the adoption of distinctive health policies by the Scottish Government, together with its desire to consult with medical representatives on policy issues.

The voluntary sector retains a Scottish focus, consisting very largely of Scottish groups or autonomous branches of UK bodies, able to take their own policy line. The Scottish Council of Voluntary Organisations (SCVO) found when it tested opinion in 1997 that its members were overwhelmingly in favour of devolution, since it held the promise of more access, more resources and more responsibilities for citizen groups. More generally, the SCVO has pursued the 'new politics', being sceptical towards political parties, professional politicians, local government and the civil service. Before devolution, the Labour government launched a Scottish Compact with the voluntary sector, promising consultation, dialogue and an encouragement to volunteering; it was renewed in 2004. The Scottish Civic Forum, an organisation charged with the task of fostering links between the devolved parliament and civic society, was seen as another important means of access, as were the committees of the Scottish Parliament. There is no doubt that, as a result, the voluntary sector has increased its role in the consultation process and, during the first session of the parliament (1999–2003) was one of the clear gainers from devolution. Since then, a certain disillusion has set in, as the political parties and the civil service have shown their resilience. Moreover, local government remains a rival to the sector in the control of public services and resources, and strongly insists on its representative and democratic credentials. During the second session of the Scottish Parliament (2003–7) the voluntary sector complained about being downgraded in favour of local government, then dominated by the Labour Party (Maxwell, 2007). Voluntary groups, for their part, bemoaned the fact that initiatives from the centre are not always carried through locally as local authorities use their discretion to set their own priorities.

There is a strong elite emphasis on Scotland's place in Europe and we found little evidence of Euroscepticism. The Scotland Act 1998 contains specific provisions for dealing with European matters. We therefore expected to find a deeper involvement in European networks. However, we found that Scottish groups tend to leave European matters to their UK counterparts or to pan-European sectoral groups, although Scotland Europa, based in Brussels, is also used to pursue specifically Scottish issues. It may be that, with the change in government in 1997 and then devolution, there was less interest in trying to by-pass domestic institutions than there had been in the 1980s and early 1990s.

Frames of reference, values and priorities

Scottish identity is so widely shared within Scotland as to be taken for granted (McCrone, 2001) and thus does not provide a discriminating factor among our groups. The meaning and implications of Scottishness, however, are contested. Like other European regions and stateless nations, Scotland has its myths and stories of village life. Scotland is often presented as a small, intimate society in which all the important people know each other, in which communication is easier and in which there is a certain consensus about values, in this case a stronger commitment to the welfare state and collectivism than is found in England. Survey evidence finds a certain limited support for the existence of these core values. People in Scotland are somewhat more inclined to egalitarianism, especially in education, but otherwise are fairly close to the British average in their attitudes (Bennie *et al.*, 1997; Brown *et al.*, 1999). This similarity arises not because of any rightward move in attitudes to welfare policy amongst Scottish people during the 1980s and 1990s, but because, for all the talk of a new Thatcherite consensus, the English and Welsh too remained tied to the old welfare values. Rather, the main difference between Scotland and England lay in the institutional articulation of these values and their reinforcement in Scotland by Scottish national identity. The same might be said of Europe. Scottish electors are at best slightly less Eurosceptic than English ones (Keating, 2009) but there is a strong elite consensus in favour of Europe.

Again, this is tied to the territorial frame of reference, the perception of Scotland as a 'European region'[4] and an object and subject of European policy.

Before devolution, these ideas of Scotland as a haven of social democracy and Europeanism were largely unchallenged and provided common ground for the parties of the centre-left, the trade unions and social interest groups. Business groups, agreeing with this perception of the nation, remained aloof from the home rule coalition, preferring to put their trust in UK Government under the Conservatives. As in other nations, the dominant stereotypes can be given very different policy implications and there is also a right-wing Scottish story in which egalitarianism is seen as the basis for meritocracy and anti-socialism (Reicher and Hopkins, 2001). There was an effort to construct such a counter-discourse in the 1980s, with Margaret Thatcher trying to exploit the legacy of Adam Smith, reinvented as a proto-Thatcherite, and appeals to the stereotypical Scottish values of hard work and financial acumen, but these made almost no headway at all.

Following devolution, groups still occasionally invoke these supposed Scottish values and the routines of village life but do so less easily. The existence of a Scottish political forum has had important effects, not all of which point in the same direction. Institutional change has strengthened an existing Scottish frame of reference. There is a shared emotive commitment to the idea of Scotland and the promotion of Scottish interests and strong pressure on groups to be seen as good citizens in the new devolved situation. The fate of the Conservative Party, which was seen during the 1980s and 1990s as 'anti-Scottish', weighs heavily on some groups and there is a concern to establish their legitimacy and defend themselves in a more exposed political environment. This is reflected in support for symbolic matters like the distinct Scottish bank notes, in instances of corporate philanthropy, and in a willingness to engage in the extensive process of consultation in which the Scottish Government and Parliament have engaged. Groups cannot opt out of Scottish politics as easily as in the past and must address each other's concerns. So business groups will accept the legitimacy of the Scottish Government's social inclusion strategy, while unions and social interest groups will accept the need for economic competitiveness. There is less evidence of old class conflicts than we found in North East England.

Nevertheless, devolution has politicised the policy process, introduced

---

4   At the risk of confusion, we must introduce this term since, from the European perspective, Scotland is treated as a region, as are other stateless nations like Catalonia or the Basque Country.

new actors, and forced actors to face conflicts of interest and competition for resources. Scottish politics before 1999 revolved to a large extent around lobbying the centre. Groups could complain about government policy and blame it on the government in power or London domination generally. From time to time they could combine to promote a shared Scottish interest on matters like public spending, industrial closures or takeovers. Now they are competing within the same policy arena and must come up with their own policy ideas. Many groups, indeed, told us that it was something of a shock to be asked what their own ideas for policy were. As a result, the village story about consensualism will no longer serve its purpose and a new one has to be learnt. Moving from the politics of managed dependency to autonomy, Scotland has become a 'normal' political society in which groups confront each other directly instead of displacing conflict to the outside. This has posed a challenge to some of the more naive analysts who hoped that the new Scottish politics could be based on consensus, banishing partisanship, ideology and lobbying.

On the other hand, there is also a distinct Scottish policy making style involving consultation and working through professional networks. This partly has an institutional explanation. The Scottish Government is descended directly from the Scottish Office, which had little developed policy making capacity since its main task was to adapt and apply Whitehall policies. The Scottish Government, in turn, relies on policy making networks and professional groups to a greater extent than is the case in UK government. It has also been committed to consultation before finalising policies and this has encouraged groups to strengthen their Scottish level of organisation and policy capacity.

We have therefore seen some consolidation of a territorial policy community in Scotland. No group or sector can completely opt out of the Scottish level as happened in the past. This, however, is only one territorial level in a complex multi-level system and different groups are oriented differently. There is some evidence of more inter-sectoral and cross-class dialogue and consultation than in the past, although this may also reflect the arrival in 1997 of the Labour government. While many professional bodies straddle the United Kingdom, adopting the same attitudes on both sides of the border, there is a certain public sector ethos in Scotland and a willingness to accept a larger role for the state and for public provision. Evidence for this is perhaps scanty, but it is consistent. Few doctors availed themselves of the provisions to become fund-holders under the Conservative government before 1997. Scottish hospital consultants in 2003 accepted a contract turned down by their English colleagues because it would interfere with their private practice. Scottish academics show a greater civic commitment and are less likely than their English counterparts to see the university as distinct from the rest of society (Paterson, 2001). The shared Scottish perspective does mean that all groups have to pay attention, at least verbally, to issues of social inclusion as well as economic competition, although we have not found evidence of a distinct Scottish capitalism, more inclined to collectivism and associationalism, such as has been identified in some of the new regionalist literature (Cooke and Morgan, 1998). Again, the linkage of social with economic priorities may reflect the change in governing party in 1997, although some groups told us that their increased standing in the policy networks since devolution had ensured that social issues had a greater salience and there is some evidence that social inclusion has penetrated a rather broad range of policies in Scotland (Keating, 2005b).

North East England

Old networks

The North East has been recognised as a region for the purposes of economic development in successive phases of government policy since the 1930s. Presently it is one of the government's standard English regions, running from the river Tees to the Scottish border. Historically the main question about its boundaries was whether to include Cumbria in the region, though there is also a tradition of localism and a lack of co-operation between the south of the region, based on Teesside, and the Newcastle conurbation. There are certain cultural and identity traits to the region, including a distinct dialect, a political culture dominated by the labour movement, a certain anti-southern sentiment, and some sense of a shared history (Tomaney, 1999). For the most part, however, regional identity has been created through public policy. Economically the region has been dominated by mining, shipbuilding and heavy manufacturing industries which have been in decline since the 1920s and which underwent massive cutbacks in the 1980s. There have not been separate interest groups as in Scotland, but business, unions and social interest groups did establish some regional presence in response to economic decline (for instance collaboration in pursuit of inward investment) (Menu, 2008) and successive government plans for the region.

Attitudes, institutional changes and orientations

A move towards re-establishing regional bodies in the North East was made by John Major's Conservative government in the 1990s. A Government Office for the region was established in 1994 with the task of co-ordinating central government regeneration policies. Calls for elected regional government received conflicting signals from the Labour Party after its election victory in 1997, with some ministers strongly in favour while others were opposed. However the new government did establish Regional Development Agencies (RDAs) in every English region (Bennett and Payne, 2000). In the North East, this built on previous agencies and adopted the name One North East in an effort to give an identity to the region as a whole. At the same time, a Regional Assembly was established, its membership consisting of local government representatives and nominees of business, labour and social organisations, charged with the task of formulating regional strategies and priorities. It was made clear, however, that RDAs were to be business-led and should not be responsible to the assemblies. Meanwhile a Constitutional Convention sought to promote the idea of an elected assembly on a cross-party basis (Tomaney, 2000a, 2000b) and a referendum was set for the autumn of 2004. The rejection of the government's proposals in that referendum[5] (which took place after our fieldwork), means the region still merely has institutions of 'governance', a range of independent agencies without any central political forum or authoritative decision maker. Indeed, the Government Office for the North East, as in England generally, has actually lost some powers and remains separate from the RDA (Mawson and Hall, 2000). Moreover, in 2007, it was announced that the English regional assemblies were to be abolished by 2010.

Nevertheless, the establishment of One North East and the Regional Assembly did lead to some organisational change, especially among groups concerned with economic development. The CBI has strengthened its regional level machinery, as has the TUC, although in both cases policy leadership still comes from London. The Chambers of Commerce within the region have come together to form the North East Chamber of Commerce, located strategically in Durham at the region's geographical centre. Some voluntary groups have also set up regional machinery, although this is rather less extensive.

In the absence of a general level of regional government, it is not

---

5   Held on 4 November 2004. On a turnout of 48 per cent, 22 per cent voted in favour of the elected Assembly, while 78 per cent voted against.

surprising that groups still operate within UK or English sectoral policy frameworks. Business groups take their lead from London, and focus their lobbying on central government as, to a large extent, do trade unions. Voluntary organisations are often tied into local government programmes or only operate at the local level. While some new networks have formed around issues of regional development – facilitated in part by the RDA, the Regional Assembly and Government Office – these are not extensive, and participation tends to be guided largely by instrumental considerations rather than by a territorial loyalty. Our interviews suggested that the nominated Regional Assembly seems to reflect these divisions rather than bringing a new pan-sectoral, territorial perspective. Business organisations are highly sceptical of the Assembly, seeing it as little more than a talking shop, or a way of hamstringing the RDA. Regionalists from the unions had more time for the Assembly, but were concerned about the presence of old Labour politicians with their localist orientation. Representatives of the voluntary sector and social groups welcomed the Assembly, since it gave them a forum for the first time, but they were frustrated at its lack of powers and action.

These attitudes spilled over into the debate about regional government. Business largely opposes political devolution, preferring the existing functional, or administrative, decentralisation, which accords them a guaranteed role (especially through the RDA) and which has a narrow focus on economic development issues. They fear that a regional government would be dominated by the left, whether old guard Labour politicians or new regionalists committed to ideas like social inclusion and sustainable development. This marks a contrast with Scotland, where an elected government has been established because of political pressure, and business groups have been forced to adapt to the new political institutions and their broader policy agendas. Institutional change and the establishment of regional machinery has thus served to strengthen the North East as a framework for interest articulation, but this is stronger in some sectors than in others. The Regional Assembly provides an outlet for voices that previously were not heard and encourages them to operate at the regional level, but the design of the machinery is such that this level of representation is separated from the economic development decisions made in the RDA. The weakness of the regional level means that strong groups, notably those in the business community, can choose whether and when to engage with it. With this exit option, they are not forced into a social dialogue or into policy compromises.

Frames of reference, values and priorities

New regional policy bodies have strengthened the North East region as a frame of reference for groups, although they still use a variety of boundaries and some do not see the region as particularly salient. There are still sharp divisions within the region as well as a marked tendency to think within a national framework. The Regional Development Agencies are overwhelmingly focused on economic development and planning, so it is not surprising that where the region features, it is above all as a framework for development policy and infrastructure planning. In this field, there has been a marked territorialisation of interest representation. There is wide agreement, inspired by experience in Scotland and in other European regions, that effective development needs a regional approach, with co-ordinated efforts in infrastructure provision, business promotion and training. The North East RDA – One North East – has become an accepted part of the institutional landscape and all the groups we interviewed wanted to keep it. This included business groups, who parted company on this issue with the Conservative Party, when it promised at the 2001 general election to abolish the RDAs. There has been some concern to promote a shared image of the region, mainly aimed at attracting inward investment. Sabine Menu (2008) found economic actors, both in business and the development agency, stressing the importance of territorial loyalty, the virtues of the workforce and the need to valorise the industrial tradition of the region. They also emphasised the small size of the region and the ease of communication as well as competition with Scotland.

Groups also share a concern about manufacturing industry and its neglect by governments dependent on votes in the south, as well as a marked resentment of the supposed advantages of Scotland in public spending. There is a strong sense of regional economic interest and of an economic development community with a shared agenda. Business and trade unions share much of the same productivist orientation, stressing investment and jobs. This does not, however, produce a shared project for society or even for the government of the region. Pro-development groups confine themselves rather carefully to a functional, economic regionalism and try to avoid commitment to broader social or environmental goals. This can bring them into conflict with environmental groups and voluntary groups who stress issues of sustainable development, social justice and redistribution. Within the dominant political party, Labour, there is a strong localism, a focus on the politics of distribution and clientelism, and a suspicion of regionalism. Some of the trade unions, notably the public sector union Unison, have an altogether broader vision, encompassing both economic and social issues and this, together with the voluntary sector, has provided the basis for the regional government movement that has sought to move beyond functional regionalism or development politics into a more expansive political agenda.

The participation of groups in the Regional Assembly and its committees was thus uneven. While the consultative mechanisms are in principle inclusive, business groups were less assiduous attenders and focused more on their direct links to central and local government, where they are already entrenched. The failure of the devolution referendum in 2004 may have owed something to the failure to construct a distinct regional civil society and shared identity. Certainly, during our fieldwork we did not detect a large degree of buy-in to this project, as opposed to narrower forms of functional regionalism. In turn the failure of the referendum has weakened the political dimension of regionalism, while the imminent demise of the Regional Assembly will remove another focus for common interest formation and intermediation.

Conclusions

Our research confirms that territory and function are now combined in complex ways in interest representation. The two cases of adaptation of territorial communities to institutional change that we have examined have served to substantiate some of our original hypotheses. The legacies of the past are important. Scotland has a civil society differentiated from that of the rest of the United Kingdom, which the North East of England lacks. This, together with a thirty-year debate about devolution, has prepared Scottish groups for change and eased adaptation to the formal devolution of political power. Devolution has stimulated organisational change, with a strengthening of the resources groups deploy at the Scottish level. At the same time, constraints of time and resources have forced groups to specialise, and especially so in Scotland where they have been drawn into the policy process. This has left less time for general lobbying, while producing a certain disengagement from wider UK matters, and a surprising neglect of the European dimension.

At the same time, devolution has altered the frames of reference of groups, albeit in somewhat different ways in the two territories. It has strengthened the territorial frame of reference in both, but this is most apparent in Scotland where the devolution settlement has left large areas of public policy regulated almost exclusively at the Scottish level by Scottish institutions. The wide responsibilities and symbolic importance of the

Scottish Parliament further encourage groups to focus attention on it, even concerning matters beyond its competence. In North East England, the Regional Development Agency and Regional Assembly have strengthened the territorial frame of reference, but this is more so in respect of economic development issues than in other policy fields.

Devolution has increased politicisation within territorial communities. Old assumptions about common values and territorial interests have been challenged as groups have to compete at the same spatial level. This is most obvious in Scotland, given the broad powers of the Parliament and the relatively self-contained policy community. In a system of full legislative devolution, as in Scotland, groups are not able to opt out or bypass the devolved institutions by going to London, as in the past, so they are forced to confront each other. This development has heightened levels of political competition, but also provided mechanisms – through the devolved institutions and associated networks – for resolving the resulting conflicts. In North East England, by contrast, the Regional Assembly has helped politicise the debate on regional development strategies by giving a platform to new actors, but it does not have the authority to resolve issues. Business, which has a privileged position within the Regional Development Agency, can opt out of broader territorial politics almost at will, and its opposition to elected regional government is an effort to prevent further politicisation of regional policy making. So it does seem that territorial *government*, elected and with broad powers, is not the same as *governance* where this notoriously vague term refers to an array of self-regulating agencies and public–private partnerships.

There is some evidence that territorial policy communities may reinforce social solidarity at the regional level, although this conclusion must remain tentative. The acceptance of social inclusion as an integral part of the regional development strategy, at least at the level of verbal commitment, may reflect a sense of shared territorial identity in Scotland that does not exist to the same extent in North East England. More likely, the explanation is institutional and related to the factor discussed above: the existence of a shared political community and the need to make social compromises at the territorial level. Actors are forced to address each others' concerns and to establish a degree of political legitimacy by accepting territorial commitments. It is also necessary to make the classic trade-offs between development and social solidarity at the territorial level in order to gain consensus on policy development. So business groups in Scotland accept, at least in principle, the legitimacy of social inclusion as an element in development policy, while their equivalents in North East England insist that their sole concern is economic growth, with issues of social inclusion, as well as environmental matters, to be taken care of by central and local governments. This is not to say that Scotland will pursue more socially inclusive forms of development in substance since that depends on other factors (see Keating, 2005b for a fuller treatment of this theme). Yet it does seem to suggest that territorial government produces different forms of politics and social dialogue from those arising in sectoralised systems of governance. The failure of the devolution referendum in North East England in 2004 has further weakened the political dimension in the region's system of functional devolution and the announcement in 2007 that the English regional assemblies are to be abolished by 2010 will reinforce the narrower vocation of the remaining institutions.

References

Bennett, R. and D. Payne (2000) *Local and Economic Regional Development: Renegotiating Power Under Labour*, Aldershot: Ashgate

Bennie, L., J. Brand and J. Mitchell (1997) *How Scotland Votes*, Manchester: Manchester University Press

Brown, A., D. McCrone and L. Paterson (1996) *Politics and Society in Scotland*, London: Macmillan

Brown, A. *et al.* (1999) *The Scottish Electorate: The 1997 General Election and Beyond*, London: Macmillan

Cooke, P. and K. Morgan (1998) *The Associational Economy: Firms, Regions and Innovation*, Oxford: Oxford University Press

Durkheim, E. (1964) *The Division of Labour in Society*, New York: Free Press

Keating, M. (1975) *The Role of the Scottish MP*, PhD thesis, Glasgow College of Technology and CNAA

Keating, M. (1998) *The New Regionalism in Western Europe: Territorial Restructuring and Political Change*, Aldershot: Edward Elgar

Keating, M. (2005a) 'Higher education policy in Scotland and England after devolution', *Regional and Federal Studies*, 14.4

Keating, M. (2005b) *The Government of Scotland: Public Policy-Making after Devolution*, Edinburgh: Edinburgh University Press

Keating, M. (2009) *The Independence of Scotland: Self-government and the Shifting Politics of Union*, Oxford: Oxford University Press

Keating, M. and D. Bleiman (1979) *Labour and Scottish Nationalism*, London: Macmillan

Kellas, J. (1989) *The Scottish Political System* (4th edn), Cambridge:

Cambridge University Press

Loughlin, J. (2001) *Subnational Democracy in the European Union: Challenges and Opportunities,* Oxford: Oxford University Press

Lynch, P. (1998), 'Reactive capital: The Scottish business community and devolution', in H. Elcock and M. Keating, eds, *Remaking the Union: Devolution and British Politics in the 1990s,* London: Frank Cass

Mawson, J. and S. Hall (2000) 'Joining it up locally? Area regeneration and holistic government in England', *Regional Studies,* 34:1

Maxwell, S. (2007) 'Social democracy and the voluntary sector in devolved Scotland', in M. Keating, ed., *Scottish Social Democracy,* Brussels: PIE-Peter Lang

McCrone, D. (2001) *Understanding Scotland: The Sociology of a Nation,* London: Routledge

Menu, S. (2008) *La Formation des Mobilisations Economiques et le Rôle de l'Identité dans Trois Régions Européennes – Nord Est Angleterre, Bretagne et Bavière (1980–2006),* PhD thesis, Institut d'Etudes Politiques de Paris

Midwinter, A., M. Keating and J. Mitchell (1991) *Politics and Public Policy in Scotland,* London: Macmillan

Moore, C. and S. Booth (1989) *Managing Competition: Meso-Corporatism, Pluralism and the Negotiated Order in Scotland,* Oxford: Clarendon

Paterson, L. (1994) *The Autonomy of Modern Scotland,* Edinburgh: Edinburgh University Press

Paterson, L. (2001) 'Higher education and European regionalism', *Pedagogy, Culture and Society,* 9:2

Raco, M. (2003) 'The social relations of business representation and devolved governance in the UK', *Environment and Planning A,* 35:10

Reicher, S. and N. Hopkins (2001) *Self and Nation,* London: Sage

Rhodes, R. A. W. (1981) *Control and Power in Central–Local Relations,* Aldershot: Gower

Rhodes, R. A. W. and D. Marsh (1992) 'Policy networks in Britain', in D. Marsh and R. A. W. Rhodes, eds, *Policy Networks in British Government,* Oxford: Clarendon

Richardson, J. and G. Jordan (1979) *Governing Under Pressure: The Policy Process in a Post-Parliamentary Democracy,* Oxford: Robertson

Scott, A. (1998) *Regions and the World Economy,* Oxford: Oxford University Press

Sharpe, L. J. (1993) 'The European meso: An appraisal', in L. J. Sharpe, ed., *The Rise of Meso Government in Europe,* London: Sage

Tomaney, J. (1999) 'In search of English regionalism: The case of the North East', *Scottish Affairs,* 28, summer

Tomaney, J. (2000a) 'Democratically elected government in England: The

work of the North-East Constitutional Convention', *Regional Studies*, 34:4
Tomaney, J. (2000b) 'The regional governance of England', in R. Hazell, ed., *The State and the Nations: The First Year of Devolution in the United Kingdom*, Thorverton: Imprint Academic
Wright, M. and S. Wilks (1987) *Comparative Government–Industry Relations: Western Europe, the United States and Japan*, Oxford: Clarendon Press

4

The politicians' response to devolution

Meg Russell and Akash Paun

Devolution to Scotland and Wales in 1999 constituted a historic redistribution of power from the centre to the periphery of the British state. At the time, expectations conferred on the new institutions in Edinburgh and Cardiff varied widely. To its proponents, devolution would lead to better policies and governance for Scotland and Wales, thereby weakening nationalism and strengthening the Union. Unionist opponents – at both ends of the political spectrum – claimed the opposite: devolution would create an unnecessary and wasteful new tier of government and could prove a slippery slope to territorial conflict and potential fragmentation of the United Kingdom. Nationalist critics also predicted that the new institutions would prove unsatisfactory, and that they would be no more than a stepping stone to further autonomy and eventual independence for Scotland and Wales.

Today, nearly a decade on, the devolved institutions are generally accepted to be permanent parts of the constitutional furniture. But opinions vary widely as to how successful they have been and what further reforms should be made to their powers and institutional design. Other chapters in this volume focus on the views of interest groups and citizens as to how devolution has worked in practice. In this chapter we pose the question of whether devolution is perceived to be a success by the politicians themselves, specifically by Members of the Scottish Parliament (MSPs) and the National Assembly for Wales (AMs) elected in 1999 and 2003. MSPs and AMs obviously have a unique inside perspective on the functioning of the devolved institutions. As a result their views may be considered important because they are better informed than the opinions of voters and pressure groups, though they may also be biased in various ways. But politicians' views – gathered here in postal surveys that covered various aspects of the operation and achievements of the new devolved bodies – are also a useful tool for explaining the political pressures around devolution that have emerged since 1999, notably the debate that led to the second Government of Wales Act in 2006, and the initiatives established after the 2007 election to review the powers of the Scottish Parliament.

Our postal surveys focused on three central research questions. The first was the extent to which members considered the devolved bodies had delivered specific benefits to the people of Scotland and Wales, such as policy improvements, better public access to government institutions, or a stronger 'voice' for Scotland and Wales. Here, we included some questions that were asked in the public attitudes surveys reported in Chapter 5, thereby allowing direct comparison between elite and popular views. The second research question was whether members believed the new institutions had improved the process of governance, for example by creating a more inclusive and open political system, an objective to which many proponents of devolution had aspired. Finally we wanted to assess devolved members' views about the powers and structure of their institutions, and whether they would support specific further reforms. Here again we draw some comparisons with public opinion.

What might we expect to find in the responses to such questions? One result that could be anticipated is a clear difference between respondents in Scotland and Wales. The original devolution legislation of 1998 created a powerful Scottish Parliament, but a Welsh Assembly with far more limited power and autonomy. We might therefore expect to see more positive responses from Scottish members about the policy achievements of their institution. The planning of the Scottish Parliament was also carefully considered long in advance, through bodies such as the Scottish Constitutional Convention (1995) and the Consultative Steering Group (1998). There were serious attempts to create a 'new politics' that was more open and participative than at Westminster. Less long-term planning went into the Welsh Assembly, which might lead us also to expect more positive responses from Scottish members about the style of politics in their institution.

Of course, MSPs and AMs are members not only of their respective legislatures but also of political parties, and their opinions are likely to reflect this in significant ways. In particular, we would expect to see differences between members of parties that supported devolution from the start (Labour and the Liberal Democrats) and those that opposed it (the Conservatives). The responses of nationalist members, meanwhile, would be expected to reflect their parties' ambivalence towards the new settlements: critical of the extent of power devolved while in favour of the trend towards more autonomy. Another significant cleavage – which largely maps onto the pro- versus anti-devolution split – is that between members of parties in government at the time of the surveys and members in opposition. On the whole, Labour and Liberal Democrat members would therefore be expected to report more positive views about the performance of the devolved bodies. The party that someone represents is especially likely to be relevant in the case of questions on openly partisan issues such as the policy performance of the devolved bodies or the need for greater autonomy in Scotland and Wales. The more interesting survey findings will often be those where members of a party are in disagreement with one another, or where members diverge from a party's public position. On matters where this occurs, or where there is unexpected cross-party consensus, the findings can more readily be taken at face value.

The following section gives further detail about our methodology. The survey findings are then discussed in detail in three substantive sections, reflecting the three core questions set out above. The first covers questions about the effectiveness of the devolved bodies in delivering improvements for the people of Scotland and Wales. The second discusses the devolved institutions' effectiveness at meeting seven key governance challenges. The last main section looks at members' views on the powers of their institutions and about future reform. A brief conclusion reflects upon the extent to which our expectations were borne out by the data, and what our results suggest about the prospects for the future.

Sources and methodology

The data in this chapter are drawn from three postal surveys sent to all MSPs and AMs in November 2000, October 2002, and June 2004.[1] Most, though not all, of the questions were included in all three surveys, enabling us to track trends in elite opinion over time. The data allow us to compare the views of MSPs and AMs, the views of members of different parties, and in some cases – due to the replication of questions asked on public opinion surveys (see Chapter 5) – the views of elected representatives with those of the general public in Scotland and Wales. However, one feature to note at the outset is the low number of cases in any survey of the members of the devolved institutions. The Scottish Parliament and Welsh Assembly are small, with 129 and 60 members respectively. Thus, while the response

---

[1] These surveys were funded by the Leverhulme 'Nations and Regions' programme and, from 2002, the ESRC's 'Devolution and Constitutional Change' programme. In 2002 the surveys were conducted by Oonagh Gay and Jonathan Bradbury (at which point some of the questions were changed slightly). We gratefully acknowledge their involvement in collecting these data.

rates to our survey were fairly good – between 36 and 55 per cent – the 'raw' number of cases is limited (ranging from 26 to 35 in the case of AMs, and 47 to 63 in the case of MSPs). The Annex shows the detailed response rates from each party in each institution. In the case of the smaller party groups in particular we inevitably only have responses from a handful of members. In the tables in this chapter, figures based on only three or four members are indicated by giving figures in parentheses, while where even fewer responses were received (principally for independents, members of minor parties, and in 2000 the Welsh Conservatives), figures are not shown. Also, because the response rates of elected members from different parties varied, the distribution of members by party in our sample did not match exactly that in the institutions themselves. Thus the 'Total' rows in the tables (which take into account all responses, including those from very small groups whose detailed figures are not shown) have been weighted to correct for this imbalance.

The delivery challenge: meeting the expectations of the voters

Perhaps the most important test for devolution is whether it manages to deliver concrete benefits to the people of Scotland and Wales. This was the promise of, for example, the Scottish Constitutional Convention whose final report claimed that 'A Scottish Parliament will be able to make a real difference to the prosperity of the Scottish people, and to the quality of the life they lead' (Scottish Constitutional Convention, 1995: 3). Complementing the public opinion data discussed in Chapter 5, our surveys asked MSPs and AMs two sets of questions about the impact of the devolved institutions. First, in 2000 only, members were asked the same question as the public about the expected impact of the Parliament/Assembly, namely whether having a Scottish Parliament or Welsh Assembly would increase or reduce Scotland/Wales's voice in the United Kingdom, the say of ordinary people in how Scotland/Wales is governed, the standard of education in Scotland/Wales and the health of Scotland/Wales's economy. The answers, including a breakdown by party, are shown in Table 4.1. The second set of questions was included in all three surveys and asked about the impact of devolution in practice. These data are presented in Table 4.2 below.

Overall, Table 4.1 shows a positive attitude among MSPs and AMs in response to all our questions. Expectations were clearly high at this point, a year and a half after the first devolved elections. Indeed, in both cases, expectations were higher than they were among the general public at this

Table 4.1   Anticipated impact of the Scottish Parliament and Welsh Assembly, 2000

		Scotland (%)	*Wales (%)*
Having a Parliament/ Assembly is going to increase:			
The strength of Scotland/Wales's voice in the UK	Labour	79	90
	SNP/Plaid Cymru	55	91
	Liberal Democrat	86	(100)
	Conservative	54	–
	Total	70	93
Ordinary people's say in how Scotland/Wales is governed	Labour	100	90
	SNP/Plaid Cymru	95	100
	Liberal Democrat	100	(100)
	Conservative	69	–
	Total	94	95
The standard of education in Scotland/Wales	Labour	100	100
	SNP/Plaid Cymru	59	100
	Liberal Democrat	100	(100)
	Conservative	23	–
	Total	78	85
The health of the Scottish/ Welsh economy	Labour	84	100
	SNP/Plaid Cymru	45	91
	Liberal Democrat	86	(100)
	Conservative	39	–
	Total	68	82

Note: Figures show the percentage of respondents who indicated that the devolved institutions would 'greatly increase' or 'increase' performance. Brackets indicate the figure is based on less than five respondents.

stage.[2] This is understandable given voter cynicism and the much greater closeness of politicians to the process. But contrary to our expectations above – given the greater strength of the Scottish devolved bodies and the higher level of public support in Scotland for devolution – Welsh members

[2]   These figures are derived from a comparison of the weighted elite opinion data in Table 4.1 with the public opinion data presented in Chapter 5. See especially Table 5.6 for equivalent data for 2000 in Scotland and 5.5 for 1999 data in Wales. Note, however, that not all wordings of the questions were exactly the same, and that, in Wales, comparison can only be made with data collected in 1999.

had higher expectations than Scottish ones. This largely reflects a more positive attitude to devolution amongst Plaid Cymru members as compared with SNP members, in line with the differing official policy positions of their parties.

Our data also show, however, the predicted pattern of difference between the parties on some questions. On the potential of the institutions to deliver better policy outcomes, opposition parties in both Scotland and Wales were less likely to hold positive views. In line with the party's public position of opposition to devolution the Conservatives in Scotland were largely negative on the question of whether the Scottish Parliament would improve the standard of education or the health of the economy. Likewise, SNP members, whose party favoured independence from the United Kingdom rather than devolution within it, were less optimistic than members of the pro-devolution Labour and Liberal Democrats. On the other hand, Plaid Cymru representatives were largely positive. Nonetheless, a majority in all parties – whether pro- or anti-devolution – stated a belief that devolution would strengthen Scotland or Wales's voice in the United Kingdom and increase ordinary people's say in how they are governed. In Wales, the support for these propositions was overwhelming in all parties, the result perhaps of a perception that the position of Wales in the Union was weak (and weaker than that of Scotland) prior to devolution. This was certainly a common view among scholars of pre-1999 territorial arrangements in the United Kingdom (e.g. Griffiths, 1999: 803–4).[3]

Providing an interesting contrast with the data on expected impact in Table 4.1, all three surveys sought members' opinions on whether the devolved bodies had in fact delivered on public expectations in four key areas. Specifically, the questions asked whether the Scottish Parliament or Welsh Assembly had 'met the expectations of those who voted for it' in terms of 'policy outputs', 'public control and participation', 'demonstrating "new politics" distinct from Westminster' and 'strengthening the voice of Scotland/Wales in the United Kingdom'. In general, these questions appear at best to have evoked an ambivalent response in both Scotland and Wales, and this mood changed little between 2000 and 2004 (Table 4.2).

---

[3] The summary figures in the table fact tend to mask the true extent of the difference between members' views in Scotland and Wales. In Wales, many more respondents thought the Assembly would 'greatly increase' the factor concerned. For example, at least half of Labour, Conservative and Liberal Democrat members thought the Assembly would 'greatly' increase Wales's voice in the United Kingdom. This contrasted with only 10 per cent of Labour members, and no Conservative or Liberal Democrat members, in Scotland.

Lying behind this overall picture are, however, significant differences between the parties, together with some key differences between Scotland and Wales.

So far as policy outputs are concerned the overall figures imply disappointment. However, they also exhibit the anticipated split between executive and non-executive parties. Opposition party members were reluctant to admit to any success in this area; in 2004, just three of 33

Table 4.2   Evaluations of the success of the Scottish Parliament and Welsh Assembly at meeting public expectations, 2000–4

		Scotland			Wales		
		2000 (%)	2002 (%)	2004 (%)	2000 (%)	2002 (%)	2004 (%)
The Parliament/ Assembly has met public expectations in terms of:							
Policy outputs	Labour	61	62	45	30	40	75
	SNP/Plaid Cymru	18	6	0	9	9	0
	Liberal Democrat	43	(25)	43	(0)	(50)	(25)
	Conservative	15	13	9	–	(25)	(0)
	Total	42	36	27	24	30	41
Public control and participation	Labour	61	46	45	56	67	69
	SNP/Plaid Cymru	27	6	27	46	18	0
	Liberal Democrat	71	(50)	71	(33)	(50)	(25)
	Conservative	15	13	18	–	(75)	(0)
	Total	48	31	40	42	52	38
New politics	Labour	74	54	40	60	73	75
	SNP/Plaid Cymru	41	17	0	45	9	0
	Liberal Democrat	57	(0)	29	(33)	(75)	(25)
	Conservative	8	13	9	–	(33)	(25)
	Total	54	31	24	52	49	45
Strengthening the voice of Scotland/ Wales in the UK	Labour	Na	62	75	Na	93	81
	SNP/Plaid Cymru	Na	17	18	Na	18	17
	Liberal Democrat	Na	(50)	71	Na	(75)	(50)
	Conservative	Na	25	0	Na	(50)	(25)
	Total	Na	44	48	Na	64	54

Note: For 2000, figures show the percentage of respondents who indicated they 'strongly agree' or 'agree' the Parliament/Assembly had met the public's expectations. For 2002 and 2004, they show the percentage who indicated the Parliament/ Assembly had met the public's expectations 'a great deal' or 'quite a lot'. Brackets indicate the figure is based on less than five respondents. Na=Not asked.

opposition MSPs agreed that the Scottish Parliament had met the public's policy expectations, as did just one opposition member in Wales (a member of the Liberal Democrats, the party having left government a year previously). However, while this split occurs in both Scotland and Wales, the trend in the two countries is different. In 2000, MSPs were more positive than AMs, but by 2004 this situation was reversed.

A major reason for this divergence was a change in the attitudes of Labour members; Labour MSPs' attitudes became more negative over time, whilst Labour AMs' views grew more positive. This may well tell a story about the respective policy agendas and political styles of Labour's leaders in Scotland and Wales. The defining metaphor of Rhodri Morgan's Welsh Assembly Government – in contrast to his predecessor Alun Michael – was to put 'clear red water' between his government and that of Tony Blair (Morgan, 2002). In practice, this involved policies such as scrapping league tables for schools, and introducing free prescriptions and eye tests, talismanic policies for Labour's traditional wing. This appears to have been appreciated by Labour AMs, while alienating other parties' members. In contrast Jack McConnell (Scottish First Minister between 2001 and 2007) was not generally regarded as being willing to advertise differences between Scottish and UK government policy, and was regarded less fondly than the 'father of devolution', Donald Dewar, who died shortly before our 2000 survey. Moreover, the best known of the policy differences that did occur in Scotland – the abolition of university tuition fees and the introduction of free long-term care for the elderly – were primarily Liberal Democrat policies to which some in the Labour party had only acceded reluctantly. Equally, perhaps the most innovative policy decision taken under McConnell's leadership, the 2004 legislation introducing proportional representation for local council elections, was a touchstone policy for the Liberal Democrats, and was forced upon Labour as a condition of the 2003 Partnership Agreement between the parties. But while this history may help account for the declining enthusiasm of Labour MSPs, it is noteworthy that the policy gains made by the Liberal Democrats in Scotland generated relatively little enthusiasm amongst the party's own MSPs.

There were also decidedly mixed views in both Scotland and Wales as to whether the devolved institutions had met expectations in respect of public control and participation, with once again a clear divide between executive and non-executive parties. Labour members (and Liberal Democrats in Scotland), who in practice were more likely to have been involved in public consultation activities as part of the Executive, were relatively positive on this point. The opposition parties tended to be more negative. As in the case of policy influence, the figures for Labour members also show an increase in confidence among Welsh members while Scottish members became more disappointed. Deteriorating opinions among Labour members could in part reflect disappointment at the performance of the Parliament's petitions procedures and the extent of public participation in committee proceedings. It is clear from the data that at the end of our survey period a majority of MSPs did not feel that the Scottish Parliament was living up to the high expectations that had been set for it in terms of increasing public involvement.

Increased public participation was intended to form one plank of the 'new politics' – more inclusive, consensual, responsive and accountable than Westminster – that devolution would create in Scotland and Wales (the reality of which was assessed, in somewhat sceptical terms, by Mitchell, 2000, and McAllister, 2000). When asked whether public expectations of 'new politics' had been met, views again revealed some apparent disappointment amongst members. In both institutions, Labour members were more positive than others, but even here there were clear signs of disappointment, particularly in Scotland. By 2004, only 40 per cent of Labour MSPs felt that expectations of 'new politics' had been met. The Conservatives and the nationalist parties had always been sceptical of this concept, so their largely negative responses are not surprising. However, after 2002, severe doubts about the ability of devolution to deliver the 'new politics' also set in among Liberal Democrat MSPs.

In 2002, a new question was added to our survey, asking whether devolution was strengthening the voice of Scotland and Wales in the United Kingdom. As already shown in Table 4.1, in 2000 expectations that this would be achieved were high, with a clear majority of members from all parties believing that devolution would have a positive impact. Our 2002 and 2004 data reveal that the reality of devolution was not thought to have lived up to these high hopes. In Scotland in both years, fewer than half our respondents felt that this had been achieved. In Wales, the figures were slightly higher but still fell well short of AMs' earlier expectations. As in the case of the other questions in Table 4.2, a clear divide is present between government and opposition members. Nationalist members were overwhelmingly negative, which is perhaps unsurprising given their parties' views that devolution granted insufficient autonomy to Scotland and Wales and their repeated claims that the predominantly Labour-run executives had been weak at defending their nations' interests in negotiations with the UK Government. Nevertheless, the 17 per cent of Plaid Cymru members who in 2004 believed that Wales's voice had been strengthened stood in remarkable contrast to the 91 per cent who in 2000 had expected this to happen. In contrast, Labour MSPs and AMs remained mostly positive. This may partly reflect the fact that intergovernmental negotiations, where the devolved nations' distinct voices should be heard, were often conducted through informal or intra-Labour party channels, a process that excluded opposition members (Trench, 2005). But of course Labour and nationalist members were also likely to have different conceptions of what public expectations were, and of how much of a 'stronger voice' was desirable.

So we have uncovered a striking discrepancy between members' generally high expectations at the outset of devolution and their disappointment with what was actually achieved. In Wales in particular, almost all members expected devolution to deliver benefits to the people of Wales; only the Conservatives did not fully share this optimism. Somewhat fewer members in Scotland had high expectations, but overall views were nonetheless positive. The perceived reality of devolution, however, appears to have fallen well short of these expectations. After 2000, MSPs grew significantly more negative in their assessment of its results, a decline that was particularly noticeable among Labour members, indicating a sense of unfulfilled potential among the party's MSPs. In Wales, the pattern was rather different, with a growing polarisation between Labour members – who became more positive – and the rest. Whether this scepticism about the outputs of devolution corresponds with a general dissatisfaction with the way the devolved institutions operated is the question to which we turn in the following section.

The governance challenge: better than Westminster?

As already mentioned, the new devolved bodies were intended not only to bring policy improvements to Scotland and Wales, but also a 'new politics' distinct from British Westminster traditions. The aspiration to a new politics was set out most clearly in the report of the Consultative Steering Group (CSG) in Scotland, which stated that four key principles would govern the operation of the new Parliament. These would be power sharing, accountability, openness and accessibility, and equal opportunities (Consultative Steering Group, 1998). Similarly, devolution in Wales was intended by Ron Davies – its chief political architect – to be driven by values such as openness, inclusiveness and co-operation (Laffin and Thomas, 2000: 559). In both Scotland and Wales, the new institutions were explicitly designed to embody these values. This in turn was expected to result in more accountable, inclusive and responsible government. Our surveys therefore included a number of questions about the style and machinery of governing used by the Parliament and Assembly, in order to gauge the extent to which these aspirations were realised. In both Scotland and Wales respondents were asked their views on the institutions' effectiveness in seven key areas of governance.

Our first set of questions address four 'internal' factors in the functioning of the Parliament and Assembly: the ability of the institutions to hold the Executive to account, to influence legislation, to initiate policy and to give backbenchers a role in policy making. As can be seen from Table 4.3, the overall responses on these points varied. Both institutions

Table 4.3 Evaluations of the 'internal governance' performance of the Scottish Parliament and Welsh Assembly, 2000–4

		Scotland			*Wales*		
		2000 (%)	*2002* (%)	*2004* (%)	*2000* (%)	*2002* (%)	*2004* (%)
The Parliament/ Assembly has been effective in:							
Holding the	Labour	95	92	90	90	81	60
Executive to	SNP/Plaid Cymru	82	61	82	45	45	17
account	Liberal Democrat	86	(75)	57	(100)	(0)	(75)
	Conservative	46	56	55	–	(75)	(0)
	Total	84	77	76	72	62	42
Influencing	Labour	84	100	84	60	56	44
legislation	SNP/Plaid Cymru	64	39	45	18	9	0
	Liberal Democrat	86	(75)	100	(100)	(50)	(25)
	Conservative	54	33	45	–	0	(0)
	Total	75	70	65	43	34	25
Initiating policy	Labour	68	62	55	50	75	63
	SNP/Plaid Cymru	18	22	27	27	25	50
	Liberal Democrat	57	(25)	43	(100)	(75)	(50)
	Conservative	67	44	18	–	(25)	(0)
	Total	51	43	39	41	54	47
Giving backbenchers	Labour	32	54	45	30	63	44
a role in policy	SNP/Plaid Cymru	9	22	9	36	18	0
making	Liberal Democrat	57	(25)	57	(100)	(50)	(25)
	Conservative	23	22	9	–	(25)	(0)
	Total	27	37	31	34	43	25

Note: For 2000, figures show the percentage of respondents who indicated that the Parliament/Assembly had been 'very effective' or 'quite effective'. For 2002 and 2004, they show the percentage who indicated the Parliament/Assembly had succeeded 'a great deal' or 'quite a lot'. Brackets indicate the figure is based on less than five respondents.

were initially seen as good at holding the Executive to account, but there was a clear decline over time in Wales. The Scottish Parliament was generally regarded as successful at influencing legislation, the Welsh Assembly far less so. In both institutions, responses on initiating policy and giving backbenchers a role were relatively negative from the outset and certainly did not become markedly more positive. However, to gain a better understanding of what lies behind these responses it is again necessary to look at AMs' and MSPs' views broken down by political party group, as the overall figures mask big differences between the parties.

In both nations, there is a clear difference between government and opposition members in perceptions of their institutions' ability to hold the Executive to account. This is particularly clear in Wales, where opposition members had relatively negative views from the beginning and simply grew more negative over time. This was a period when relations between the government and opposition parties on the cross-party Business Committee broke down, and Labour controversially decided to reduce the frequency of Assembly committee meetings (Osmond and Mugaseth, 2003: 17–21). But the opposition parties' attitudes are not enough to explain the sharp overall decline seen in Wales between 2000 and 2004. The perception of unaccountable government was increasingly shared by at least some on the Labour benches; the proportion of Labour AMs believing the Assembly effective in holding the government to account fell from 90 per cent in 2000 to 60 per cent in 2004. The increasingly negative views of AMs across all parties may tally with the realisation that the original Welsh devolution model, which combined the Assembly and Executive in a single 'corporate body' and where Assembly ministers sat on subject committees alongside 'backbenchers', did not make for effective accountability (Richard Commission, 2004: paragraph 36). Indeed, the consensus on this issue led to the formal division of the Assembly and Assembly Government in the 2006 Government of Wales Act.

In Scotland, views on this question remained relatively upbeat. Significantly, members of the SNP – and to a lesser extent the Conservative Party – remained largely positive about the Parliament's success in holding the Executive to account. This suggests that non-executive MSPs considered themselves able to perform effectively the traditional 'Westminster' role of the opposition – that is, to oppose, if not necessarily to make a constructive contribution to, the government's agenda. Curiously, the one party amongst whom concerns about accountability seem to have grown somewhat was the Liberal Democrats; perhaps this reflects some concern among the party's backbenchers about their ability as junior coalition partners to influence the Executive's agenda.

There is an important distinction between the next two subjects covered by our surveys: the effectiveness of the devolved bodies in influencing legislation and initiating policy. The latter relates to the proactive ability of the Scottish Parliament and Welsh Assembly to set the policy agenda, the former to reacting to initiatives of the Executive. However, our figures show that the Scottish Parliament was deemed far more effective at influencing legislation than at initiating policy. In Wales, by contrast, views incline to the opposite. The low rating of the Assembly on influencing legislation is unsurprising given its lack of primary legislative powers and difficulties in influencing legislation passed at Westminster (though this may not necessarily explain why the views of AMs became more negative over time). Legislative dependence on the UK Parliament has been a consistent concern of Welsh politicians (e.g. Richard Commission, 2004) and was addressed, at least in part, in the Government of Wales Act 2006. What is perhaps more noteworthy is that despite its limited legislative role and sphere of policy competence, by 2002 the Assembly was just as likely as the Scottish Parliament to be deemed effective by its members at initiating policy.

Members were also asked whether devolution had been effective at giving backbenchers a role in policy making. The Scottish Parliament in particular was explicitly intended to ensure 'that a positive and constructive role will be played in its business by all its elected members' (Scottish Constitutional Convention, 1995: 8). Great emphasis was placed on the devolved legislatures' strong committee systems, in which executive and legislative scrutiny were brought together, and committees had more powers than their counterparts at Westminster. For example the Scottish parliamentary committees were given the ability – not available at Westminster – to initiate legislation (Arter, 2004: 74–6).

However, there seems to have been disappointment among MSPs and AMs about backbenchers' policy influence. Overall, only around a third of members had a favourable view on this point, with members of opposition parties even less positive. For example, in 2004, a positive response was received from only one of fourteen opposition AMs and four of 33 opposition MSPs. Such a pattern of responses may of course simply be motivated by partisan considerations. Or it may reflect efforts by the respective executives to include their backbench members in intra-party discussions, and the greater ability of government party members to influence committee recommendations. But whatever the reason, it hardly suggests that this element of 'power-sharing' between executive and legislature has been a huge success in either Scotland or Wales.

We also questioned members about three aspects of their institution's external relations: the ability of the institutions to involve ordinary people in policy making, to involve outside bodies in policy making, and to communicate their achievements to the public. As noted above, one of the ways in which the new institutions were intended to be different from Westminster was in their openness to outside actors. Public participation in the policy process was to be channelled through the submission of petitions that were automatically considered by a petitions committee, the provision for committees to meet outside the metropolitan centre, and a greater willingness to hear non-professional voices in committee hearings. In Wales, a system of 'regional committees' represented a further attempt to bring government closer to the people.

With respect to involving ordinary people in policy making, Table 4.4 shows that neither institution was considered by its members to be a particular success. Only between one-quarter and one-third responded positively on this point. Once again, however, in both institutions the overall figures mask a sharp split between executive and opposition parties. Members of executive parties were more likely to regard public consultation as a success, though even here the response was at best mixed. Only a bare majority of Labour members ever considered public involvement to be successful. Nonetheless, in both institutions the views of Conservative and nationalist members were more negative still.

In contrast, in all three surveys, a majority of MSPs and AMs considered their legislature effective at involving outside bodies in policy making. Although executive party members were again more positive, on this question there was a greater degree of cross-party agreement; even around half the respondents from opposition parties felt their institution was effective. Whatever doubts members may have had about the ability of their institution to involve the general public in its affairs, those doubts apparently do not extend to organised civil society, whose representatives are, for example, often called upon to give evidence at committee hearings.

But by far the most negative impression of the new bodies' external relations concerned their ability to communicate their achievements to the public. Here the results are little short of disastrous. In Wales, after a year of being in operation, just one in ten of the Assembly's members thought it a success at communicating its achievements. There was little improvement during the subsequent four years. In Scotland, those regarding the Parliament as effective fell from one in four in 2000 to one in eight in 2004. Doubtless this is a result of the bad publicity the Parliament received, for instance because of the unexpectedly high cost of the new parliament building, and the 'Officegate' affair that led to the downfall of First Minister Henry McLeish in 2001. In any event, the poor public image of the new

Table 4.4 Evaluation of the 'external governance' performance of the Scottish Parliament and Welsh Assembly, 2000–4

		Scotland			Wales		
		2000 (%)	*2002* (%)	*2004* (%)	*2000* (%)	*2002* (%)	*2004* (%)
The Parliament/ Assembly has been effective in:							
Involving ordinary people in policy making	Labour	42	54	50	40	56	50
	SNP/Plaid Cymru	14	22	18	9	18	0
	Liberal Democrat	43	(0)	43	(67)	(50)	(0)
	Conservative	31	22	18	–	(0)	(0)
	Total	34	34	34	28	36	25
Involving outside bodies in policy making	Labour	58	85	75	70	81	75
	SNP/Plaid Cymru	32	44	45	55	46	50
	Liberal Democrat	71	(75)	57	(100)	(50)	(75)
	Conservative	69	56	46	–	(25)	(50)
	Total	55	69	65	58	60	65
Communicating its achievements to the public	Labour	32	0	10	20	6	31
	SNP/Plaid Cymru	18	0	9	9	0	0
	Liberal Democrat	29	(0)	43	(0)	(0)	(0)
	Conservative	31	0	18	–	(50)	(0)
	Total	27	0	14	12	9	16

Note: See the note to Table 4.3.

institutions was one thing at least on which in both institutions executive and non-executive parties were largely able to agree.

The constitutional challenge: towards a stable settlement?

In addition to creating better forms of governance and delivering specific benefits to the Scottish and Welsh people, devolution was also seen by many advocates as a strategy to defuse the territorial issue in British politics and undercut support for nationalism. Events since 1999 have demonstrated that this was not a wholly successful strategy, culminating in the Richard Commission and Government of Wales Act 2006 on the one hand, and the electoral success of the SNP in Scotland in 2007 on the other. In both Scotland and Wales, there has been pressure for the devolved bodies to be given greater powers, as reflected in late 2007 by the creation in Wales of a convention to pave the way to full legislative devolution, and the establishment in Scotland in 2008 of a commission under the chairmanship of Sir Kenneth Calman to review the devolution settlement there. Indeed, the minority SNP government in Scotland even hopes to be able to hold a referendum on independence in 2010.

To examine attitudes towards the institutional capacity of the devolved bodies, in 2000 and 2002 we asked elected members which tier of government they believed *did* have the most influence on the way Scotland/Wales was run and then which tier of government they believed *ought* to have the most influence. Respondents were allowed to choose between the devolved institutions, the UK Government at Westminster, local councils and the European Union. Since few nominated either local councils or the European Union, we focus on the figures for the devolved bodies and Westminster only

A large majority of Labour and Liberal Democrat MSPs believed that Holyrood had the most influence over Scotland (see Table 4.5). Further, and less predictably, in both surveys this view was shared by at least half of Conservative respondents, despite their party's opposition to devolution. Only SNP members were more doubtful about the degree of influence wielded by the Scottish Parliament. This is hardly surprising given the party's claim that devolution was an insufficient recognition of Scotland's distinctiveness; most SNP members believed Westminster retained the

Table 4.5   Views on policy influence in Scotland and Wales, 2000–2

| | 2000 | | | | 2002 | | | |
| | *Westminster* | | *Devolved body* | | *Westminster* | | *Devolved body* | |
	Does have most influence	*Ought to have most influence*	*Does have most influence*	*Ought to have most influence*	*Does have most influence*	*Ought to have most influence*	*Does have most influence*	*Ought to have most influence*
Scotland								
Labour	23	13	77	88	22	0	78	100
SNP	71	0	29	94	90	0	10	83
Liberal Democrat	0	20	100	80	(0)	(0)	(100)	(100)
Conservative	50	29	50	57	14	0	71	50
Total	29	12	71	84	38	0	60	88
Wales								
Labour	56	0	44	83	56	10	44	80
Plaid Cymru	100	0	0	100	75	0	25	100
Liberal Democrat	(67)	–	(33)	–	(33)	–	(67)	–
Conservative	–	–	–	–	(67)	–	(0)	–
Total	76	0	24	92	55	5	40	91

Note: Brackets indicate the figure is based on less than five respondents.

dominant influence. Equally unsurprisingly, perhaps, there was agreement across the parties that the Scottish Parliament ought to have the greatest influence over the way Scotland is run, though there was rather less enthusiasm for this proposition amongst Conservative members.

The equivalent figures for Wales show, in contrast, that a majority of members continued to believe that Westminster was the most influential tier of government. While over 90 per cent believed the Welsh Assembly should be in this position, only a minority thought it already was. This large disparity suggests widespread dissatisfaction among AMs of all parties with the powers accorded to the Assembly in the original devolution settlement. Since these surveys were conducted, further legislative powers have been transferred to the Assembly by means of the Government of Wales Act 2006; time will tell whether this reform proves satisfactory to AMs.

The equivalent public opinion data in Chapter 6 (see Tables 6.7 and 6.8), provide an interesting contrast. The Welsh public appeared largely to agree with their elected representatives that Westminster does exercise most influence but that the Assembly in Cardiff should be in this position. People in Scotland, by contrast, appear to be much more negative than MSPs in their judgement about the relative power of the Scottish Parliament. Between 2000 and 2004 a majority consistently believed that Westminster was more powerful, while two-thirds or more thought Holyrood ought to wield the greatest influence. The views of non-nationalist MSPs about the effectiveness of the constitutional settlement therefore appear to be out of step with the views of the public.

Having asked elected members for their broad views on the capacity of their institution, we then asked for their opinions on more specific reforms to the devolution settlement. In Wales, each of the surveys asked members whether the size of the Assembly ought to be increased beyond its current 60 members, and whether – like the Scottish Parliament – it should have primary legislative powers, and/or tax raising powers. These issues were considered by the Richard Commission set up by the Welsh Assembly Government in 2002. In its 2004 report the Commission recommended an increase in the Assembly's size and the granting to it of primary legislative powers, while concluding that the power of taxation was 'desirable but not essential' (Richard Commission, 2004: 258). As our surveys first canvassed these issues long before the Commission was set up, and last asked AMs' views after it had reported, they can help explain the political dynamic that surrounded the Richard Commission and the response to its recommendations.

The possibility of increasing the size of the Assembly consistently received majority support among AMs, as shown in Table 4.6, but with significant differences between the parties.[4] All Liberal Democrat and Plaid Cymru members repeatedly expressed their support for a larger Assembly, a reflection of party policy. The Labour Party was more divided on this issue, with support peaking in 2002. At the time the 2004 survey was being conducted, the Labour Party was in the process of rejecting the Richard

Table 4.6 Support amongst Assembly Members for reforms to the Welsh Assembly, 2000–4

		2000 (%)	2002 (%)	2004 (%)
The Assembly should:				
Have more elected members	Labour	40	69	44
	Plaid Cymru	100	100	100
	Liberal Democrat	(100)	(100)	(100)
	Conservative	–	(25)	(25)
	Total	65	74	57
Have primary legislative powers	Labour	50	75	75
	Plaid Cymru	100	100	100
	Liberal Democrat	(100)	(100)	(100)
	Conservative	–	(50)	(0)
	Total	62	81	69
Have tax raising powers	Labour	30	Na	25
	Plaid Cymru	100	Na	100
	Liberal Democrat	(100)	Na	(100)
	Conservative	–	Na	(0)
	Total	52	Na	43

Note: For most questions the figures represent those who said 'strongly agree' or 'agree'. The one exception is the number of elected members, where in 2002 and 2004, the question was whether the size of the Assembly should increase, decrease or stay the same, with the figures showing the percentage of respondents saying it should increase. Brackets indicate the figure is based on less than five respondents. Na=Not asked.

[4] We did also ask MSPs about a possible change in the size of the Scottish Parliament. As originally enacted, the Scotland Act envisaged a reduction in its size, but this provision was subsequently reversed. As a result, the figures are not shown here. In fact, in 2002, two-thirds of members said the Parliament should remain at its current size. All of those seeking a smaller parliament were Conservatives, whilst a small number of SNP and Labour members supported a larger parliament.

Commission recommendation for an 80–member Assembly, not least because the proposed change would have made it more difficult for the party to win a majority in the Assembly. Our data suggest that, in fact, a large minority of Labour members were unhappy with this decision. Conservative members, on the other hand, were generally negative about enlarging the Assembly. This again reflects party policy.

On whether the Assembly should have primary legislative powers, Plaid Cymru and Liberal Democrat members were unanimously in favour from the start, in line with party policy. In both 2002 and 2004, three-quarters of Labour AMs favoured primary legislative devolution, too, as recommended by the Richard Commission. In holding this view, Labour AMs were probably at odds with other sections of their party. The eventual government policy response to the Commission's report reflected the split inside the party, with Labour's pro-devolutionist wing having to settle for the curious compromise of the Government of Wales Act 2006 under which the Assembly can be granted legislative powers on a case-by-case basis. Under the terms of the Act, full legislative devolution will only be granted following a referendum at some unspecified future date.[5]

With respect to the Assembly being given tax raising powers equivalent to those devolved to Scotland, opinions were largely predictable. All nationalist members and all Liberal Democrats were in favour of 'fiscal devolution'. Labour and Conservative members in contrast were predominantly hostile. Members of all parties appeared to back party policy. In addition Scottish members were asked in 2004 whether they favoured further tax raising powers for Holyrood. The responses reveal a similar pattern to that in Wales: unanimous support among SNP and Liberal Democrat MSPs and scepticism among Labour and Conservative members (with just 25 and 36 per cent respectively backing fiscal devolution). It is therefore interesting that in 2007 both these latter parties decided to back the establishment of the Calman Commission to review the Scottish devolution settlement, including not least its financial provisions.

The attitudes of MSPs and AMs towards the terms of the original devolution settlement largely, but not wholly, have reflected the policy positions of their parties. A clear majority of AMs were dissatisfied with the balance of power between the UK Government and the Welsh Assembly. Consistent with this was the widespread support among (non-Tory) AMs for the devolution of primary legislative powers. Only Liberal Democrats and Plaid members, however, consistently favoured fiscal devolution to

---

[5] The provisions of this piece of legislation are discussed at length by the House of Lords Constitution Committee (2006).

Wales and a larger Assembly. In Scotland, only the SNP appeared seriously dissatisfied with the balance of power between Westminster and Holyrood, although the Liberal Democrats were also strongly in favour of greater fiscal devolution. There is little in our data, therefore, to suggest that devolution has succeeded in resolving the territorial question in the United Kingdom so far as members of the devolved institutions are concerned.

Conclusion

The evidence presented in this chapter has been discussed through various lenses, with comparisons drawn between parties, across time, between MSPs and AMs, and among the various indicators of perceived institutional performance. A number of general conclusions emerge. At the highest level of generalisation, it can clearly be seen that the performance of the new elected bodies did not – in their first five years at least – live up to the initial high expectations of their members. To the extent that trends can be ascertained, opinion clearly grew more negative in a number of significant ways.

Given the far more extensive set of powers devolved to Scotland than to Wales we hypothesised that MSPs would be more satisfied than AMs with the performance of their institution. However, this expectation has largely not been borne out; indeed sometimes the very opposite has been true. On several important issues, AMs were more positive in their assessment of devolution than were MSPs. Most notably perhaps, by 2004, more AMs than MSPs believed that their institution had succeeded in initiating policy and in meeting public expectations for policy improvements. However, MSPs were more positive than AMs about their legislature's ability to hold the Executive to account and influence legislation. This suggests that the Scottish Parliament is seen as more successful than the Welsh Assembly (and maybe Westminster) at traditional parliamentary tasks. But both institutions were seen as less successful in creating the much heralded 'new politics' in any tangible sense. While members felt they had managed to engage civil society organisations, they were clearly disappointed with the level of backbench influence and wider public participation.

We also anticipated that there would be clear variation in members' opinions according to party affiliation. As expected, Labour and Liberal Democrat members were generally more positive in their assessments than Conservative and nationalist members. It is impossible to disentangle whether this discrepancy is due to the latter parties being in opposition in Scotland and Wales or to their critical attitude towards the devolution settlement. (This is an area which could be fruitfully explored in future research now that the Labour Party is out of power in Scotland and the nationalists in office in both countries.) At the same time, we also ascertained a pattern we had not expected. Labour AMs were inclined to rate the Welsh Assembly more highly over time, whereas Labour MSPs appear to have become more disillusioned with the Scottish Parliament. This may well reflect differences in the perceived performance of the respective First Ministers.

So far as the constitutional framework is concerned, a clear and unsurprising difference between Scotland and Wales is revealed by our data. There was cross-party consensus in Wales that the Assembly had insufficient power and that the balance of power should be shifted away from Westminster and towards the Assembly. In contrast in Scotland, only the SNP were strongly dissatisfied with the status quo though they had some support from the Liberal Democrats for further fiscal devolution.

As devolution enters a new era – with nationalists in government in both Edinburgh and Cardiff – a major question will be how these views develop, and whether MSPs and AMs grow more or less satisfied with devolution. Inevitably, devolution will lose some of its sheen for Labour members in Scotland now that they are in opposition, and it remains to be seen how SNP members will respond having taken ministerial responsibility for the first time. They may well remain critical of the capacity of the devolution settlement, but equally a taste of power could help reconcile nationalist members to the constitutional status quo. In Wales, the major question is whether the enhanced legislative powers for the Assembly will satisfy those (principally Labour) AMs who were unhappy with the balance of power between UK and Welsh institutions but not yet convinced of the need for full primary legislative devolution. Plaid Cymru members will continue to press for primary legislative and fiscal powers, but now that they sit in government, they may also come to hold more positive views on the operation of the Welsh Assembly. Our surveys have provided a picture of elite opinion during the formative years of devolution and have helped explain some of the political developments that have occurred. Continuing to monitor the views of those engaged directly with the devolved institutions will be essential in evaluating the future performance of devolution.

References

Arter, D. (2004) 'The Scottish committees and the goal of a "New Politics": A verdict on the first four years of the devolved Scottish

parliament', *Journal of Contemporary European Studies*, 12:1
Consultative Steering Group (1998) *Report on the Scottish Parliament*, Edinburgh: The Scottish Office
Griffiths, D. (1999) 'The Welsh Office and Welsh autonomy', *Public Administration*, 77:4
House of Lords Constitution Committee (2006) *Government of Wales Bill*, HL 142, 8th Report of Session 2005–6, London: House of Lords
Laffin, M. and Thomas, A. (2000) 'Designing the National Assembly for Wales', *Parliamentary Affairs*, 53:3
McAllister, L. (2000) 'The new politics in Wales: Rhetoric or reality?', *Parliamentary Affairs*, 53:3
Mitchell, J. (2000) 'New Parliament, new politics in Scotland', *Parliamentary Affairs*, 53:3
Morgan, R. (2002) 'Speech to the National Centre for Public Policy', University of Wales, Swansea, 11 December
Osmond, J. and Mugaseth, J. (2003) 'The Assembly', in J. Osmond, ed., *Wales Unplugged: Monitoring the National Assembly for Wales*, June–August, London: The Constitution Unit
Richard Commission (2004) *Report of the Richard Commission*, Commission on the Powers and Electoral Arrangements of the National Assembly for Wales, Cardiff: National Assembly
Scottish Constitutional Convention (1995) *Scotland's Parliament, Scotland's Right*, final report, available at: www.almac.co.uk/business_park /scc/scc-rep.htm (accessed 5 January 2008)
Trench, A. (2005) 'Intergovernmental relations within the UK: The pressures yet to come', in A. Trench, ed., *The Dynamics of Devolution: The State of the Nations 2005*, Thorveton: Imprint Academic

Annex: details of the surveys

Questionnaires were distributed by post in November 2000, October 2002 and June 2004. Between four and six weeks later, reminder letters were sent to non-respondents, together with a second copy of the questionnaire. The tables below show for each survey: (i) the total number of responses from each party group, (ii) the percentage of all responses that came from that group, and (iii) the percentage of that group's members responding to the survey. In addition, the tables show for each party group the total number of group members elected at the preceding election and the percentage of all elected members this represents.

Annex   Details of surveys

	1999 election seats		2000 survey responses			2002 survey responses			2003 election seats		2004 survey responses		
	No.	% of total	No.	% of total	% of party group	No.	% of total	% of party group	No.	% of total	No.	% of total	% of party group
Scotland													
Labour	56	43.4	20	31.7	35.7	14	29.8	25.0	50	38.8	20	33.3	40.0
SNP	35	27.1	22	34.9	62.6	18	38.3	51.4	27	20.9	11	18.3	40.7
Conservative	18	14.0	13	20.6	72.2	9	19.1	50.0	18	14.0	11	18.3	61.1
Liberal Democrat	17	13.2	7	11.1	41.2	4	8.5	23.5	17	13.2	7	11.7	41.2
Other	3	2.3	1	1.6	33.3	2	4.3	66.7	17	13.2	11	18.3	64.8
Total	129	100.0	63	100.0	48.8	47	100.0	36.4	129	100.0	60	100.0	46.5
Wales													
Labour	28	46.7	10	38.5	35.7	16	45.7	57.1	30	50.0	16	53.3	53.3
Plaid Cymru	17	28.3	11	42.3	64.7	11	31.4	64.7	12	20.0	6	20.0	50.0
Conservative	9	15.0	2	7.7	22.2	4	11.4	44.4	11	18.3	4	13.3	36.4
Liberal Democrat	6	10.0	3	11.5	50.0	4	11.4	66.7	6	10.0	4	13.3	66.7
Other	–	–	–	–	–	–	–	–	1	1.7	–	–	–
Total	60	100.0	26	100.0	43.3	35	100.0	58.3	60	100.0	30	100.0	50.0

5
The citizens' response: the performance of the devolved bodies[1]

Ben Seyd

Devolution in Britain represented an attempt to fashion a new relationship between political authority and citizens. New tiers of government were intended to forge closer relations between citizens and political institutions through more effective policy decisions, improved policy outcomes, more representative and responsive political elites and the expression of stronger national identities. In a variety of ways, then, the establishment of the Scottish Parliament and Welsh Assembly was a response to anxiety with the previous governing arrangements, and an attempt to deliver political and democratic benefits that, it was hoped, would strengthen the bonds between citizens and political institutions.

One of these bonds was clearly partisan in nature. As Chapter 2 sets out clearly, one reason for the push towards devolving political authority to Scotland was the Labour Party's concern with its own electoral base in that country. Yet, alongside this partisan motivation lay a perception among political elites of an increasing disquiet among people in Scotland and, to a lesser extent, Wales, with the centralised nature of political authority in Britain. The public rationale for devolution thus emphasised the demand among citizens for reform of the British state. The final report of the Scottish Constitutional Convention confidently asserted that 'The first and greatest reason for creating a Scottish Parliament is that the people of Scotland want and deserve democracy' (Scottish Constitutional Convention, 1995: 2). The chief architect of Scottish devolution, and the country's initial First Minister, Donald Dewar, also stressed public demands in commending the Scottish Parliament to the House of Commons. The Parliament, Dewar argued, was intended to establish 'a new covenant with the people', going on to express his hope that devolution would 'earn the

[1] I would like to thank Ann Mair of Strathclyde University's Social Statistics Laboratory and the Scottish Centre for Social Research for the provision of some of the data reported here.

trust of Scotland's peoples, and it is the people who have played the key role in making change possible' (HC Debs, 12 January 1998, cols 19, 21). Public opinion was also used to justify the establishment of devolved bodies in Wales, although less in meeting public aspirations and demands, and more in providing for public accountability of government agencies and reducing a perceived 'democratic deficit' (Welsh Office, 1997: 7).

The views of the public thus occupied, in rather different ways, central positions in the official narrative around devolution. Many in Scotland identified a public demand for devolution to deliver more effective and responsive public policies; to the extent that these demands existed, the Scottish Parliament would be judged by how far they were met. The rather weaker public appetite for devolution in Wales did not mean that the new institutions could proceed without reference to public reactions. On the contrary, in not being the product of overwhelming popular demand, the Welsh Assembly was founded on extremely shallow roots. It was thus important for the Assembly to create public support and establish some legitimacy, as opposed to meeting existing demands and reinforcing legitimacy, the task arguably facing the Scottish Parliament.

In this chapter and the next, we consider public reactions to devolution to Scotland and Wales. We explore how citizens have evaluated the performance of the Scottish Parliament and Welsh Assembly, going on to examine how these evaluations might have shaped public attitudes towards the position of Scotland and Wales within the Union. The results across the two chapters cast light on popular acceptance of the devolved institutions, and on the popular legitimacy of Britain's post-devolution constitutional arrangements.

This chapter focuses on public reactions to the performance of the devolved institutions in Scotland and Wales. In order to establish a baseline against which subsequent evaluations can be set, we begin by identifying the level and nature of public demand for devolution. We explore how far citizens in Scotland and Wales favoured devolution, and whether this support was long-standing or of more recent vintage. We then go on to consider what people were looking for from a devolved tier of government. Did people favour devolution primarily because it was seen to yield more effective policy outcomes, or because it was seen to enhance the responsiveness and accountability of political agents? Put starkly, was devolution favoured for its contribution to policy outcomes or to democratic ones?[2] Having established this baseline, we then move on to consider whether

---

[2] Devolution might also be favoured for providing institutions that embody various forms of social or political identity, a frequent demand of nationalist movements. The relationship between devolution and national identity is considered in Chapter 6.

these public expectations and demands have subsequently been met. Are public evaluations of the devolved institutions broadly positive or negative? If, as we might anticipate, reactions are mixed, on which areas are the institutions perceived to have performed well, and on which issues is performance judged to be poor?

Our task in this chapter is thus to provide a detailed evaluation of how citizens have evaluated the performance of the devolved institutions in Britain. The task of considering what these evaluations mean for the stability of the devolution programme, and for the coherence of the Union, is taken up in the following chapter.

In identifying the historical public demand for devolution and public evaluations of the devolved bodies in Scotland and Wales since 1999, our basic sources are public opinion surveys. Public attitudes to devolution were first systematically analysed via population surveys in the early 1970s. Similar surveys have been conducted ever since, although these vary in frequency in different parts of Britain. Details of these surveys are shown in the Appendix at the end of this book. In Scotland, a number of studies were conducted between 1970 and 1999, including four dedicated surveys of the Scottish population (the Scottish Election Study of 1979, 1992 and 1997 and the Scottish Referendum Study of 1997). These studies allow us to trace the historical level of demand for devolution. Since the first election to the Scottish Parliament in 1999, annual surveys of attitudes to devolution has been conducted (the Scottish Social Attitudes series), providing detailed information on how citizens have reacted to devolution.[3] The survey coverage is less extensive in Wales, with two dedicated studies prior to 1999 (the Welsh Election Study of 1979 and the Welsh Referendum Study of 1997), and periodic, rather than regular, studies thereafter.

The public demand for devolution

In order to understand how citizens across Britain have reacted to devolution, we need first to clarify the initial level of public support for devolution, and what the main expectations of the devolved institutions were. While we have measures of public attitudes to devolution stretching back almost four decades, it is not always easy to accurately gauge levels of public support for different constitutional options. This is because the

[3] Modules of questions on devolution in 2001 and 2003 were funded by the Leverhulme Trust under its 'Nations and Regions' programme. The funding also covered the costs of analysing the resulting data, of which this chapter and the next are among the principal results.

survey questions probing attitudes have often been worded in different ways or have offered different response options. In reporting the data between 1970 and 1997, we allocate the various survey responses into one of four categories: opposition to devolution, support for the limited decentralisation of power to the regions, support for a stronger assembly in Scotland and Wales and support for outright independence (all question wordings are set out in the Annex at the end of this chapter, so readers can see how these groupings have been constructed).

It is usually clear what proportion of people favour the two extreme options, of either no change to (what was then) the unitary status quo or full independence from the rest of the United Kingdom. Among people in Scotland, the proportions favouring the constitutional status quo or outright independence for the country remained fairly constant over the period (Table 5.1). Between one-fifth and one-third of people opposed any devolution of power to Scotland, while between one-fifth and one-quarter would have liked to see Scotland gain independence from England and Wales. It is often less clear how many people favoured the intermediate option, devolution, and in what form. Early surveys – those from 1970 to 1979 – offered respondents some variations in the degree of autonomy they could choose for Scotland, although the wordings of these questions were rather vague (referring in broad terms to greater decision making being concentrated within Scotland). Later surveys – those from 1992 – offered a more clearly defined set of constitutional options (explicitly mentioning an Assembly or Parliament). Nonetheless, even taking into account the rather loose wording of early survey questions, it appears as though the proportion of people in Scotland who favour at least some decentralisation of decision making capacity has consistently run between four and five in ten of the population. To that extent, devolution – whether limited or extensive in form – appears to be a long-standing preference of many people in Scotland.

The demand for devolution in Wales has always been lower than in Scotland (Table 5.2). The Kilbrandon Commission survey in 1970 allowed respondents to select the rather vague constitutional options of having 'more decisions' or 'as many decisions as possible' taken in Wales, potentially inflating levels of support for devolution. Aside from this, there is clear evidence from the end of the 1970s up to the end of the 1980s of firm public opposition to devolution.[4] Only in the 1990s did support for devolution pick up, although as late as 1992, the constitutional status quo retained the support of a plurality of Welsh citizens. When it came to the referendum in 1997, support

----

[4] Although the low Welsh samples in the British Election Survey for 1983, 1987 and 1992 (the maximum number of Welsh interviewees being just over 200) should make us cautious about over-interpreting the data from these years.

Table 5.1 Constitutional preferences in Scotland, 1970–97

	1970 (%)	1974 (%)	1975 (%)	1979 (%)	1992 (%)	1994 (%)	1996 (%)	1997 (%)
No devolution	25	34	26	34	25	21	26	18
Greater regional decision making	26	44	27	44	–	–	–	–
Regional assembly	24	–	19	–	50	55	46	51
Independence	23	21	24	21	23	22	26	26
Don't know	1	1	3	1	2	1	3	5

Note: The samples are of people in Scotland only.
Sources: Commission on the Constitution, 1970; Scottish Election Study, 1974, 1979, 1992, 1997; Opinion Research Centre, 1975; British Election Panel Study, 1994 and 1996.

for a Welsh Assembly only fractionally outweighed opposition to it. Thus, to the extent that devolution to Wales reflected public demand, this demand was relatively limited and of recent origin.

Public expectations of devolution

Historical variations in public demand might help explain the very different forms of devolution granted to Scotland and Wales, but they are an unreliable guide to how citizens might have responded to their new institutions. A more plausible guide to these reactions can be found by examining the public's expectations of devolution. What did citizens hope for – or fear – from the new institutions? And did they look to the devolved bodies primarily as means of securing more favourable policy outcomes or as forums through which more representative and democratic political

Table 5.2 Constitutional preferences in Wales, 1970–97

	1970 (%)	1979 (%)	1983 (%)	1987 (%)	1992 (%)	1997 (%)
No devolution	42	71	79	70	45	37
Greater regional decision making	21	7	–	–	–	–
Regional assembly	23	12	12	22	40	43
Independence	13	5	6	6	13	12
Don't know	0	5	3	3	2	7

Note: The samples are of people in Wales only.
Sources: Commission on the Constitution, 1970; Welsh Election Survey, 1979; British Election Study, 1983, 1987, 1992; Welsh Referendum Study, 1997.

decisions could be achieved? To answer these questions, we rely on surveys conducted in 1997 and 1999. The 1997 survey – the Scottish and Welsh Referendum Study – provides us with a first extensive battery of questions measuring public expectations of devolution in Scotland and Wales. These questions were followed up by a survey in Scotland – the first of the annual Scottish Social Attitudes surveys – in 1999, which asked respondents for their expectations of the nascent Scottish Parliament. In Wales, the Welsh Assembly Election Study in 1999 asked about expectations of the Welsh Assembly, although a more limited set of expectations were explored than in Scotland (for which reason, we mainly use the 1997 survey in Wales).

We can examine public expectations of devolution in Scotland through survey questions that asked respondents what they anticipated the impact of a Scottish Parliament would be. These expectations can be divided into two categories. The first relates to the Scottish Parliament's impact on policy outcomes, such as the level of unemployment, the state of education and of the economy, the quality of the NHS, and the standard of social welfare and of general living standards. The second category of expectations relates to the Parliament's impact on representative and democratic outcomes, such as Scottish 'voice' within the United Kingdom and Europe and the responsiveness of decision making in Scotland to public concerns.

Popular expectations of the Scottish Parliament in 1997 and 1999 are set out in Table 5.3. Three main points emerge. The first is that expectations of the Parliament were generally positive. In the main, more people believed the Parliament would have a positive impact than believed it would have either a negative or a neutral effect. Expectations were higher in 1997 than immediately after the first devolution election in 1999. Asked what the impact of the Parliament would be on the Scottish economy, in 1997 six in ten (64 per cent) saw the Parliament as playing a positive role, while seven in ten (71 per cent) believed it would stimulate improvements in education. By 1999, the proportion anticipating that devolution would benefit the economy had fallen to 43 per cent, while on education it had dropped to 56 per cent. The main exception to the public's rosy expectations of the Scottish Parliament is taxation, where far more people believed the Parliament would increase, rather than reduce, levels of taxation.[5] On

[5]   Note, however, that a belief that a parliament would increase taxes is not neces-
       sarily a negative judgement; many people in Scotland may well have favoured
       higher taxes if this entailed higher levels of public spending. Analyses of voting
       in the 1997 Scottish referendum confirm that even among those who believed
       a parliament would entail additional taxes, aggregate opinion was favourable
       towards the establishment of the Parliament (Brown *et al.*, 1999: 118–21;
       Denver *et al.*, 2000: 162).

Table 5.3   Expectations of a Scottish Parliament, 1997 and 1999

	Higher/better/ stronger		Lower/worse/ weaker		No difference	
	1997 (%)	1999 (%)	1997 (%)	1999 (%)	1997 (%)	1999 (%)
The impact of a Scottish Parliament on:						
Unemployment	18	15	44	28	38	50
Economy	64	43	12	13	24	37
Taxes	76	64	4	4	20	26
Standard of NHS	66	49	6	4	28	41
Standard/quality of education	71	56	3	3	19	36
Standard of social welfare	59	Na	5	Na	36	Na
Standard of living	56	38	16	9	29	48
People's say in how Scotland is governed	81	64	2	2	17	32
Scotland's voice in Britain	73	70	10	7	17	20
Scotland's voice in Europe	65	Na	12	Na	24	Na

Note: Figures are row percentages. Those responding 'don't know' are not included in the totals, meaning rows may not sum exactly to 100 per cent. Na=Not asked.
Sources: Scottish Referendum Study, 1997; Scottish Social Attitudes Survey, 1999.

one further issue, public expectations of the Parliament were finely balanced. This issue was unemployment where, in 1997, only slightly more people believed the Parliament would help reduce unemployment (44 per cent) than thought it would make no difference (38 per cent), while by 1999 more people thought devolution would make no difference.

A second point about the data reinforces the generally benign impression we have of Scottish attitudes towards a devolved government. Very few people believed a parliament would have a negative impact on outcomes. To the extent that people had reservations about the Parliament, it was on the grounds of failing to make any impact, rather than making things worse. Only on economic outcomes (the standard of living, unemployment and the Scottish economy) did more than one in ten people in Scotland in either 1997 or 1999 anticipate the Parliament would have a negative effect. Far more people believed that the Parliament would simply make no difference to outcomes at all.

A third observation to make is that devolution was anticipated to deliver on democratic criteria as much as on policy ones. The Scottish and

Welsh Referendum Study asked respondents whether they believed a Scottish Parliament would give Scotland a stronger or weaker voice within the United Kingdom, and whether it would give Scottish people more or less say in the way Scotland was governed. On Scotland's representation within the United Kingdom, in 1997 seven in ten people (73 per cent) anticipated the Parliament would help to strengthen this voice, while eight in ten (81 per cent) believed the Parliament would enhance people's say in how Scotland was governed (these proportions were rather lower by 1999). That voters hoped devolution would make a difference to democratic as well as to policy outcomes is also apparent if we examine the areas identified by people in Scotland in 1997 as the priority for a Scottish Parliament (Table 5.4). While many hoped devolution would increase the standard of living and improve education, a large number also wanted it to give ordinary people greater say in political decisions.[6]

In comparison with Scotland, expectations of devolution among people in Wales were somewhat low. In Table 5.5, we report data from 1997, along with the more limited range of expectations examined in the 1999 Welsh Assembly Election Study (the data from which appear in brackets). Recall from Table 5.3 that on all policy areas bar one – the level of taxation – people in Scotland believed a Scottish Parliament would improve outcomes. In contrast, on only one policy area – education – did as many people in Wales in

Table 5.4   Priorities for a Scottish Parliament and Welsh Assembly, 1997

Most important thing for devolution to bring about:	Scotland (%)	Wales (%)
Improve education	23	28
Increase standard of living	27	24
Give Scotland/Wales stronger voice in UK	11	14
Give Scotland/Wales stronger voice in EU	4	7
Give people more say in how Scotland/Wales is governed	28	21

Source: Scottish and Welsh Referendum Study, 1997.

[6] A similar result can be seen from the 1992 Scottish Election Study, which asked respondents what outcome they believed would be the most important advantage of a Scottish Parliament. Of the six response options, giving people more say in Scottish government was by far the most popular response (32 per cent), followed by helping the Scottish economy (18 per cent) and enabling Scots to solve their own problems (17 per cent). Expectations that a Scottish Parliament would trigger improvements in policy and democratic outcomes has also been found to play a strong role in explaining support for the government's devolution proposals at the 1997 Scottish referendum (Brown *et al.*, 1999: chapters 6–7; Denver *et al.*, 2000: 162–5).

1997 believe the Assembly would have a positive effect as believe it would make no difference or make things worse (and by 1999, the combined proportions anticipating no change or a negative effect were actually greater). When it came to democratic processes, people in Wales were slightly more optimistic, with majorities – a bare one in 1997, a slightly more substantial one in 1999 – believing an Assembly would give people more say in decision making and strengthen Wales's voice within the United Kingdom. However, the Assembly was not seen as likely to deliver on one of its prime rationales, namely providing democratic oversight of unelected executive bodies. Only slightly more people expected the Assembly to afford them more control over quangos (38 per cent) than expected it to make no difference (36 per cent). Still, a crumb of comfort for the architects of Welsh devolution could have been taken from the fact that, as in Scotland, few believed devolution would do active harm. Meanwhile, if we examine the public's priorities for a Welsh Assembly (Table 5.4), we find that, as in Scotland, people hoped it would give them more say in government as well as improve living standards and the quality of education (albeit that people in Wales placed slightly less emphasis than did those in Scotland on the role of the devolved bodies in extending popular control of decision making).

Table 5.5   Expectations of a Welsh Assembly, 1997 and 1999

	Higher/better/ stronger (%)	*Lower/worse/ weaker (%)*	*No difference (%)*
The impact of a Welsh Assembly on:			
Unemployment	13	26	60
Economy	41	16	41
Taxes	41	2	55
Standard of NHS	46	9	43
Standard of education	50 (43)	5 (4)	37 (47)
Standard of living	29 (28)	12 (6)	51 (61)
People's say in how Wales is governed	54 (56)	4 (2)	36 (40)
Wales's voice in Britain	50 (62)	12 (4)	33 (33)
Wales's voice in Europe	44	10	39
Give the Welsh more control over quangos	38	7	36

Note: The data are for 1997; data for 1999 are in brackets. Figures are row percentages. Those responding 'don't know' are not included in the totals, meaning rows may not sum exactly to 100 per cent.
Sources: Welsh Referendum Study, 1997; Welsh Assembly Election Study, 1999.

So where did devolution stand in the eyes of the public prior to the first elections to the Scottish Parliament and Welsh Assembly in 1999? The first thing to note is the strong historical demand for devolution among the Scottish population, and the weaker historical demand among the Welsh population. In the years before the 1997 referendum, support for devolution in Wales had begun to catch up with that in Scotland, yet a Welsh Assembly never commanded the popularity among people in Wales that a Scottish Parliament did among those in Scotland. The second thing to note is the very different expectations that people in Scotland and Wales had of their devolved institutions. While people in Scotland had high expectations of a parliament, at least in 1997, people in Wales were less convinced of the ability of the proposed assembly to effect favourable outcomes. Only in relation to democratic processes – enhancing public 'voice' in decision making and securing stronger representation within the United Kingdom – were people in Wales relatively sanguine about the role of an assembly. Clearly, the devolved institutions started their lives with very different patterns of public support and expectations.

Public evaluations of devolution

This was the backdrop of public expectations against which the new devolved institutions were established in Scotland and Wales. What has the public made of devolution since then? Our analysis focuses on two key questions. First, have public reactions to the performance of the devolved institutions been positive or negative? Second, is there any evidence that these institutions are thought to have achieved more in respect of policy outcomes than democratic processes, or vice versa? In Scotland we consider public reactions up to and including 2007, the latest point for which survey data are available (surveys were conducted in Scotland in each year between 2000 and 2007); in Wales, equivalent data are only available for 2001 and 2003.[7]

To assess how the public has judged the performance of the devolved institutions, we draw principally on a question that asks respondents what effects they think the Scottish Parliament and Welsh Assembly are having. The issues on which performance evaluations are sought include the standard of education, the standard of the National Health Service, the

[7] The Life in Wales Today Survey 2007 contained no measures of the direct impact of the Welsh Assembly. The next section reports alternative performance evaluations, which ask how far the Assembly is responsible for various policy outcomes.

economy, the nation's voice within the United Kingdom and the extent of public 'voice' in decision making. The list of issues thus covers both policy outcomes and democratic processes. In the analysis that follows, we contrast people who think devolution has led to improvements in outcomes with those who think it has made things worse or that it has simply not made any difference.[8]

In both Scotland and Wales, popular evaluations of devolution appear not to have kept up with initial assessments. So far as Scotland is concerned, on each area reported in Table 5.6, evaluations are less positive at the end of the period than they were at the beginning. However, people's responses to survey questions are highly sensitive to the way questions are worded, and this might help explain some of the decline.[9] In 2000, respondents were asked to judge the performance of the Scottish Parliament in prospective terms on all measures.[10] But, in the case of education, voice in the United Kingdom and people's say in government, respondents were asked from 2001 onwards to evaluate the current performance of the Scottish Parliament. In contrast, in the case of the National Health Service and the economy, the question continued to be a prospective one until after 2003. It is possible that people will be more critical of current performance than of future performance, and we note that in the case of both education and health, evaluations became far more critical immediately after the question was switched to current performance. It may thus be more instructive to note that in the case of education, at least, the perceived performance of the Scottish Parliament has not declined since 2001, even if, at the same time, a rather larger proportion consistently believes the Parliament has made no difference to outcomes than believes it has improved things.

Evaluations of the impact of devolution on Scotland's voice within the United Kingdom, and on people's say in government, have fluctuated considerably, but not evidently in response to changes of question wording. Rather, more people evaluated the Parliament favourably on these criteria in the immediate wake of the devolved elections in 2003 and (especially) in

---

[8] Recall from Tables 5.3 and 5.5 that, prior to 1999, few people in Scotland and Wales believed the devolved institutions would lead to worse performance; rather they feared that they would have no impact on outcomes at all.

[9] My thanks to John Curtice, and to the analysis in Ormston and Sharp (2007), for pointing this out.

[10] Worded in prospective terms, the survey questions are arguably a measure of people's expectations of future performance, rather than of evaluations of actual performance. However, since the 2000 survey meant respondents had at least one year's worth of real experience of devolution against which to judge outcomes, the resulting data are treated as evaluations rather than expectations.

Table 5.6   Evaluations of the performance of the Scottish Parliament, 2000–7

	2000 (%)	2001 (%)	2002 (%)	2003 (%)	2004 (%)	2005 (%)	2006 (%)	2007 (%)
Impact of the Scottish Parliament on:								
Standard of education								
Improve	43	27	25	23	Na	Na	30	28
Reduce	3	5	6	7	Na	Na	6	3
Make no difference	49	59	58	59	Na	Na	53	54
Balance	-9	-37	-39	-43			-29	-29
Standard of NHS								
Improve	Na	45	Na	37	Na	Na	22	26
Reduce	Na	9	Na	10	Na	Na	9	6
Make no difference	Na	42	Na	46	Na	Na	63	59
Balance		-6		-19			-50	-39
Scotland's economy								
Improve	36	43	Na	35	Na	Na	Na	Na
Reduce	13	10	Na	12	Na	Na	Na	Na
Make no difference	45	43	Na	46	Na	Na	Na	Na
Balance	-22	-10		-23				
Scotland's voice in the UK								
Improve	52	52	39	49	35	41	43	61
Reduce	6	6	7	7	7	6	6	4
Make no difference	40	40	52	41	55	50	48	32
Balance	+6	+6	-20	+1	-27	-15	-11	+25
People's say in government								
Improve	44	38	31	39	31	37	37	47
Reduce	3	4	4	4	6	5	5	3
Make no difference	51	56	62	54	60	55	55	35
Balance	-10	-22	-35	-19	-35	-23	-23	+9

Note: 'Balance' represents the proportion of respondents judging the Scottish Parliament to be improving outcomes minus the proportions judging it to be worsening outcomes or not making a difference to outcomes.

Question wording for 2000: 'From what you have seen and heard so far, do you think that having a Scottish Parliament is going to increase/reduce/make no difference to the standard of education [other outcome] in Scotland?'

Question wording for education, voice in the United Kingdom and say in government from 2001: 'From what you have seen and heard so far, do you think that having a Scottish Parliament is increasing/reducing/making no difference to the standard of education [other outcome] in Scotland?'

Question wording for NHS standards and the economy in 2001 and 2003: 'From what you have seen and heard so far, do you think that as a result of having a Scottish Parliament the standard of the National Health Service in Scotland/Scotland's economy will become better/worse/make no difference?'. In 2006 and 2007, the question about the NHS asked whether the Parliament 'is increasing/reducing/making no difference to the standard of the NHS'.

Na=Not asked.

Source: Scottish Social Attitudes Surveys, 2000–7.

2007. Evidently, devolved elections help to renew popular faith in the democratic performance of the Parliament.

In Wales, we only have survey evidence for 2001 and 2003, making it more difficult to draw firm conclusions. So far as policy outcomes are concerned – the standard of education, health and the economy – most people believed the Welsh Assembly was making little difference (Table 5.7). The same was true of the democratic criterion of increasing popular say in government. But no less than one half of respondents thought the Assembly was enhancing Wales's voice within the United Kingdom.

Thus, in Scotland and Wales, public opinion appears to be underwhelmed by the performance of the devolved institutions in their early years. On most performance evaluations, more people judge the Scottish Parliament and Welsh Assembly not to have made any difference than consider them to be improving things. In both Scotland and Wales, we find that evaluations of the devolved bodies' contribution to democratic processes (representation within the United Kingdom and people's voice in government) are slightly more positive than their perceived contribution to policy outcomes (such as education and health). Nevertheless, taking into account potential question wording effects in Scotland, and the limited number of years for which data are available in Wales, there is little sense that the public is becoming more critical of the devolved institutions over time. True, evaluations of actual performance have not matched expectations of what devolution would achieve. But people's experience of devolution has not made them consistently more negative about the devolved bodies. Meanwhile, strikingly in 2003, evaluations were broadly similar in Wales to those in Scotland; the greater institutional powers of the Scottish Parliament have evidently not yielded a bigger dividend in the eyes of its citizens.

Which tier of government is responsible?

So far, we have explored what impact citizens in Scotland and Wales believe their devolved bodies are having on key policy and democratic outcomes. The survey questions we have drawn on direct respondents' attention to the impact of the Scottish Parliament and Welsh Assembly. But maybe most people in Scotland and Wales do not believe that these bodies truly determine outcomes. In spite of powers having been devolved to the Parliament and Assembly, perhaps people perceive outcomes in areas like education, health and the economy to remain primarily shaped by central government. If so, this might explain why so many people in Scotland and Wales seem

Table 5.7   Evaluations of the performance of the Welsh Assembly, 2001 and 2003

	2001 (%)	2003 (%)
Impact of the Welsh Assembly on:		
Standard of education		
Improve	22	27
Reduce	3	6
Make no difference	64	53
Balance	–45	–32
Standard of NHS		
Improve	30	41
Reduce	5	9
Make no difference	61	45
Balance	–36	–13
Wales's economy		
Improve	33	36
Reduce	8	7
Make no difference	54	51
Balance	–29	–22
Wales's voice in the UK		
Improve	49	52
Reduce	3	4
Make no difference	45	42
Balance	+1	+6
People's say in government		
Improve	34	38
Reduce	3	6
Make no difference	60	54
Balance	–29	–22

Note: 'Balance' represents the proportion of respondents judging the Welsh Assembly to be improving outcomes minus the proportions judging it to be worsening outcomes or not making a difference to outcomes.

Question wording for education, voice in the UK and say in government: 'From what you have seen and heard so far, do you think that having a Welsh National Assembly is increasing/reducing/making no difference to the standard of education [other outcome] in Wales?'.

Question wording for NHS and economy: 'From what you have seen and heard so far, do you think that as a result of having a Welsh National Assembly the standard of the National Health Service in Wales/Wales's economy will become better/worse/make no difference?'.

Source: Wales Life and Times Surveys, 2001–3.

to believe that their devolved bodies will make no difference to outcomes; the key decisions are seen to be taken in London.

To gauge how far the devolved bodies are perceived to shape policy outcomes, we draw on survey questions that ask respondents to attribute institutional responsibility for certain policy outcomes. The precise wording of the questions – asked in Scotland every year between 2001 and 2007 – and in Wales in 2001, 2003 and 2007 – was:

> Thinking back over the last twelve months[11] would you say the standard of the health service/quality of education/general standard of living in Scotland [Wales] has increased or fallen?

> What do you think this has been mainly the result of? Mainly the result of the UK Government's policies at Westminster, the Scottish Executive's[12] policies [administration of the Welsh Assembly[13]] or for some other reason?

It is the answers to the second part of this sequence that particularly interest us here. Are policy outcomes perceived to be primarily influenced by the devolved institutions, or by central government in London?[14] The answers to this question so far as Scotland is concerned are shown in Table 5.8. Westminster is evidently still seen as important, but the Scottish Executive (now Government) is becoming more significant in the public's eyes. In 2001, just over one in ten people believed that policy outcomes in health and living standards were primarily due to decisions made by the devolved tier, while less than one in five (19 per cent) said the same in relation to standards of education. By 2006, the proportion of people in Scotland who believed that the devolved tier was primarily responsible for what was happening to health and education had increased to one quarter or more. Indeed, in the case of education, by 2005 more people believed the devolved tier was responsible for outcomes than the government in London, the gap becoming even greater in 2006. This finding should not surprise us; after all, responsibility for education policy is a matter devolved to the Scottish Parliament. It is noticeable, however, that the public still sees health – also a devolved matter – as primarily driven by central government.

---

[11] In Scotland and Wales, the reference point in the 2001 surveys was the 1997 general election; in the 2003 surveys it was the devolved election in 1999. In Wales in 2007, the reference point was the previous devolved election in 2003.

[12] Until 2004, the question referred to the 'Scottish Parliament'.

[13] In 2007, the question referred to the 'Welsh Assembly Government'.

[14] Clearly, people might attribute policy outcomes to neither tier of government. In fact, between 10 and 20 per cent believe that neither the Scottish nor Westminster parliaments are responsible for health and education outcomes in Scotland, and up to 24 per cent in the case of the standard of living.

Table 5.8   Attributions of responsibility in Scotland, 2001–7

	2001 (%)	2003 (%)	2004 (%)	2005 (%)	2006 (%)	2007 (%)
Standard of NHS						
Who primarily responsible:						
UK Government	53	38	42	39	32	34
Scottish Executive	11	21	20	23	25	23
Quality of education						
Who primarily responsible:						
UK Government	40	30	29	28	20	22
Scottish Executive	19	25	28	30	33	28
General standard of living						
Who primarily responsible:						
UK Government	53	43	38	42	33	37
Scottish Executive	11	18	18	17	21	19

Note: The data for those giving a variety of other responses, especially 'for some other reason' and 'don't know', are not shown.
Source: Scottish Social Attitudes Surveys, 2001–7.

We do not know why attributions for policy responsibility have shifted over time. This may reflect changes in popular awareness of the role and capacity of the devolved institutions and of the division of responsibility between devolved and central tiers. It may reflect perceptions of how distinctive the policy agenda of Scottish politicians has been. What is clear is that, since the early years of devolution, there has been a fairly steady increase in the proportion of the Scottish population that believes the devolved tier of government is responsible for policy outcomes, and a decline in the proportion that identifies the Westminster Government as responsible. This shift has been most noticeable when it comes to education, but is also apparent in relation to perceived outcomes in health and living standards. Thus, the devolved institutions in Scotland are steadily becoming recognised for shaping outcomes in key areas of public policy.

In the cases of education and health – both devolved matters – this attribution of responsibility is the first step in ensuring the democratic accountability of the devolved tiers of government (the potential benefits are less clear in relation to the standard of living, which is arguably as much shaped by decisions reserved to Westminster as by those devolved to Scotland). Whether citizens in Scotland actually employ these attributions of responsibility when they vote – the sine qua non of electoral accountability – is considered in Chapter 7. Yet the growing perception among people in

Scotland that the devolved tier is primarily responsible for policy outcomes is not unalloyed good news for actors in the devolved institutions. This is because responsibility can be used by citizens to attribute blame for poor outcomes as well as credit for good ones. Granted, in any one year, the devolved tier is more likely to be credited by people who perceive policy outcomes to have improved than it is to be blamed by people who perceive outcomes to have worsened. For instance, in 2001, among those people who perceived standards in education to have increased, 35 per cent saw this as resulting from the actions of the Scottish Executive (45 per cent credited the UK Government), whereas among those people who thought education had worsened, only 18 per cent thought the Scottish Executive was to blame (with 51 per cent blaming the UK Government). However, over time, the devolved tier appears to be taking more of the brickbats as well as the plaudits. By 2006, far more people in Scotland gave the credit for perceived improvements in education to the Scottish Executive (50 per cent) than to the UK Government (22 per cent). But the proportions blaming the devolved tier for perceived falling educational standards had also increased, to 28 per cent in 2006 (against 37 per cent blaming the UK Government) (Ormston and Sharp, 2007: Table 9; see also Park and McCrone, 2006). This may help explain why, as we saw earlier, there has not been any increase over time in the proportions thinking that the Scottish Parliament has been beneficial for policy outcomes.

In Wales, as in Scotland, the key policy actor two years into the life of the devolved institutions was seen to be the UK Government in London; in 2001, around six in ten people in Wales saw this tier as responsible for policy outcomes, as against around one in ten who saw the Welsh Assembly as the dominant actor (Table 5.9). Since then, however, the role of the devolved institutions has increasingly been recognised, so that by 2007, three in ten respondents saw the Welsh Assembly Government as responsible for health and education outcomes, while one quarter saw it as responsible for living standards. Interestingly, the devolved institutions in Wales are accorded as much responsibility for policy outcomes as those in Scotland, despite the greater policy powers enjoyed by the latter.

Again, as in Scotland, the growing identification of the devolved institutions with policy outcomes means the Welsh Assembly is both credited with good performance and blamed for bad performance. Thus, among people who perceived standards in education to have increased in 2001, less than two in ten – 15 per cent – credited the Welsh Assembly with these outcomes, while six in ten – 61 per cent – believed the UK Government was responsible. By 2007, these positions had virtually reversed; now, 58 per cent of people believed the Welsh Assembly was responsible for

Table 5.9 Attributions of responsibility in Wales, 2001–7

	2001 (%)	2003 (%)	2007 (%)
Standard of NHS			
Who primarily responsible:			
UK Government	58	39	34
Welsh Assembly	10	22	31
Quality of education			
Who primarily responsible:			
UK Government	52	34	29
Welsh Assembly	8	20	30
General standard of living			
Who primarily responsible:			
UK Government	58	42	43
Welsh Assembly	8	17	24

Note: The data for those giving a variety of other responses, especially 'for some other reason' and 'don't know', are not shown.
Source: Wales Life and Times Survey, 2001–7.

improvements in education, while just 25 per cent credited the UK Government. But whereas, in 2001, just 6 per cent believed that falling educational standards could be attributed to the Welsh Assembly, six years on, this proportion had risen to 26 per cent (although far more – 47 per cent – continued to blame the UK Government for poor educational performance).

Thus, if devolution is intended to grant sub-national governments a degree of policy autonomy, and for these administrations to take public responsibility for their decisions, the evidence from Scotland and Wales suggests growing success. At the outset of the devolved institutions' life, policy outcomes were primarily attributed not to actors in Edinburgh or Cardiff, but to those in London. Although the UK Government is still seen as a significant actor, policy responsibility for health and education are increasingly being attributed to the devolved administrations. However, while the devolved actors were initially shielded from criticism over poor policy performance, they are now taking not only some credit for improvements, but also some of the blame for failure.

Conclusion

Devolution to Scotland and Wales represented a major reform of the British state. This chapter has sought to review how people in Scotland and Wales have responded to this change. We have seen that, prior to 1999, devolution was keenly anticipated in Scotland. For people in Scotland, some form of self-government had been a long-standing demand, and the Scottish Parliament was overwhelmingly backed in the 1997 referendum. Expectations immediately before and after the establishment of the Parliament in 1999 were high, with the new body seen as likely to deliver both policy and democratic improvements. In Wales, the demand for devolution was lower, and expectations of what the Assembly would achieve were more cautious, with large sections of the Welsh population anticipating that devolution would make no difference to outcomes.

However, the perceived performance of the Scottish Parliament and Welsh Assembly since 1999 has failed to match expectations. This decline is most noticeable in Scotland, although it may be that, here, early expectations of what a Scottish Parliament might achieve were rather inflated. However, since 2000, there has been little further decline in the way people have evaluated the performance of the devolved bodies. While, admittedly, the data in Wales are too limited to allow for firm judgments, it appears as though the performance of the devolved institutions has reached a steady state in the eyes of the Welsh public too. Few people believe the Scottish Parliament and Welsh Assembly are doing much harm on issues such as education, health, their country's voice within the United Kingdom or people's influence on decisions. Instead, popular doubts appear to lie in a lack of conviction that the bodies are making any difference at all to outcomes, even though there appears to be a growing recognition of their role in matters such as health and education. If the devolved institutions face a challenge from the public, it is not that they are damaging to economic, social and democratic outcomes, but that they are simply not delivering what the public anticipated at their inception.

Maybe this should not be held too strongly against the devolved institutions. After all, even by the endpoint of our data, these institutions are less than a decade old. Performance may well improve as the devolved bodies accumulate further experience (and possibly powers). But our data highlight a growing challenge for the devolved bodies in Scotland and Wales. We have suggested that people in Scotland and Wales are adjusting to the exercise of power under devolution, and attributing greater responsibility for outcomes to the devolved bodies. This may allow the devolved institutions to claim greater credit for policy improvements, but will also entail the apportionment of blame when things are seen to go wrong.

Having explored the way people have evaluated the performance of the Scottish Parliament and Welsh Assembly since 1999, a further question arises. This is how people's experience of the early years of devolution has shaped their views on the nature and powers of the devolved bodies. Have the rather lukewarm assessments of performance we have identified among people in Scotland and Wales impelled them to seek reforms to these institutions? Have they lost faith with the idea of self-government to the extent of seeking the end of devolution? Or would they like to increase the powers wielded by the devolved bodies, even to the extent of breaking up Britain into separate states? The implications of devolution's early years for the wider constitutional stability of the United Kingdom are the subject of the following chapter.

References

Brown, A. *et al.* (1999) *The Scottish Electorate: The 1997 General Election and Beyond*, Houndmills, Basingstoke: Macmillan

Denver, D. *et al.* (2000) *Scotland Decides: The Devolution Issue and the 1997 Referendum*, London: Frank Cass

Ormston, R. and C. Sharp (2007) *Scottish Social Attitudes Survey 2006: Core Module Report One – Attitudes to Public Services in Scotland*, Edinburgh: Scottish Government Social Research

Park, A. and D. McCrone (2006) 'The devolution conundrum?', in C. Bromley *et al.*, eds., *Has Devolution Delivered?* Edinburgh: Edinburgh University Press

Scottish Constitutional Convention (1995) *Scotland's Parliament, Scotland's Right*, Edinburgh: Scottish Constitutional Convention

Welsh Office (1997) *A Voice for Wales: The Government's Proposals for a Welsh Assembly*, Cm 3718, London: The Stationery Office

Annex Question wordings on attitudes to devolution

Scotland

	No devolution	More regional decisions	Regional assembly	Independence
1970: Royal Commission on the Constitution				
1975: Survey on Scottish Attitudes to Devolution				
For running Scotland as a whole, which of these five alternatives would you prefer overall?				
Leave things as they are at present	✓			
Keep things much the same as they are now but make sure that the needs of the region are better understood by the government	✓			
Keep the present system but allow more decisions to be made in the region		✓		
Have a new system of governing the region so that as many decisions as possible are made in the area			✓	
Let the region take over complete responsibility for running things in the area				✓
1974, 1979: British/Scottish Election Study				
There has been a lot of discussion recently about giving more power to Scotland (1974). Which of these statements comes closest to what you yourself feel should be done (1979: about the governing of Scotland)?				
Keep the governing of Scotland much as it is now	✓			
Make sure the needs of Scotland are better understood by the government	✓			
Allow more decisions to be made in Scotland		✓		
Scotland should completely run its own affairs				✓

	No devolution	More regional decisions	Regional assembly	Independence
1991: State of the Nation				
1992: Scottish Election Study				
1994, 1996: British Election Panel Study				
Now thinking about the running of Scotland, which of these options would you most like to see? (1991)				
An issue in Scotland is the question of an elected assembly – a special Parliament for Scotland dealing with Scottish affairs. Which of these statements comes closest to your view? (1992, 1994, 1996)				
There should be no change from the present system	✓			
Scotland should remain part of the UK but with its own elected Assembly that has some taxation and spending powers			✓	
Scotland should become independent, separate from the UK (1991: England and Wales) but part of the European Community				✓
Scotland should become independent, separate from the UK (1991: England and Wales) and the European Community				✓
1997: Scottish Election Study				
An issue in Scotland is the question of an elected parliament – a special Parliament for Scotland dealing with Scottish affairs. Which of these statements comes closest to your view?				
Scotland should remain part of the UK without an elected parliament	✓			
Scotland should remain part of the UK with its own elected parliament which has no taxation powers			✓	
Scotland should remain part of the UK but with its own elected parliament which has some taxation powers			✓	

	No devolution	More regional decisions	Regional assembly	Independence
Scotland should become independent, separate from the UK but part of the European Union				✓
Scotland should become independent, separate from the UK and the European Union				✓

Wales

	No devolution	More regional decisions	Regional assembly	Independence
1970: Royal Commission on the Constitution				
For running Wales as a whole, which of these five alternatives would you prefer overall?				
Leave things as they are at present	✓			
Keep things much the same as they are now but make sure that the needs of the region are better understood by the government	✓			
Keep the present system but allow more decisions to be made in the region		✓		
Have a new system of governing the region so that as many decisions as possible are made in the area			✓	
Let the region take over complete responsibility for running things in the area				✓
1979: Welsh Election Study				
Which option comes closest to your view of the ideal form of government for Wales?				
No change, keeping the governing of Wales much as it is now	✓			
An Assembly as proposed at the referendum		✓		
A stronger Assembly with its own law making powers, like the one proposed for Scotland			✓	

	No devolution	More regional decisions	Regional assembly	Independence
Complete self-government for Wales				✓

1983, 1987: British Election Survey

An issue in Wales is the question of an elected assembly – a special Parliament for Wales dealing with Welsh affairs. Which of these statements comes closest to your view?

	No devolution	More regional decisions	Regional assembly	Independence
Keep the governing of Wales much as it has been	✓			
Some other way should be found to make sure the needs of Wales are better understood by the government in London	✓			
There should be an elected assembly for Wales			✓	
Wales should become completely independent				✓

1992: British Election Study

An issue in Wales is the question of an elected assembly – a special Parliament for Wales dealing with Welsh affairs. Which of these statements comes closest to your view?

	No devolution	More regional decisions	Regional assembly	Independence
There should be no change from the present system	✓			
Wales should remain part of the UK but with its own elected assembly which has some taxation and spending powers			✓	
Wales should become independent, separate from the UK but part of the European Community				✓
Wales should become independent, separate from the UK and the European Community				✓

1997: Welsh Referendum Study

An issue in Wales is the question of an elected assembly – a special Parliament for Wales dealing with Welsh affairs. Which of these statements comes closest to your view?

Wales should remain part of the UK without an elected assembly	✓
Wales should remain part of the UK with its own elected assembly which has limited law making powers only	✓
Wales should remain part of the UK with its own elected assembly which has law-making and taxation powers	✓
Wales should become independent, separate from the UK but part of the European Union	✓
Wales should become independent, separate from the UK and the European Union	✓

6
The citizens' response: devolution and the Union

John Curtice and Ben Seyd

In the previous chapter we examined the impact the devolved institutions are thought to have had on the governance of Scotland and Wales. In so doing we considered in particular whether devolution was thought to have delivered some of the instrumental benefits it was hoped it would bring. Now we turn to a broader question: what impact has devolution had on attitudes towards the Union? Has devolution helped cement the Union by meeting the aspirations of people in Scotland and Wales for a measure of self-government? Or has it set the United Kingdom on a course that will eventually result in its dissolution?

Dissolution is certainly what many critics feared would be the ultimate consequence of devolution. By providing people in Scotland and Wales with political institutions that symbolised their distinctive national identity instead of their Britishness, devolution would fuel nationalist sentiment (Thatcher, 1998). By giving politicians in Scotland and Wales the opportunity to govern effectively, devolution would encourage the feeling in those countries that they could go it alone. Meanwhile, the highly asymmetric nature of a devolution settlement that granted a significant measure of self-rule to Scotland and Wales but denied it to England would generate an 'English backlash'. Such a backlash would, at best, put additional strains on the Union as people in England sought some form of devolution for themselves and would, at worst, lead to the Union's demise as they demanded that Scotland and Wales should fend for themselves.

In contrast, many advocates of devolution argued the very opposite case (see, for example, Mackintosh, 1998; Bogdanor, 1999; Davies, 1999; Aughey, 2001). The creation of devolved institutions in Scotland and Wales would demonstrate to the people of those countries that their distinctive aspirations and identities could be accommodated within the framework of the Union. As a result, devolution would, in the memorable words of the former Shadow Scottish Secretary, George Robertson, kill nationalism 'stone dead'. Instead of fuelling demands for independence, the separatist cause would be denied the oxygen of discontent and resentment that was generated by the previous arrangements for governing Scotland and Wales.

Our aim in this chapter is to establish which of these two perspectives is the more accurate, now that the public has had nearly a decade of experience on which to judge the merits of devolution. We begin by examining trends in national identity in each of Scotland, Wales and England. Has the advent of devolution served to undermine whatever sense of Britishness existed hitherto in Scotland and Wales (Paterson *et al.*, 2001: 101–2)? And has the creation of separate institutions in Scotland and Wales generated a reaction amongst people in England, encouraging them to think of themselves as English rather than British? We then consider people's constitutional preferences. Has support for independence risen or declined in Scotland and Wales? Has the absence of devolved institutions in England generated resentment towards Scotland and Wales, or alternatively a demand that England should enjoy some form of devolution too? Finally, we consider possible pressures for change short of dismantling the framework of the current asymmetric devolution settlement. Do people in Scotland and in Wales want to see significant changes in the powers of their devolved institutions? And how far do people in England want to see some of the apparent anomalies thrown up by the asymmetric settlement removed?

The decline of Britishness?

National identity is often thought to provide the emotional 'glue' that helps keep a country together. People who share the same national identity are likely to be willing – indeed will positively wish – to be governed by the same set of political institutions (Gellner, 1983). They are also more likely to accept that they have an obligation to support each other in time of need (Miller, 2000). So if people's sense of Britishness were to decline, this would seem to pose a threat to their willingness to maintain the United Kingdom.

There are two slightly different measures of national identity available to us in our surveys. One measure simply asks respondents to examine an extensive list of possible national identities and to state which apply to themselves. Respondents may choose more than one, but in that event they are then asked to state which single one best applies to themselves. Although the list is extensive, most people choose British or one of the three sub-state national identities, that is English, Scottish or Welsh. So in

Table 6.1, we show for each of England, Scotland and Wales, how many people have, when forced to choose a single identity, said they are British and how many said they are English/Scottish/Welsh as appropriate.

The results show different patterns in each of the three countries. In Scotland, adherence to a British national identity declined considerably during Mrs Thatcher's tenure as Prime Minister. By the time people in Scotland were being asked in 1997 to vote in the devolution referendum, no more than one in five chose 'British' as their principal identity. However, since the creation of the Scottish Parliament in 1999 there has not been any consistent trend. Annual readings have simply shown trendless fluctuations around a position where three-quarters of people in Scotland say they are Scottish and somewhat less than one in five say they are British. As one of us has suggested elsewhere, devolution in Scotland was more a product of, than a contributor to, a strengthening of a distinctive sense of national identity (Curtice, 2006).

In Wales, too, there is little sign that the creation of devolved institutions has been accompanied by a decline in British national identity. But in contrast to Scotland, it appears that Britishness did not decline either in the period before the introduction of devolution. As a result, although they are still a minority, the proportion of people in the principality who say they are British is, at around three in ten, substantially larger than the equivalent group in Scotland. Meanwhile, the proportion of people who say they are Welsh is typically close to twice that figure.

It is in England, however, that a sense of British national identity is at its strongest. But it is also in England where Britishness does seem to have declined since the advent of devolution. As can be seen from Table 6.1, in two readings taken before 1999, around one in three said that they were English while around three in five said they were British. But in 1999, in the weeks after the first devolved elections were held, the two groups proved to be of equal size. Although thereafter, those saying they are British have again outnumbered those claiming they are English, the imbalance was never as large as before 1999. Typically in recent years, around two in five have said they are English, while one half say they are British. It seems possible that, to some degree, people may have been made aware of their distinctive English national identity by the creation of separate political institutions in Scotland and Wales.

Still, it may be felt that forcing people to choose a single national identity is potentially misleading. Perhaps people hold, say, their Scottish identity in combination with a British identity. Failure to recognise that fact may lead us to understate the level of adherence to British national identity and to exaggerate the significance of the apparent decline we have identi-

Table 6.1 Trends in 'forced choice' national identity in Scotland, Wales and England, 1979–2007

	1979 (%)	1992 (%)	1997 (%)	1999 (%)	2000 (%)	2001 (%)	2002 (%)	2003 (%)	2004 (%)	2005 (%)	2006 (%)	2007 (%)
Scotland												
Scottish	56	72	72	77	80	77	75	72	75	79	78	72
British	38	25	20	17	13	16	18	20	19	14	14	19
Wales												
Welsh	59	Na	63	57	Na	57	Na	60	Na	Na	Na	56
British	34	Na	26	31	Na	31	Na	27	Na	Na	Na	32
England												
English	Na	31	34	44	41	43	37	38	38	40	47	39
British	Na	63	59	44	47	44	51	48	51	48	39	48

Note: Data for Wales in 1997 were obtained after the devolution referendum; those for Scotland and England were obtained after the UK general election. Na=Not asked.
Sources: Scottish Election Studies, 1979–97; Scottish Social Attitudes, 1999–2007; Welsh Election Study, 1979; Welsh Referendum Study 1997; Welsh Assembly Election Study 1999; Wales Life and Times Surveys, 2001–7; British Election Studies, 1992 and 1997; British Social Attitudes, 1999–2007.

fied in England. Our second measure, known as the Moreno scale (Moreno, 1988), recognises the existence of dual identities by allowing people to choose one of a number of options that both permit people to deny they are British at all and to state that they feel both British and Scottish/Welsh/English. The measure reads:

> Which, if any, of the following best describes how you see yourself?
>
> Scottish/Welsh/English not British
> More Scottish/Welsh/English than British
> Equally Scottish/Welsh/English and British
> More British than Scottish/Welsh/English
> British not Scottish/Welsh/English

In practice, as Table 6.2 shows, the pattern of responses received in response to this question largely confirms the impression given by our first measure. In Scotland, a British identity clearly plays second fiddle to a Scottish one, but this is no more true now than it was when the Scottish Parliament was first created. Typically around two-thirds say they are wholly or mostly Scottish. In Wales, the proportion saying they are wholly or mostly Welsh, is typically rather lower, at between two-fifths and a half, but this group still clearly outnumbers those who say they are wholly or mostly British. One trend that we can discern that was not evident in Table 6.1 is an apparent increase between 1999 and 2001

Table 6.2 Trends in Moreno national identity in Scotland, Wales and England, 1992–2007

	1992 (%)	1997 (%)	1999 (%)	2000 (%)	2001 (%)	2003 (%)	2005 (%)	2006 (%)	2007 (%)
Scotland									
Scottish not British	19	23	32	37	36	31	32	33	27
More Scottish than British	40	38	35	31	30	34	32	32	30
Equally Scottish and British	33	27	22	21	24	22	22	21	28
More British than Scottish	3	4	3	3	3	4	4	4	5
British not Scottish	3	4	4	4	3	4	5	5	6
Wales									
Welsh not British	Na	17	17	Na	24	21	Na	Na	24
More Welsh than British	Na	26	19	Na	23	27	Na	Na	20
Equally Welsh and British	Na	34	37	Na	28	29	Na	Na	32
More British than Welsh	Na	10	8	Na	11	8	Na	Na	9
British not Welsh	Na	12	14	Na	11	9	Na	Na	9
England									
English not British	Na	7	17	19	17	17	Na	Na	19
More English than British	Na	17	15	14	13	19	Na	Na	14
Equally English and British	Na	45	37	34	42	31	Na	Na	31
More British than English	Na	14	11	14	9	13	Na	Na	14
British not English	Na	9	14	12	11	10	Na	Na	12

Notes: Data for Wales in 1997 were obtained after the devolution referendum; those for Scotland and England were obtained after the UK general election. Na=Not asked.
Sources: Scottish Election Studies, 1992-97; Scottish Social Attitudes, 1999-2007; Welsh Referendum Study 1997; Welsh Assembly Election Study 1999; Wales Life and Times Surveys, 2001–7; British Election Study, 1997; British Social Attitudes, 1999–2007.

in the proportion who say they are 'Welsh, not British', an increase that has apparently been sustained thereafter. But even so, there is no sign of a consistent secular trend since 2001. In England, meanwhile, only around one in three say they are wholly or mostly English, but again this group has consistently been larger since 1999 than it was beforehand.

One conclusion is clear. The advent of devolution has not been accompanied by any strengthening of a sense of Britishness. But the more apocalyptic claims about its likely negative impact have not been fulfilled either. It certainly seems to be the case that Britishness has not been eroded in Scotland, not least because, by 1999, there were already so few who strongly adhered to that identity. In Wales, the evidence is somewhat inconsistent but certainly does not suggest a process of continuous decline. It is, ironically, in England where adherence to British national identity seems to have declined somewhat just as the devolved institutions were being created in 1999. But even here the change seems to have been a one-off event rather than the beginning of a continued fall.

Still, while British national identity might potentially be a glue that helps maintain public support for the Union, it is far from inevitable that those who say they are Scottish or Welsh want to leave the United Kingdom (Rosie and Bond, 2003). They may find it sufficient that their national identity is recognised in the form of devolved institutions. We thus now turn to more direct measures of people's preferences for how the United Kingdom should be governed.

A slippery slope to independence?

The first survey measures we have capture attitudes towards the constitutional debate in Scotland and Wales. The measures differ slightly in the two countries. In Scotland, surveys ask people which of five possible constitutional positions they prefer, two of which refer to independence – either inside or outside the European Union – two to some form of devolution – either with or without taxation powers – while the last refers to staying inside the United Kingdom without having a devolved parliament. In Wales, the survey measures reflect the fact that, when established in 1999, the Welsh Assembly was denied primary legislative authority (as well as taxation powers). Thus, among the constitutional options offered to people in Wales, the first of the two devolution options refers to having a parliament with primary law making powers, while the second refers to an assembly with only 'limited' law making powers. The three remaining options are, however, the same as those in Scotland.

One important pattern is found in both Scotland and Wales (Table 6.3). Opposition to the creation of separate political institutions fell away as soon as they were established in 1999, and has remained relatively low ever since. This is particularly true in Wales, where the opposition to the creation of the Assembly came very close to being victorious in the 1997 referendum. Immediately after that referendum, over one-third of people in Wales still said they opposed the creation of any kind of assembly. But by 1999, that figure had halved and has continued to fluctuate at around one in five ever since. In Scotland, the level of opposition has fallen from just under one in five to around one in ten. There seems to be little doubt that the idea of having distinctive political institutions has secured widespread assent within both Scotland and Wales.

But what form of distinctive institutions do people in those countries want? In particular, has the advent of devolution fostered or quelled the demand for independence? In truth, what has been notable in both countries is the stability of support for independence over the last decade. In

Table 6.3   Constitutional preferences for Scotland and Wales, 1999–2007
(Scottish and Welsh samples)

	1997 (%)	1999 (%)	2000 (%)	2001 (%)	2002 (%)	2003 (%)	2004 (%)	2005 (%)	2006 (%)	2007 (%)
Scotland										
Independent in/out EU	28	28	30	27	30	26	32	35	30	24
Devolution with tax powers	44	50	47	54	44	48	40	38	47	54
Devolution without tax powers	10	8	8	6	8	7	5	6	7	8
No devolution	18	10	12	9	12	13	17	14	9	9
Wales										
Independent in/out EU	13	9	Na	12	Na	13	Na	Na	Na	12
Devolution with legislative/ tax powers	18	35	Na	37	Na	36	Na	Na	Na	42
Devolution with limited legislative powers	25	35	Na	25	Na	25	Na	Na	Na	26
No devolution	37	18	Na	23	Na	20	Na	Na	Na	16

Note: Na=Not asked.
Sources: Scottish Election Study 1997; Scottish Social Attitudes, 1999–2007; Welsh
Referendum Study, 1997; Welsh Assembly Election Study, 1999; Wales Life and Times
Surveys, 2001–7.

Scotland, the level of support for independence has rarely varied much
from 30 per cent since 1997. Not even the success of the SNP in the 2007
Scottish election signified any marked increase in support for independence; rather, it was accompanied by the lowest level of support yet for
independence. Meanwhile in Wales, support for independence has varied
little from around one in eight. While devolution has certainly not killed
support for independence 'stone dead' – in Scotland, at least, independence continues to be supported by a substantial minority – there is no
evidence that devolution has fostered constitutional nationalism. On this
measure at least, the Union seems neither stronger nor weaker than it was
when devolution was first introduced.

With support for independence largely steady, but opposition to the
creation of any kind of assembly or parliament lower from 1997 onwards,
it comes as little surprise to learn that some form of devolution has consistently been the most popular option in both Scotland and Wales. Indeed,
it has usually been backed by a majority. Although for a while, in 2004 and
2005, it looked as though support for devolution was declining in Scotland, by 2007 its popularity had been restored. Moreover, the vast majority
of those in favour of devolution believe that the parliament should have
some taxation powers. In Wales, by contrast, opinion has been more evenly
divided between having an assembly without legislative and taxation
powers and a parliament that does have such powers, albeit with opinion

gradually moving in favour of the latter. We will return to the implications of this trend later in this chapter.

But what does England think about the way that Scotland and Wales should be governed? Survey questions on people's preferred constitutional status for Scotland and Wales have been asked not only in these countries, but also among people in England. This gives us an indication of any wish in England for Scotland or Wales to leave the Union, as well as public willingness to tolerate the existence of devolved bodies in Edinburgh and Cardiff.

The relevant data are set out in Table 6.4. First, we should note that there is little apparent appetite for ending the Union. Only around one in five people in England say that Scotland should become independent, while just one in six believe the same about Wales.[1] Moreover, there is no sign of either figure increasing over time. True, we should not presume that this commitment to preserving the Union is necessarily deeply felt; in 2003, only 49 per cent of people in England said that they would be sorry if England, Scotland and Wales were all to become separate countries, while in 2007 only 44 per cent did so. Nevertheless, it seems that support for the Union remains as strong in England now as it was at the outset of the devolution settlement.

Table 6.4 Constitutional preferences for Scotland and Wales, 1999–2007 (English sample)

	1997 (%)	1999 (%)	2000 (%)	2001 (%)	2003 (%)	2007 (%)
Scotland						
Independent in/out EU	14	20	20	19	17	19
Devolution with tax powers	38	44	44	53	51	36
Devolution without tax powers	17	10	8	7	9	12
No devolution	23	13	17	11	13	18
Wales						
Independent in/out EU	13	20	17	17	16	17
Devolution with legislative/tax powers	37	34	35	39	37	29
Devolution with limited legislative powers	18	22	17	19	20	18
No devolution	25	15	20	14	15	20

Sources: British Election Study, 1997; British Social Attitudes, 1999–2007.

[1] These figures receive further support from the answers given to an additional question asked in 2007 only. This found that just 16 per cent of people in England believed it would be in England's interest to become independent of the rest of the United Kingdom.

Nor are people in England unhappy with the devolution of power to Scotland and Wales. Indeed, since 1999, attitudes in England towards how Scotland and Wales should be governed have been remarkably similar to public opinion within those two countries. Usually a majority has expressed support for some form of devolution, with most backing taxation powers for the Scottish Parliament, while opinion on the best form of devolution for Wales is more evenly divided. However, there is one exception to this generalisation. In 2007, support in England for Scottish and Welsh devolution appears to have dropped somewhat, falling to a little below half in both cases. Perhaps this is a first sign of England's patience beginning to wear a little thin. But we might note that, while the support for Scottish devolution fell between 2003 and 2007 by twelve points, and for Welsh devolution by ten, opposition to the existence of any kind of separate institutions for Scotland and Wales only increased by five points. The difference is accounted for by an increase in the proportion saying, 'Don't Know' to our survey question. So instead of being a sign of growing resentment, the recent decline in support in England for Scottish and Welsh devolution may simply reflect a growing lack of interest.

There is also little sign that any growing resentment in England has fuelled a demand that England should have devolution too. In contrast to Scotland and Wales, in England two very different models of devolution have vied with each other for pre-eminence. One is that there should be a system of assemblies in each of England's regions, a policy backed by the UK Labour government until the first attempt to create such an assembly in the North East was defeated in a referendum in November 2004. The other is to create a parliament for the whole of England, with powers and responsibilities not dissimilar to those enjoyed by the Scottish Parliament, an idea spearheaded by the Campaign for an English Parliament. Thus in asking people in England how they would like to be governed, our surveys have presented both of these options together with the status quo of England being 'governed as it is now, with laws made by the UK Parliament'.

It is this last option, of no devolution, that has consistently proved the most popular (Table 6.5). On each of the nine occasions during the last decade when attitudes towards devolution for England have been surveyed, over half have supported the status quo. There were some signs of growing support for regional devolution up to, and including, 2003, but this seems to have fallen away again in the wake of the referendum defeat in the North East. Meanwhile, support for the idea of an English Parliament has never been much above 20 per cent. While there is substantial minority support for some form of devolution for England, the fact that this support is

Table 6.5 Constitutional preferences for England, 1999–2007

	1999 (%)	2000 (%)	2001 (%)	2002 (%)	2003 (%)	2004 (%)	2005 (%)	2006 (%)	2007 (%)
Governed as now from UK Parliament	62	54	59	56	55	53	54	54	58
English regional assemblies	15	18	21	20	24	21	20	17	14
English Parliament	18	19	13	17	16	21	18	22	17

Note: In 2004–6, the regional assemblies were described as bodies that make 'decisions about the region's economy, planning and housing', while in other years they were introduced as bodies that run 'services like health'. The 2003 survey carried both versions of this option and demonstrated that the different wording did not make a material difference to the response pattern.
Source: British Social Attitudes, 1999–2007 (respondents in England only).

divided between two very different options helps to dissipate its potential influence. In any event, overall it seems that the pattern of asymmetric devolution introduced in 1999 reflects and respects the varying contours of public opinion across the United Kingdom, in which there is widespread support for devolved institutions in Scotland and Wales, but little enthusiasm for their introduction in England.

We might at this stage be wondering how it is possible for there to be continued apparent support for the maintenance of the United Kingdom given the far from overwhelming commitment to a common British national identity we identified earlier. How, for example, can Scotland remain relatively content with remaining in the Union when four out of five prioritise their Scottish identity over any British one they may feel? Why is England apparently so little interested in devolution given that, even there, around two in five prioritise their sense of Englishness?

The answer is reasonably straightforward. People's constitutional preferences are not tied to their national identity as strongly as is sometimes supposed. This is illustrated in Table 6.6, which shows people's preferred form of government for their part of the United Kingdom amongst those who, in response to the first of our two measures of national identity, indicated they felt British or Scottish/Welsh/English. As we would expect, those in Scotland and Wales who prioritise their Scottish or Welsh identity are more likely to favour independence than are those who primarily regard themselves as British (this effect is particularly noticeable in Scotland). Equally, opposition to any form of separate political institutions is higher amongst those who say they are British. But in neither case are these associations sufficiently strong to stop a majority of both groups supporting some form of devolution. For most people who feel Scottish or Welsh, it is

Table 6.6 Constitutional preferences by national identity in Scotland, Wales and England, 2007

	National identity	
	Scottish/Welsh/ English (%)	British (%)
Scotland		
Independent in/out EU	28	6
Devolution with tax powers	52	60
Devolution without tax powers	7	9
No devolution	7	21
Wales		
Independent in/out EU	13	9
Devolution with legislative/tax powers	49	31
Devolution with limited legislative powers	22	32
No devolution	11	23
England		
Governed as now from UK Parliament	50	69
English regional assemblies	16	12
English Parliament	27	11

Sources: Scottish Social Attitudes, 2007; Wales Life and Times, 2007; British Social Attitudes, 2007.

sufficient that their country's distinctive sense of identity is recognised in the form of devolved institutions, while most of those who feel British do not regard the existence of such institutions as an affront to their unionist identity (for similar conclusions, see Paterson *et al.*, 2001: 112–13; Rosie and Bond, 2003; Curtice, 2006). The result is a remarkable consensus across the two identities.

Equally, in England, those with different national identities largely agree on how England should be governed. True, those who prioritise their English identity are rather more likely to favour a separate English Parliament, while those who say they are primarily British are more likely to favour the status quo of rule from Westminster. Nevertheless, even amongst those who say they are English, half also back the status quo. Evidently, many of those who regard themselves as English regard rule from Westminster as perfectly compatible with their sense of identity. In short, it seems that the maintenance of a strong sense of Britishness may not be essential to the maintenance of public support for the Union, even in its current asymmetric form.

Need for adjustment?

Still, the fact that the broad architecture of the asymmetric devolution settlement seems to fit the contours of public opinion across the United Kingdom does not necessarily mean that pressure for change is absent. We have already seen that, in Wales, more people now want to have a parliament with legislative and taxation powers than an assembly that largely lacks such powers. Indeed, this mood has already been reflected in changes to the devolution settlement in Wales. Under the terms of the Government of Wales Act 2006, the Westminster Parliament can grant the Welsh Assembly the right to legislate in specific areas, while provision is also made for a future referendum on giving the Assembly legislative powers similar to those of the Scottish Parliament. Perhaps in Scotland, too, there is pressure to increase the powers of the parliament; certainly a cross-party commission established under the chairmanship of Sir Kenneth Calman has recommended new tax powers in particular. Meanwhile, although people in England may be broadly supportive of devolution for Scotland and Wales – albeit not wanting it for themselves – they may still feel unhappy about some of the apparent anomalies that arise as a result.

The first question to ask in examining whether there is popular pressure for further change in Scotland and Wales is to consider how powerful the current devolved institutions are thought to be. In Table 6.7, we show how people have responded when asked which tier of government they thought had most influence over the way their country was run. Consistently in both countries, more people have identified the UK Government as having the most influence than have identified their devolved administration. True, the devolved institutions have gradually been making their mark in the two countries. By 2007, 28 per cent of people in Scotland felt that their devolved body had the most influence, nearly double the 15 per cent who felt that way in 2001; in Wales the equivalent figures were 33 per cent and 17 per cent.[2] Nevertheless, the devolved institutions still clearly lag behind Westminster in their perceived level of influence.

Moreover, this perception is at odds with what people feel should be the case. As Table 6.8 shows, in both countries most people feel that their devolved government should have most influence over what happens in their country. In Scotland, around seven in ten seem to take that view, with an apparent slight decline by 2006 being reversed in the 2007 survey. In

---

[2] It is notable that, despite its weaker powers, the Welsh Assembly is as likely to be regarded as having the most influence in Wales as the devolved institutions are in Scotland.

Table 6.7 Perceptions of influence in Scotland and Wales, by tier of government, 2000–7

	2000 (%)	2001 (%)	2003 (%)	2004 (%)	2005 (%)	2006 (%)	2007 (%)
Which tier has most influence in Scotland:							
Scottish Parliament[a]	13	15	17	19	23	24	28
UK Government at Westminster	66	66	64	48	47	38	47
Local councils in Scotland	10	9	7	20	15	18	8
European Union	4	7	5	6	8	11	9
Which tier has most influence in Wales:							
Welsh Assembly	Na	17	21	Na	Na	Na	33
UK Government at Westminster	Na	61	53	Na	Na	Na	50
Local councils in Wales	Na	14	13	Na	Na	Na	5
European Union	Na	3	4	Na	Na	Na	5

Note: [a] Since 2005, the question referred to the 'Scottish Executive' rather than the 'Scottish Parliament'. The 2004 survey carried both versions of this option and demonstrated that the different wording did not make a material difference to the response pattern; the figures for 2004 are the results for the two wordings combined. Na=Not asked.
Sources: Scottish Social Attitudes, 2000–7; Wales Life and Times Surveys, 2001–7.

the early years of devolution, support in Wales for the devolved institution having the pre-eminent role was rather lower at just over one half, but by 2007, it had risen to the same level as in Scotland. This seems to corroborate our earlier evidence that opinion in Wales has gradually swung towards wanting a legislative parliament rather than an administrative assembly. In any event, it seems that there is potential public support in both countries for more powerful devolved institutions than the current settlement is thought to provide.

Further evidence that people in Scotland would like the Scottish Parliament to be strengthened is to be found in Table 6.9. This shows that, ever since the Parliament was first created in 1999, consistently around two-thirds have agreed with the statement 'The Scottish Parliament should be given more powers'. Only around one in five appears to be opposed.[3] True, the strength of this feeling should not be exaggerated – most simply 'agree' with the proposition rather than 'strongly agree' – but it does seem that the current devolution settlement fails to meet the

---

[3] Unfortunately, a similar question has not been asked on the Welsh surveys.

Table 6.8 Desired influence in Scotland and Wales, by tier of government, 1999–2007

	1999 (%)	2000 (%)	2001 (%)	2003 (%)	2004 (%)	2005 (%)	2006 (%)	2007 (%)
Which tier ought to have most influence in Scotland:								
Scottish Parliament[a]	74	72	74	66	67	67	64	71
UK Government at Westminster	13	13	14	20	12	13	11	14
Local councils in Scotland	8	10	8	9	17	15	19	9
European Union	1	1	1	1	1	1	1	1
Which tier ought to have most influence in Wales:								
Welsh Assembly	59	Na	54	54	Na	Na	Na	72
UK Government at Westminster	24	Na	25	27	Na	Na	Na	17
Local councils in Wales	11	Na	16	13	Na	Na	Na	8
European Union	1	Na	1	1	Na	Na	Na	*

Notes: [a] See note to Table 6.7. *Less than 1 per cent. Na=Not asked.
Sources: Scottish Social Attitudes, 1999-2007; Welsh Assembly Election Study, 1999; Wales Life and Times Surveys, 2001–7.

desire of many people in Scotland for the way they would like to be governed.

We can acquire some idea of how far those aspirations extend beyond Scotland to Wales from the answers given when people in the two countries were asked in 2007 which tier of government should make most of the important decisions in their part of the United Kingdom. Two of the areas of decision making we asked about were the National Health Service and schools, both areas where primary responsibility already lies in the hands of

Table 6.9 Attitudes towards the powers of the Scottish Parliament, 1999–2007

The Scottish Parliament should be given more powers	1999 (%)	2000 (%)	2001 (%)	2003 (%)	2005 (%)	2007 (%)
Strongly agree	14	23	20	13	17	24
Agree	42	43	48	46	47	42
Neither agree/disagree	20	15	14	18	17	17
Disagree	18	12	13	17	13	13
Strongly disagree	4	5	4	6	5	3

Source: Scottish Social Attitudes, 1999-2007.

the devolved administrations. In both Scotland and Wales, around three in five people said that the NHS and schools were indeed areas where their devolved body should be pre-eminent (Table 6.10). The two remaining areas we asked about are ones where responsibility clearly still lies in the hands of the UK Government: welfare benefits, and defence and foreign affairs. In the case of the latter the status quo accords with public preferences, albeit more clearly so in Wales than in Scotland. But so far as welfare benefits are concerned, there is just as much support for responsibility being assigned to the devolved institutions as there is in the case of health and schools.

For many of a unionist persuasion, especially those on the left, the idea that decisions about welfare benefits might be devolved is an anathema. To do so would cut across the notion that all citizens of the United Kingdom are entitled to the same social rights of citizenship. It would certainly constitute a radical change to the current devolution settlement. Yet this seems to be what people in Scotland and Wales want. In saying they do not favour outright independence for their country (see Table 6.3), people in Scotland and Wales may simply be saying they do not see merit in their country having its own armed forces and pursuing its own foreign policy. So far as domestic affairs are concerned, however, they may still have an appetite for Scotland and Wales taking their own decisions that extends well beyond the boundaries of the current devolution settlement.

So far as England is concerned, the current asymmetric devolution settlement is often thought to result in two unfair features in particular.

Table 6.10   Who should make most of the important decisions for Scotland/Wales, 2007

	Scottish Parliament/ Welsh Assembly Government (%)	UK Government (%)
Scotland		
NHS	63	25
Schools	63	14
Welfare benefits	63	18
Defence and foreign affairs	34	58
Wales		
NHS	61	26
Schools	56	18
Welfare benefits	58	22
Defence and foreign affairs	21	72

Sources: Scottish Social Attitudes, 2007; Wales Life and Times, 2007.

The first is the so-called West Lothian Question. As a result of the creation of the Scottish Parliament, laws for Scotland on devolved matters such as health and education are now made by that body rather than by Westminster. Nobody from England is represented in the Scottish Parliament. At the same time, the laws that apply in England to matters such as health and education are made by the UK Parliament in which MPs from Scotland do have a vote (for an extensive discussion of this issue, see Hazell, 2006). Moreover, the votes of Scottish MPs may even on occasion prove decisive, as they did, for example, in the passage of legislation on 'top-up' fees in higher education and the creation of foundation hospitals, neither of which policy was pursued in Scotland (Russell and Lodge, 2006). In short, MPs from England no longer have any say on devolved issues in Scotland, yet MPs from Scotland still have a say – and potentially a vital one – on equivalent matters in England. This would appear to be an anomaly that could easily cause resentment amongst people in England.

To establish whether this is the case we can examine the answers people in England have given when faced with the statement:

> Now that Scotland has its own parliament, Scottish MPs should no longer be allowed to vote in the House of Commons on laws that only affect England.

The responses in Table 6.11 clearly show that ever since the advent of devolution, people in England have consistently opposed the right of Scottish MPs to shape decisions on issues that only affect England. Around three in five seem to be of this view, while only one in five dissent. Moreover, there is some suggestion that support for the proposition has grown a little over time, though it remains an issue that for the most part simply secures agreement rather than strong agreement. Feelings may not therefore be as strong as some Conservative politicians such as William Hague, Lord Baker and Kenneth Clarke have assumed in proposing (in 1999, 2006 and 2008 respectively) that the right of Scottish MPs to vote on English laws should be limited.

In any event, this is not an issue that sets public opinion in England against that in Scotland. For, as we show in the bottom half of Table 6.11, people in Scotland also believe – albeit less strongly than those in England – that Scottish MPs should not vote on matters that only affect England. So the commitment of people in Scotland to the Union would not necessarily be undermined if such a change were introduced. That, of course, does not mean that restricting the voting rights of Scottish MPs would not be politically controversial, given that it would probably hinder the ability of a Labour government to secure the passage of English legislation more than the ability of a Conservative administration to do so.

Table 6.11   Attitudes towards barring Scottish MPs from voting on English laws, 2000–7

	2000 (%)	2001 (%)	2003 (%)	2007 (%)
People in England				
Strongly agree	18	19	22	23
Agree	46	38	38	37
Neither agree nor disagree	19	18	18	16
Disagree	8	12	10	10
Strongly disagree	1	2	1	1
People in Scotland				
Strongly agree	14	15	14	14
Agree	39	36	34	36
Neither agree nor disagree	17	21	29	26
Disagree	19	16	18	18
Strongly disagree	4	8	5	4

Sources: British Social Attitudes, 2000–7; Scottish Social Attitudes, 2000–7.

A second apparent unfairness suffered by England is the fact that public expenditure per head in Scotland is some 20 per cent or so higher than in England, a difference not matched by higher tax receipts in Scotland. This disparity predates the current devolution settlement, but arguably it is potentially more salient now that the Scottish Parliament is free to determine the distribution of public expenditure in Scotland while having no responsibility under the devolution settlement to raise the money it spends.[4] If, as has happened, Scotland introduces a benefit, such as 'free' personal care for older people, that is denied to people in England, it can be argued that the money of English taxpayers is being used to pay for a benefit that they themselves are denied. Such an argument might be expected to persuade people in England that Scotland gets more than its fair share of public expenditure.

In practice, people in England seem, so far at least, surprisingly tolerant of this situation. Between 2001 and 2003, only between a fifth and a quarter said that Scotland got more than its fair share of public spending (Table 6.12). One likely explanation is that few people in England are aware of the disparity; only around three-quarters of people in England feel able to respond at all when asked if Scotland receives more or less than its

[4]   The Scottish Parliament does have the ability to vary the basic rate of income tax by up to 3p in the pound. However, in 1999, the estimated revenue of an extra 3p in the pound was just £450m, well short of the then £16bn annual budget of the Parliament (Heald and McLeod, 2003: 76).

**Table 6.12	Perceptions of Scotland's share of UK Government spending, 2000–7**

	2000 (%)	2001 (%)	2003 (%)	2007 (%)
People in England				
More than fair	20	24	22	32
Pretty much fair	42	44	45	38
Less than fair	12	9	9	7
People in Scotland				
More than fair	10	10	11	16
Pretty much fair	37	36	35	37
Less than fair	58	47	48	36

Sources: British Social Attitudes, 2000–7; Scottish Social Attitudes, 2000–7.

fair share of public spending. Nevertheless, more recently the balance of opinion amongst those who do feel able to give an answer has swung towards the perception that Scotland does receive more than its fair share. Even so, this perception is still only shared by one in three people in England.

Intriguingly, however, this change of perception has not been confined to England. It seems that the public in Scotland, too, have become more inclined to think that their country does relatively well out of the distribution of public expenditure. In 2000, nearly three in five (58 per cent) of people in Scotland felt that their country received less than its fair share; by 2007, only just over one in three (36 per cent) shared that view. While people in Scotland are still only half as likely as their counterparts in England to believe that Scotland gets more than its fair share, perceptions on the two sides of the border are much closer to each other than they were in the early days of devolution.

This convergence suggests it might be possible to address concerns in England about the current financial settlement without necessarily creating a great degree of antagonism amongst the public in Scotland. One means of achieving this might be to ensure that at least some of Scotland's public expenditure was financed directly out of taxes raised in Scotland rather than, as at present, financing the work of the Scottish Parliament entirely out of a block grant from Westminster. This certainly seems to be a popular idea with people in England, amongst whom, as Table 6.13 shows, around three-quarters agree with the proposition that 'Now that Scotland has its own parliament, it should pay for its services out of taxes collected in Scotland'. Moreover, the proportion that strongly agrees with this proposition seems to have increased somewhat. Meanwhile, in tune with the mood in

Table 6.13   Attitudes to the funding of services in Scotland, 2001–7

Scotland should pay for its services out of taxes collected in Scotland	2001 (%)	2003 (%)	2007 (%)
People in England			
Strongly agree	20	22	28
Agree	53	52	47
Neither agree nor disagree	12	12	14
Disagree	11	10	5
Strongly disagree	1	0	1
People in Scotland			
Strongly agree	7	5	8
Agree	45	46	49
Neither agree nor disagree	18	16	16
Disagree	24	25	20
Strongly disagree	3	4	2

Sources: British Social Attitudes, 2001–7; Scottish Social Attitudes, 2001–7.

Scotland that the Scottish Parliament should have more powers, a little over half of people there are inclined to the same view, albeit with rather less enthusiasm. Given this symmetry of view, it is little wonder that an examination of ways of financing the Scottish Parliament was placed particularly high on the agenda of the Calman Commission on Scottish devolution.

So while the broad architecture of the current devolution settlement appears to fit the varying contours of public opinion in Britain, this does not mean that the fit is a perfect one. Although the devolved institutions are now making a bigger impression, many people in both Scotland and in Wales still feel that their devolved institutions are insufficiently powerful. People in Wales appear to support granting primary legislative powers to their Assembly, an issue on which they have been promised a vote by 2011 in the coalition agreement formed between Labour and Plaid Cymru after the 2007 election. In both Scotland and Wales, people are prepared to extend the competence of their devolved institutions to areas of domestic policy, such as welfare benefits, that are currently regarded as central to the remit of the UK Government.

Meanwhile, although people in England may not want devolution for themselves, this does not mean they are unconcerned about the apparent anomalies thrown up by asymmetrical devolution. This is certainly true of the West Lothian Question. There are also indications that debates about the distribution of public spending across the United Kingdom are beginning to have some influence on public opinion in England, albeit that, unprompted at least, only a minority appears to feel that the current distribution is unfair. Yet it does not seem that any attempt to resolve these anomalies will necessarily place a strain on public support for the Union. Many in Scotland, too, find it a little odd that their MPs are voting on purely English laws, while proposals to give the Scottish Parliament more freedom – and also responsibility – to raise the money it spends may be capable of securing public support north of the border too.

Conclusion

We began this chapter by presenting two very different perspectives on the likely impact that devolution to Scotland and Wales would have on public support for the Union. One suggested that devolution would weaken that support, the other that it would strengthen it. Our analysis has not given much credence to either proposition.

Neither Scotland nor Wales seems any keener on independence now than it was in 1999. Nor is there any evidence that England has come to the view that the Union should be dissolved. Dismantling the Union remains the view of a minority, albeit a larger one in Scotland than elsewhere. Equally, there is no evidence that willingness to uphold a British identity has weakened in Scotland, in part because relatively few prioritised their British, over their Scottish, identity even before the Scottish Parliament was established. In Wales the evidence is inconsistent. Only in England does adherence to a British, rather than an English, identity clearly seem to have suffered a clear drop. But in any event, the view that British identity is an essential glue for the maintenance of the Union seems to be mistaken.

Equally, however, adherence to a British national identity has certainly not become more common since the advent of devolution. There has been no decline in support for independence for Scotland or Wales. Moreover, although most people in Scotland and Wales seem to want to stop short of independence, the appetite in both countries for extending the areas over which the devolved institutions have competence appears to be considerable. And although England continues to show little interest in devolution for itself, this does not mean that public support cannot be aroused for proposals to 'correct' some of the apparent anomalies of the current devolution settlement.

In short, the fit between the current devolution arrangements and the shape of public opinion is not sufficiently precise to end all debate about the future shape of the United Kingdom. Scotland and Wales want more devolution than they have at present, while England is showing some signs of greater awareness of the alleged disadvantages that it suffers. Thus, we should not be surprised that the constitutional future of Scotland and Wales, together with their relationship with England, remains the subject of considerable debate, and that both countries currently face the prospect of further referendums on the subject in the near future. As Donald Dewar, the inaugural First Minister of Scotland famously quipped, 'Devolution is a process, not an event'. What remains to be seen is whether that process can eventually uncover a set of constitutional arrangements with which all parts of the United Kingdom are sufficiently content.

References

Aughey, A. (2001) *Nationalism, Devolution and the Challenge to the United Kingdom State*, London: Pluto Press

Bogdanor, V. (1999) *Devolution in the United Kingdom*, Oxford: Oxford University Press

Curtice, J. (2006), 'A stronger or weaker Union? Public reactions to asymmetric devolution in the United Kingdom', *Publius: The Journal of Federalism*, 36:1

Davies, R. (1999) 'Preface', in B. Taylor and K. Thomson, eds, *Scotland and Wales: Nations Again?* Cardiff: University of Wales Press

Gellner, E. (1983) *Nations and Nationalism*, Oxford: Blackwell

Hazell, R., ed. (2006) *The English Question*, Manchester: Manchester University Press

Heald, D. and A. McLeod (2003) 'Revenue raising by UK devolved administrations in the context of an expenditure-based financing system', *Regional and Federal Studies*, 13:4

Mackintosh, J. (1998) 'A parliament for Scotland', in L. Paterson, ed., *A Diverse Assembly: The Debate on the Scottish Parliament*, Edinburgh: Edinburgh University Press

Miller, D. (2000) *Citizenship and National Identity*, Cambridge: Polity Press

Moreno, L. (1988) 'Scotland and Catalonia: The path to home rule', in D. McCrone and A. Brown, eds, *The Scottish Government Yearbook 1988*, Edinburgh: Unit for the Study of Government in Scotland

Paterson, L. *et al.* (2001) *New Scotland, New Politics?* Edinburgh: Polygon

Rosie, M. and Bond, R. (2003), 'Identity matters: The personal and political significance of feeling Scottish', in C. Bromley *et al*, eds, *Devolution: Scottish Answers to Scottish Questions?*, Edinburgh: Edinburgh University Press

Russell, M. and G. Lodge (2006) *Westminster and the English Question*, London: The Constitution Unit

Thatcher, M. (1998) 'Don't wreck the heritage we all share', in L. Paterson, ed., *A Diverse Assembly: The Debate on the Scottish Parliament*, Edinburgh: Edinburgh University Press

7
At the ballot box

John Curtice

The story of devolution in Britain did not begin in 1999. Separate governmental institutions had long since existed in Scotland and Wales, above all the Scottish Office (created in 1885) and the Welsh Office (created in 1964). However, these institutions simply constituted a form of administrative devolution. While the Scottish and Welsh Offices had their own ministers who were responsible for (some of) the domestic affairs of their part of the United Kingdom, those ministers were in post because their party had secured election in a UK-wide contest rather than because it had demonstrated its popularity in Scotland or Wales. So if England voted one way, but Scotland and Wales another, as repeatedly happened from 1979 onwards, Scotland and Wales could be administered by a party that had 'lost' the last general election within their part of the United Kingdom. Equally, the people of Scotland and Wales were unable to express dissatisfaction with a party's performance locally by voting it out of office; that could only happen if people in England concurred with their view.

A crucial feature of the new devolution settlement was the removal of this apparent 'democratic deficit'. In creating the Scottish Parliament and Welsh Assembly, the settlement established bodies whose membership was determined by the votes of the people of Scotland and Wales alone. Now if those responsible for those countries' affairs were deemed to have performed poorly, they could be held accountable at the ballot box, irrespective of the views and votes of people of England. Equally, the people of Scotland and Wales were free to decide for themselves whom to elect into office in the first place, and thus could ensure that the views of those who ran their affairs were in tune with public opinion locally.

However, the fulfilment of this vision depends on how the people of Scotland and Wales behave in devolved elections. Such elections will hardly succeed in holding those responsible for Scotland's and Wales's domestic affairs to account if, when deciding how to vote, voters do not take any notice of how well or badly they think the incumbent devolved administration has performed. Equally, there is little chance that those elected to the devolved institutions will be representative of the views of their electorate if voters do not take into consideration the policy proposals put forward by the parties.

There is, of course, no guarantee that voters will behave in this way in any election. How far voters in mature democracies in general vote on the basis of their policy preferences or their views on the performance of the incumbent government is the subject of considerable controversy (Kiewet, 1983; Popkin, 1991; Page and Shapiro, 1992; Bartels, 1996; Delli Carpini and Keeter, 1996; Whitten and Palmer, 1999; Evans and Andersen, 2006; Anderson, 2007). But there is particular reason why we might wonder whether voters will behave in this way in a devolved election. In part this is because the task of doing so may well be harder in a system of multi-level governance (Gélineau and Bélanger, 2005; Anderson, 2006). Voters have to establish in their minds which tier of government is responsible for any disappointment they might have experienced; the UK Government at Westminster or the devolved institution in Edinburgh or Cardiff? Equally, they have to be aware which tier is able to implement any particular policy proposal; there is little point in their voting in a devolved election on the basis of policy proposals that fall (primarily) within the remit of the UK Government. In short, casting an effective vote is arguably a more demanding task when governmental responsibilities are scattered across two or more institutional tiers.

There is another reason why voters may not behave in a devolved election in the desired fashion. The theory of 'second order' elections suggests that voters do not in fact vote in elections for lower tiers of government on the basis of the issues confronting that tier. Instead they vote on the basis of their views about what is happening in the state-wide political arena (Reif and Schmitt, 1980; Reif, 1984). According to this argument, what happens in the Scottish Parliament or Welsh Assembly is of less interest to voters than what happens in Whitehall and Westminster. As a result, rather than becoming occasions for the people of Scotland and Wales to hold their devolved politicians to account or to express their views about devolved matters, devolved elections are regarded as an opportunity to express a judgement about the performance of the government in London – assuming, indeed, that voters consider it sufficiently worthwhile to vote in devolved elections at all.

Ensuring accountability and delivering representation does not, however, exhaust the possible functions that an election might perform. They both rather emphasise the role of the voter as a rational, calculating individual. Instead, elections can be occasions on which voters express a sense of belonging to, or identification with, a particular group or section of society. It was, for example, once commonplace (e.g. Butler and Stokes, 1974) to suggest that some people voted Labour as a way of expressing a sense of working-class identity. In so doing they might also have anticipated that the Labour Party would be more likely to pursue policies that collectively advantaged the working class. This suggests a rather different perspective on how voters might behave in a devolved election. Asking voters to vote in a purely Scottish or Welsh contest might stimulate them to regard it as an occasion to express a distinctive sense of national identity. As a result, national identity comes to play a greater role in accounting for how people vote in a devolved election as compared with a UK-wide contest. Equally, people may also be more concerned to support a party that will best advocate the interests of their part of the United Kingdom. After all, in a system of multi-level governance, lower tier institutions can play an important role in defending and promoting the interests of their part of the wider state. As a result, instead of simply voting for the party on the basis of how they would use the devolved powers within Scotland or Wales, voters may be concerned in a devolved election to support a party that will lobby the UK Government to make decisions beneficial to Scotland or Wales.

This chapter assesses how voters behave in devolved elections in Scotland and Wales in the light of these arguments. It begins by asking whether voters' behaviour in devolved elections thus far has been consistent with the objective that such elections should hold to account those in charge of decision making in Scotland and Wales. It then asks how behaviour in devolved elections reflects voters' views about issues of devolved policy, and thus helps ensure that elections produce a parliament or assembly that is representative of public opinion on the key issues that fall within that body's competence. Thereafter, and finally, it considers whether voters behave differently in devolved elections from the way they do in a UK-wide general election because they are more concerned in a devolved election to express their national identity or to vote for a party that they think will promote the interests of their part of the United Kingdom.

For much of the chapter, our focus is on how voters behaved in the second and third devolved elections, held in 2003 and 2007. We leave aside the first election in 1999 for one simple reason: on that occasion there was no incumbent devolved administration whose record could be held to account. In 2003 and 2007, in contrast, voters could form a judgement on how good or bad a job the incumbent administration had done and vote accordingly. Thus we can compare the importance that such judgements had on the way that people voted as compared with their opinion of the performance of the incumbent UK Government. In the last section of the chapter, however, our interest lies in comparing how people vote in devolved elections with the way in which they behave in UK general elections. We thus compare what happened in the first three devolved elections with the pattern of behaviour in the two intervening UK general elections held in 2001 and 2005. Our data come from a series of Scottish and Welsh surveys, details of which are given in the Appendix to this book.

Preliminaries

If devolved elections in Scotland and Wales are to be primarily about what is happening in these countries, then voters need to have the issues and concerns of their particular country uppermost in their minds. As compared with a general election at least, this does seem to be the case. In Table 7.1, we show the responses voters in Scotland and Wales gave when, after each general and devolved election since 1999, they were asked to state whether they had decided how to vote mainly on the basis of what was 'going on' in their part of the United Kingdom, or on the basis of what was happening across Britain as a whole. As can be seen, voters were consistently more likely in a devolved election than they were in a general election to say that they took into account what was happening in Scotland/Wales in particular. Indeed, in each case after a devolved election, a plurality said that they had focused on their part of the United Kingdom,

Table 7.1   What is uppermost in voters' minds?

	Devolved election 1999 (%)	*UK election 2001 (%)*	*Devolved election 2003 (%)*	*UK election 2005 (%)*	*Devolved election 2007 (%)*
Scotland					
Mostly what is going on in:					
Scotland	52	34	54	32	56
Britain as a whole	34	44	27	43	29
Wales					
Mostly what is going on in:					
Wales	45	22	50	Na	58
Britain as a whole	32	62	32	Na	28

Note: Na=Not asked.
Sources: Scottish Social Attitudes, 1999–2007; Welsh Assembly Election Study, 1999; Wales Life and Times, 2001–7.

whereas after a general election, most said they voted on the basis of what was going on across Britain as a whole.

This suggests the possibility that people vote in devolved elections on the basis of the devolved government's record and on the particular policy issues confronting their part of the United Kingdom. But of course, the evidence is far from conclusive. The pattern in Table 7.1 is also consistent with the possibility that national identity and perceptions of Scotland's or Wales's interests matter more in devolved elections. And, of course, even if they are focusing more on what is happening in their part of the United Kingdom, if voters think the UK Government has been primarily responsible for those developments, they may still be using devolved elections to express a judgement about the performance of the UK Government. We thus need to undertake a more nuanced analysis.

Accountability

We begin by analysing the degree to which people seem to use devolved elections to hold the devolved administrations to account. If they do, then we should find that their willingness to vote for the party or parties in power in Edinburgh or Cardiff depends on how well they think the devolved administration has performed, while ideally their views on the performance of the UK Government should not make much, if any, difference to how they vote. In particular, we might expect to find that those who, at the previous devolved election, voted for a party that formed part of the devolved administration over the last four years should be more likely to remain loyal to that party if they think it has performed well, but be less likely to do so if they believe it has performed badly. In contrast, their views about the performance of the UK Government should make little difference to their degree of loyalty.

In order to assess this possibility, our 2007 surveys in Scotland and Wales asked people how good or bad a job of running Britain the UK Government had done in recent years, and equally how good or bad a job the devolved administration in their part of the United Kingdom had done. In Scotland, of course, the previous devolved administration had been a coalition between Labour and the Liberal Democrats and so respondents were asked separately about the performance of these two parties' ministers in the Scottish Executive. However, as Labour were the senior partner in the coalition and in order to keep the analysis in Scotland comparable with that in Wales, our analysis of Scotland simply focuses on people's evaluations of the performance of Labour ministers.

Table 7.2 Overall evaluations of the performance of the UK Government and devolved administrations, 2007

	Scotland (%)	Wales (%)
Scottish Executive/		
Welsh Assembly Government		
Very/fairly good	39	46
Neither good nor bad	33	26
Very/fairly bad	20	15
UK Government		
Very/fairly good	48	46
Neither good nor bad	25	26
Very/fairly bad	23	24

Note: In Scotland, figures are for the Labour ministers in the Scottish Executive.
Source: Scottish Social Attitudes, 2007.

Table 7.2 summarises how well the various governments were thought to have performed. In Scotland, it appears that the UK Government was evaluated rather more favourably than the Scottish Executive; nearly half felt that the UK Government had done a good job, whereas less than two-fifths felt that Labour ministers in the Scottish Executive had done so. In contrast, in Wales, the same proportion of people reckoned the Welsh Assembly Government had done a good job as felt the UK Government had done so, while rather fewer believed the devolved government had done badly.

These are, however, very broad assessments. They do not tell us in what ways the various governments are thought to have done a good or bad job. Moreover, they are unable to tell us whether the devolved administrations are in fact judged on the basis of those policy areas for which they are primarily responsible. At the same time, we have to bear in mind that in asking how well various governments have performed we may simply be encouraging voters to provide a post hoc justification of why they voted as they did. Those who did not vote Labour may be reluctant to declare that Labour had in fact performed well in office, for fear of appearing inconsistent.

These potential problems are addressed by a different, more complex line of questioning that was adopted in both our 2003 and 2007 surveys. First, respondents were asked whether they thought the standard of the NHS in Scotland/Wales had increased or fallen. Then they were asked whether they felt the trend they perceived was the result of the policies of the UK Government, or the devolved administration, or for some other reason. The responses to this question enable us to ascertain how far the devolved administrations are actually thought to be responsible for recent trends in the state of the health service; the more that is the case, the more that voters would seem to have reason to vote in devolved elections on the basis of those outcomes. Much the same line of questioning was then also pursued in respect of both the quality of education and the 'general standard of living'. However, whereas education is, like health, primarily a devolved responsibility, many of the levers that affect the standard of living are in the hands of the UK Government. We would thus anticipate that fewer people would assign responsibility for the standard of living to the devolved administration than would in the case of the health service or education.

As Table 7.3 shows, the one policy area to receive a predominantly negative rating in 2003 from the public in both Scotland and Wales was the National Health Service. In both cases, approaching half felt that standards had fallen. However, by 2007 the reputation of the NHS had recovered somewhat in both countries, and the most common response then was simply that standards had remained much the same. Indeed, this was also the predominant feeling in both countries in 2007 about the quality of education, though in this case in 2003 opinion was more or less evenly

Table 7.3 Evaluations of policy performance, 2003 and 2007

Outcome	*Evaluation*	*Scotland*		*Wales*	
		2003 (%)	*2007 (%)*	*2003 (%)*	*2007 (%)*
Standard of NHS	Increased	20	19	24	25
	Stayed the same	25	45	26	40
	Fallen	46	26	44	25
Quality of education	Increased	25	20	31	25
	Stayed the same	27	45	24	43
	Fallen	29	12	26	11
General standard of living	Increased	34	29	38	37
	Stayed the same	36	41	33	31
	Fallen	24	20	22	26

Note: In Scotland, in 2007, the question asked about trends over the previous 12 months. In 2003, and in both years in Wales, it asked about trends over the previous four years.
Sources: Scottish Social Attitudes, 2003 and 2007; Wales Life and Times, 2003 and 2007.

divided between all three possible responses. In contrast, attitudes towards the general standard of living were much the same in 2007 as they were in 2003, with those thinking that standards had increased outnumbering those who thought they had fallen on both occasions in both countries.

Meanwhile, Table 7.4 reveals that people were indeed more likely to regard the devolved administrations as responsible for recent trends in health and education than they were for the general standard of living. Indeed, by 2007, people were at least as likely to regard their devolved administration as primarily responsible for trends in education as they were the UK Government. Nevertheless, we might still consider it remarkable that after eight years of devolution less than one person in three in either Scotland or Wales regards the devolved administration as primarily responsible for either the quality of education or the standard of the NHS in their part of the United Kingdom.

However, our principal interest here is not in whether people's evaluations were positive or negative, or which government they considered responsible for recent trends, but whether those evaluations were reflected in their behaviour in the polling station. Were those who thought that, overall, the devolved administration had done a bad job of running their part of the United Kingdom less likely to vote Labour again? And was the same true of those who felt that recent trends in health, education or the

Table 7.4 Attributions of responsibility, 2003 and 2007

Outcome	Who primarily	Scotland		Wales	
	responsible	*2003 (%)*	*2007 (%)*	*2003 (%)*	*2007 (%)*
Standard of NHS	Scottish Executive/				
	Welsh Assembly	21	23	22	31
	UK Government	38	34	39	34
Quality of education	Scottish Executive/				
	Welsh Assembly	25	28	20	30
	UK Government	30	22	34	29
General standard of living	Scottish Executive/				
	Welsh Assembly	18	19	17	24
	UK Government	43	37	40	43

Note: In Wales, in 2003, the question referred to the Welsh Assembly; in 2007, it referred to the Welsh Assembly Government.
Sources: Scottish Social Attitudes, 2003 and 2007; Wales Life and Times, 2003 and 2007.

Table 7.5 Logistic regression of impact of overall evaluations on voting Labour in 2007

	Scotland	*Wales*
Recall vote 2003:		
Conservative	–0.64 (.81)	–1.38 (1.51)
Labour	2.69 (.25)*	2.67 (.32)*
Liberal Democrat	0.36 (.43)	–1.42 (1.31)
Nationalist	–0.26 (.50)	0.09 (.60)
Other	1.59 (.55)*	–
(Abstained)		
Evaluation of:		
Devolved government	Ns	0.78 (.22)*
UK Government	0.86 (.12)*	0.52 (.19)*
Nagelkerke R^2	48%	53%

Note: Dependent variable is respondent reporting Labour as their first preference party in the devolved election versus not (including abstained). Recall vote is recalled constituency vote in 2003. Evaluation of devolved government and UK Government are both treated as interval level variables in which the higher the score, the more positive the evaluation.

Main cell entries for recall vote are simple contrast parameter estimates. Those who abstained represent the default category. Main cell entries for evaluations represent the effect of a one point increase in the evaluation score on the log odds of voting Labour. Figures in brackets represent the associated standard errors. Note that there were too few respondents in Wales who recalled voting for an Other party in 2003 to make it possible to produce a stable estimate.
* Significant at the 5 per cent level.
Ns=Not included in model because not significant at 5 per cent level.
Sources: Scottish Social Attitudes, 2007; Wales Life and Times, 2007.

general standard of living had been adverse, and especially so if they regarded the devolved administration as principally responsible for this?

Table 7.5 provides us with an answer to the first of these two questions. It shows the results of a logistic regression analysis where the dependent variable is whether someone supported Labour in 2007 or not.[1] The independent variables are, first, how people said they had voted in the last devolved election, in 2003, and, second, where statistically significant, their

---

[1] The measure used is voters' report of the party for whom they would have voted as their first choice if they had been given a single ballot paper to indicate their first and second choice. Use of this measure rather than actual constituency or list vote reduces the danger that our measure of support is affected by strategic considerations.

evaluation of how good or bad a job the devolved administration and the UK Government had done. By including how people voted in the last devolved election as an independent variable, our model effectively becomes one of what influenced people to switch to or away from Labour between the 2003 and 2007 elections. Respondents' evaluations of the performance of a government will only be included in the model if they are associated with such switching.

In the case of Wales, our results provide some support for the argument that devolved elections do help to hold devolved administrations to account. Whether people felt the Welsh Assembly Government had done a good or bad job of running Wales was clearly associated with the chances of someone switching to or away from Labour. Not that this was the only consideration; people also seem to have acted on their evaluations of the performance of the UK Government, but at least this seems to have been a somewhat less important influence. On the other hand, in Scotland, evaluations of the performance of Labour ministers in the Scottish Executive are not significantly associated with vote switching at all. Here, it seems that evaluations of the UK Government were the predominant influence.

In Table 7.6, meanwhile, we show the results of a similar analysis based on the answers obtained to our more complex line of questioning. Once again, we first of all include how people said they voted in the previous devolved election. Then we identify whether switching to or away from Labour was significantly associated with evaluations of any of our three policy areas, irrespective of who was thought to be responsible. Then in order to assess whether those who felt that their devolved administration was responsible[2] for an outcome were particularly likely to act on their evaluation, we include an interaction term that identifies separately the evaluations of this particular group. The argument that people use devolved elections to hold their devolved administration to account will be strongest if one or more such interaction terms proves to be significant.

So far as Scotland is concerned, we can see that evaluations of education appear to have had some influence on people's voting behaviour in 2003, while in 2007 it seems to have been the health service that was particularly important. After taking into account how they voted in 1999, in 2003 those who felt that the quality of education had fallen were less likely to vote Labour than were those who believed the quality of education had increased. In 2007, those who believed the standard of the

---

[2] This includes both those who said that their devolved administration was principally responsible and those who said that their devolved administration and the UK Government were equally responsible.

Table 7.6 Logistic regression of impact of policy evaluations on voting Labour in 2003 and 2007

	2003	*2007*
Scotland		
Recall vote 1999/2003:		
Conservative	−0.82 (.51)	−0.94 (.80)
Labour	2.87 (.22)*	3.04 (.32)*
Liberal Democrat	−0.09 (.44)	0.45 (.42)
Scottish National Party	−0.80 (.44)	−0.43 (.46)
Other	−0.04 (1.20)	1.29 (.52)*
(Abstained)		
Evaluation of education:		
(Increased)		
Stayed same	−0.22 (.23)	Ns
Fallen	−0.66 (.23)*	Ns
Don't know	0.29 (.25)	Ns
Evaluation of health:		
(Increased)		
Stayed same	Ns	−0.36 (.22)
Fallen	Ns	−0.77 (.25)*
Don't know	Ns	−0.90 (.40)*
Nagelkerke R2	43%	43%
Wales		
Recall vote 1999/2003:		
Conservative	−1.29 (.75)	−2.00 (1.50)
Labour	2.33 (.23)*	3.26 (.31)*
Liberal Democrat	−0.63 (.76)	−1.32 (1.30)
Plaid Cymru	0.35 (.38)	0.07 (.59)
(Abstained)		
Evaluation of health:		
(Increased)		
Stayed same	-0.48 (.25)*	Ns
Fallen	-0.89 (.23)*	Ns
Don't know	-2.09 (.77)*	Ns
Evaluation of standard of living:		
(Increased)		
Stayed same	Ns	0.10 (.35)
Fallen	Ns	−0.56 (.39)
Don't know	Ns	−0.20 (.56)

Evaluation of standard of living and Welsh Assembly responsible (Increased)		
Stayed same	Ns	−1.04 (.36)*
Fallen	Ns	−1.54 (.61)*
Don't know	Ns	−2.38 (.97)*
Nagelkerke R^2	33%	43%

Note: Dependent variable is respondent reporting Labour as their first preference party in the devolved election versus not (including abstained). Recall vote is recalled constituency vote at previous devolved election. Reference categories for independent variables are given in brackets. Main cell entries are simple contrast parameter estimates. Figures in brackets represent the associated standard errors.
* Significant at the 5 per cent level.
Ns=Not included in model because not significant at 5 per cent level.
Sources: Scottish Social Attitudes, 2003 and 2007; Wales Life and Times, 2003 and 2007.

NHS had fallen were less willing to vote Labour than were those who claimed the NHS had improved. However, in neither case does the relevant interaction term make an appearance. People seem to have been just as likely to have acted on these evaluations if they felt the UK Government was responsible as if they believed the Scottish Executive was.

In Wales, the picture in 2003 is not dissimilar. Evaluations of the health service appear to have had an impact on how people voted, with those who felt the standard of the NHS had remained the same, together with those who believed it had fallen, being less likely to vote Labour. The relevant interaction term is not significant. However, in 2007, when evaluations of the general standard of living emerge as particularly influential, the interaction term is significant. It suggests that support for Labour was significantly lower among those who felt the general standard of living had stayed the same or had fallen, and who also believed that the Welsh Assembly Government was responsible for this state of affairs, than it was among those who believed the Assembly Government was responsible for an improvement in the standard of living. In contrast, support for Labour was not affected by perceptions of the standard of living amongst respondents who felt the UK Government was responsible; indeed such people seem to have been relatively reluctant to support Labour at all.

We have, then, uncovered only limited evidence that people use devolved elections to hold their devolved administration to account. The strongest evidence that they do so comes from the 2007 Welsh election, when the likelihood of voting Labour seems to have been affected by how well people felt the Welsh Assembly Government had performed in general, and their views about its impact on the standard of living in particular. Even so, it is rather curious that the Assembly Government appears most likely to have been held to account for a policy area for which relatively few people think that it is responsible, while it should be remembered that overall evaluations of the performance of the UK Government seem to have mattered in 2007 too. Meanwhile, we have not uncovered any clear evidence that voters in Scotland used their evaluations of the performance of the Scottish Executive when deciding how to vote, while equivalent evidence is also lacking for the 2003 election in Wales.

Leaders

Still, it might be felt that so far we have focused on a rather abstract notion of accountability. Evaluating the state of a public service or the economy, and then deciding who is primarily responsible for that state, is a relatively demanding task for any voter. More visible and immediately present are the utterances and behaviour of those who occupy the principal offices of state. Perhaps what matters to how people vote in devolved elections is not what they think of the overall performance of their devolved administration or its particular policy successes and failures, but rather the impression they form of the effectiveness of their leaders. Equally, however, we might find voters use devolved elections to express their views about the performance of the incumbent Prime Minister in London rather than their devolved leaders.

We asked respondents to our 2003 and 2007 surveys to give Scotland's First Minister, Jack McConnell, and his counterpart in Wales, Rhodri Morgan, a mark out of ten that reflected how good or bad a job they had done as First Minister. At the same time, we also asked respondents to give Tony Blair a mark out of ten for his performance as Prime Minister. Respondents were also invited to give a mark out of ten to the leader of the principal opposition party in both countries – the Scottish National Party in Scotland and Plaid Cymru in Wales – to show how good a job they would do as First Minister. This means we can assess the possibility that voters were not simply holding the incumbent First Minister to account, but were comparing his perceived merits with those of his principal challenger.

Table 7.7 summarises the range of scores each leader received. It shows the proportion of people who gave a leader a 'good' score (seven points or more), those who gave him a more modest score (between four and six points), and how many marked him as performing badly (three points or

Table 7.7   Evaluations of party leaders, 2003 and 2007

	2003 *(%)*	*2007* *(%)*
Scotland		
Tony Blair		
Good (7-10 points)	41	39
Middle (4-6)	39	35
Bad (0-3)	18	24
Don't know	2	2
Jack McConnell		
Good (7-10 points)	20	23
Middle (4-6)	48	45
Bad (0-3)	18	22
Don't know	14	10
John Swinney/Alex Salmond		
Good (7-10 points)	9	39
Middle (4-6)	37	35
Bad (0-3)	32	14
Don't know	22	13
Wales		
Tony Blair		
Good (7-10 points)	45	39
Middle (4-6)	38	41
Bad (0-3)	16	19
Don't know	1	1
Rhodri Morgan		
Good (7-10 points)	31	27
Middle (4-6)	37	43
Bad (0-3)	15	17
Don't know	17	13
Ieuan Wyn Jones		
Good (7-10 points)	11	17
Middle (4-6)	31	28
Bad (0-3)	20	12
Don't know	40	43

Sources: Scottish Social Attitudes, 2003 and 2007; Wales Life and Times, 2003 and 2007.

less). The table also indicates how many felt unable to rate each leader at all. Two points are immediately apparent. First, the Prime Minister, Tony Blair, was more likely to receive a good score than was either of the two First Ministers, Jack McConnell and Rhodri Morgan. This even proved to be the case in 2007, by which time opinion polls suggested that Tony Blair had lost much of his former popularity across Britain as a whole. Second, far fewer people felt unable to give the Prime Minister a score than failed to mark the card of their First Minister. Mr Blair apparently put his devolved counterparts in the shade.

Still, for the most part, both First Ministers made more of an impression upon the public than did their opposition counterparts. To this though there is one clear exception, Alex Salmond, the SNP leader in 2007.[3] Not only did more people in Scotland give Mr Salmond a good score than they did Mr McConnell, but as many did so as did for Mr Blair in that year. In addition, the proportion unable to give Mr Salmond a score at all was barely any greater than was the case for Mr McConnell. Here, perhaps, is one opposition personality who might well have influenced the way that voters behaved.

In order to establish what impact people's views of the party leaders might have had on how they voted in their devolved election, we follow a similar strategy to that in the previous section. Once again, we undertake a logistic regression of whether people voted Labour or not, and include as our first independent variable how people said they voted in the previous devolved election. We then allow evaluations of both the Prime Minister and the First Minister to enter the model, using the full range of marks from one to ten (with those saying they did not know how good a job they had done being given a score of five). This is our principal means of establishing whether voters seem primarily to have been holding their First Minister to account, or whether in practice the performance of the Prime Minister was uppermost in their minds. Then, however, to help ensure that we have not underestimated the importance of evaluations of devolved leaders in influencing how people voted, we also add evaluations of the principal opposition leader in Scotland and Wales to each model.

Table 7.8 shows the results of this analysis. It suggests that, in 2003 at least, what people thought about the Prime Minister made more difference to how they voted than what they thought of Jack McConnell or Rhodri Morgan. In Wales, evaluations of Mr Morgan were not significantly associated with switching to or from Labour at all, while in Scotland evaluations of Mr Blair had a considerably greater effect on voting than did what

---

[3] At the time of writing, Salmond is the First Minister of Scotland.

Table 7.8 Logistic regression of impact of leadership evaluations on voting Labour in 2003 and 2007

	2003		2007	
	Model 1	*Model 2*	*Model 1*	*Model 2*
Scotland				
Recall vote 1999/2003:				
Conservative	–0.68 (.49)	–0.77 (.51)	–0.66 (.80)	–0.78 (.81)
Labour	2.55 (.22)*	2.51 (.22)*	2.89 (.24)*	2.89 (.24)*
Liberal Democrat	–0.16 (.45)	-0.21 (.45)	0.46 (.42)	0.52 (.43)
Scottish National Party	–0.83 (.44)	-0.73 (.45)	–0.18 (.47)	0.22 (.48)
Other	0.67(1.23)	0.65 (1.27)	1.80 (.54)*	1.91 (.54)*
(Abstained)				
Evaluation of:				
McConnell	0.11 (.05)*	0.15 (.06)*	0.16 (.05)*	0.19 (.05)*
Blair	0.32 (.05)*	0.31 (.05)*	0.20 (.04)*	0.20 (.04)*
Swinney/Salmond	–	–0.09 (.05)	–	–0.19 (.04)*
Nagelkerke R²	50%	50%	47%	49%
Wales				
Recall vote 1999/2003:				
Conservative	–1.26 (.82)	–1.23 (.82)	–1.49 (1.51)	–1.50 (1.51)
Labour	2.16 (.23)*	2.11 (.24)*	2.83 (.31)*	2.82 (.31)*
Liberal Democrat	–1.31 (.99)	–1.91 (.99)	–1.43 (1.31)	–1.43 (1.31)
Plaid Cymru	0.30 (.40)	0.45 (.40)	0.21 (.60)	0.30 (.61)
(Abstained)				
Evaluation of:				
Morgan	0.04 (.05)	0.10 (.06)	0.21 (.07)*	0.22 (.07)*
Blair	0.28 (.05)*	0.27 (.05)*	0.27 (.07)*	0.27 (.07)*
Wyn Jones	–	–0.19 (.06)*	–	–0.06 (.07)
Nagelkerke R²	39%	41%	46%	53%

Notes: Dependent variable is respondent reporting Labour as their first preference party in the devolved election versus not (including abstained). Recall vote is recalled constituency vote at previous election. Main cell entries for recall vote are simple contrast parameter estimates. Those who abstained represent the default category. Main cell entries for evaluations represent the effect of a one point increase in the evaluation score on the log odds of voting Labour. Figures in brackets represent the associated standard errors.

* Significant at the 5 per cent level.

Sources: Scottish Social Attitudes, 2003 and 2007; Wales Life and Times, 2003 and 2007.

people thought of Mr McConnell. Even if we bear in mind that evaluations of the Welsh Nationalist leader, Ieuan Wyn Jones, appear to have played some role in Wales in 2003, it is far from clear that voters were using the 2003 devolved elections to hold their devolved politicians to account.

In 2007, however, the position seems to have been somewhat different. In both Scotland and Wales evaluations of the Prime Minister and the First Minister appear to have had more or less the same impact on voters' choice. While voters' decisions in the 2007 election were hardly unaffected by what they thought of the UK Prime Minister, those contests do at least seem to have served in part as a judgement on the perceived performance of the two First Ministers. Meanwhile, as we anticipated earlier, in Scotland people's voting choice also seems to have been guided by what they thought of the principal opposition leader, Alex Salmond.

So it seems that voters may be able to use devolved elections to hold devolved politicians to account even if they are little inclined to use them to pass judgement on the performance of their policies. Of course, it remains to be seen whether what happened in 2007 proves to be the more typical of devolved elections in future, a better indication, perhaps, of what will happen once voters become more accustomed to the operation of devolution and those in power in the devolved institutions. But at least our 2007 results suggest that some degree of accountability might be provided by devolved elections.

Representation

The second main role that devolution's advocates hoped devolved elections would fulfil was to ensure that the views of those elected to the Scottish Parliament and the Welsh Assembly were representative of the public they served. No longer would it be possible for Scotland and Wales to have foisted on them a government that reflected a rather different pattern of public opinion in England, as was argued in the case of the Conservative administration between 1979 and 1997. But does the way that people vote in devolved elections reflect their views about the policy issues confronting the devolved institutions? Or do they use their vote to reflect their views on apparently more important matters that fall within the remit of the UK Government?

We are able to address these questions using data from our surveys in Scotland in both 2003 and 2007. In these surveys we asked respondents their views about a number of devolved issues on which the parties in Scotland presented clearly different positions. At the same time, we also included some issues 'reserved' to Westminster that were the subject of political dispute at the time. This enables us to establish, across a range of policy issues, how likely it was that people voted for a party whose policy position reflected their own views. If devolved elections do succeed in enabling domestic public opinion to be reflected in the Scottish Parliament, we should find that people in Scotland are markedly more likely to vote for a party if they agree with that party's views on key devolved issues.

Table 7.9 shows the pattern of responses to the questions we included. In 2003, Labour and the Liberal Democrats favoured the introduction of a Scotland-wide free bus pass for all those aged over 60, while both the SNP and the Conservatives backed a reduction in business taxes. Both proposals were apparently relatively popular. This remained true of reducing business taxes in 2007. In 2007, we also examined three further issues: the introduction of a local income tax, the abolition of any form of university tuition fee and the abolition of all prescription charges, all of which were supported by the SNP and the Liberal Democrats and opposed by both Labour and the Conservatives. While the principle of basing local

Table 7.9   Policy preferences in Scotland, 2003 and 2007

	Agree (%)	*Disagree (%)*
2003		
Cut business taxes to strengthen Scotland's economy	60	16
Free bus passes to all over 60 even though most could afford to pay	74	18
Britain was wrong to go to war with Iraq	42	40
2007		
Cut business taxes to strengthen Scotland's economy	57	14
Introduce local income tax[a]	83	11
No student should have to pay fees[b]	30	69
Abolish all prescription charges	46	40
Britain was wrong to go to war with Iraq	64	19
Agree with British Government decision to renew Trident	34	42

Note: [a] Question asked respondents whether it was better for local taxation to be based on people's income or on the value of their property. Those who said income are classified as 'agree', while those who said property are classified as 'disagree'.

[b] Question asked respondents to choose between all students paying tuition costs, some paying costs or none at all paying costs. Those giving one of the first two answers are classified as 'disagree'.

Source: Scottish Social Attitudes, 2003 and 2007.

taxation on income rather than property seems to have been overwhelmingly popular, only three in ten people felt that no student should have to make a contribution towards the cost of their tuition. Meanwhile, opinion on the abolition of prescription charges was split down the middle.

So far as reserved issues were concerned, both the 2003 and (to a lesser extent) the 2007 contests were fought under the shadow of the Iraq war. In 2003, shortly after the war had concluded, public opinion in Scotland was divided as to whether Britain was right to have taken part in the conflict. By 2007, opinion was overwhelmingly opposed. On the other hand, the public was evenly divided in its attitude towards the UK Government's decision, announced only a few weeks before the 2007 election, to renew the country's independent nuclear weapon capability based on the Trident missile system.

But were the public's views about devolved issues reflected in the ballot box? Given that in each case there were clear differences of view between the political parties on most of these issues, there was certainly plenty of opportunity for people to use their vote to express their views. In Table 7.10, we address this question by showing what proportion of those who favoured each of the policy positions outlined in Table 7.9 voted for a party whose policy position at that election accorded with their own views. Thus, for example, in the first row of the table it shows that amongst those who favoured cutting business taxes in 2003, 45 per cent voted for a party that included that policy in their manifesto. Equally, 57 per cent of those who rejected cutting business taxes voted for a party that opposed that policy.

Looking at the top half of Table 7.10, a striking pattern emerges. In most cases, there was only around a 50 per cent chance that people would vote for a party whose policy position on a devolved issue reflected their views on that issue. This, of course, is no more than would be the case if voters were to vote purely at random. Only on the issue of cutting business taxes is there some exception to that generalisation. It seems that devolved elections are indeed poor instruments for discerning the balance of public opinion on a devolved issue.

In contrast, how people voted in the devolved elections does seem to have partially reflected their views on reserved issues such as Iraq and Trident. Typically, around three in five of those taking a particular stance on one of those issues voted for a party whose position accorded with their own views. This, of course, makes the lack of correspondence between people's views on devolved issues and their voting behaviour even more striking.

Our analysis of what happened in Scotland in 2003 and 2007 casts serious doubt on the ability of devolved elections to ensure that those who

Table 7.10   Policy preferences and vote choice in Scotland, 2003 and 2007

	% vote for party consistent with position amongst those who:	
	Support policy	*Oppose policy*
Devolved issues		
2003		
Cut business taxes to strengthen Scotland's economy	45	57
Free bus passes to all over 60 even though most could afford to pay	50	53
2007		
Cut business taxes to strengthen Scotland's economy	59	64
Introduce local income tax[a]	49	57
No student should have to pay fees[a]	49	52
Abolish all prescription charges	47	48
Reserved issues		
2003		
Britain was wrong to go to war with Iraq	52	64
2007		
Britain was wrong to go to war with Iraq	56	64
Agree with British Government decision to renew Trident	61	62

Note: [a] For explanation of these measures, see the notes to Table 7.9.
Source: Scottish Social Attitudes, 2003 and 2007.

are responsible for making decisions about devolved matters are representative of public opinion in the country. Even though the political parties took clearly divergent views on a number of key devolved issues, and especially so in 2007, those positions largely do not seem to be reflected in the way in which people voted. In this respect at least, devolved elections do not seem to have proved effective in fulfilling the hopes invested in them.

National identity and nationhood

So far, then, it seems that devolved elections have only been a limited success as a mechanism that enables voters to bring their devolved administration to account, while they do not appear to have proved effective at all in ensuring that the devolved assemblies are representative of public opinion. But as we remarked at the beginning of this chapter, perhaps devolved elections play a different role. Maybe they are a mechanism for people in Scotland and Wales to express a distinctive sense of national identity and to support parties that they think will promote the interests of their nation vis-à-vis the rest of the United Kingdom.

If national identity does matter more to people in devolved elections then one likely consequence would seem to be a higher level of support for nationalist parties. After all, if people wish to express their sense of feeling Scottish or Welsh, the most obvious way of doing so would be to vote for a nationalist party. Indeed, the nationalist parties in Scotland and Wales have proved more successful in devolved elections than in UK general elections, and in this respect the pattern of behaviour in devolved elections in the United Kingdom appears to be similar to that in other sub-state elections held in territories that have a distinctive sense of national identity (Jeffery and Hough, 2003). In fact, if people in both Scotland and Wales are asked how they would vote in different elections on the same day, more say they would vote for a nationalist party in a devolved election than in a UK-wide contest. Thus, for example, whereas a third of people said that the SNP was their first preference party in the 2007 Scottish election, only 23 per cent said they would have voted for the nationalists in a UK general election held on the same day. In Wales, the equivalent figures are 22 per cent and 12 per cent respectively.

So it is clear that people in both Scotland and Wales are more willing to vote for a nationalist party in a devolved election than in a UK general election. But – crucially – does this happen because people are more likely to express a distinctive sense of national identity in devolved elections? Table 7.11 examines this possibility by showing how the level of support for the two main nationalist parties in Scotland and Wales at recent devolved and general elections has varied according to people's sense of national identity. In this case, national identity is measured using the so-called Moreno question that was introduced in Chapter 6.

Notice first of all that in Scotland, the level of support for the SNP varies little from one election to another amongst those whose national identity is exclusively or primarily British rather than Scottish. Even amongst those who say they are equally British and Scottish there seems to be little more than random fluctuation. But amongst those who say they are primarily or exclusively Scottish, there is a clear pattern. The SNP consistently performed better amongst these two groups (and especially so amongst those who feel exclusively Scottish) in the three Scottish elections held to date than it did in either of the two intervening UK general elec-

Table 7.11   National identity and support for nationalist parties, 1999–2007

	Devolved election 1999 (%)	*UK election 2001 (%)*	*Devolved election 2003 (%)*	*UK election 2005 (%)*	*Devolved election 2007 (%)*
Scotland					
(Vote for SNP)[a]					
Scottish not British	43	24	40	25	58
More Scottish than British	27	16	27	19	42
Equally Scottish and British	18	8	6	9	15
More British than Scottish	6	9	2	4	11
British, not Scottish	6	3	1	2	7
Wales					
(Vote for Plaid Cymru)[a]					
Welsh, not British	53	28	45	Na	39
More Welsh than British	48	15	22	Na	29
Equally Welsh and British	25	9	11	Na	14
More British than Welsh	13	6	5	Na	13
British, not Welsh	13	8	10	Na	13

Note: [a] Support for the nationalist parties is measured at the devolved elections by whether the respondent reported the SNP or Plaid Cymru as their first preference party in the devolved election. For UK elections, support is measured by reported vote for either the SNP or Plaid Cymru.
Na=Not asked.
Sources: Scottish Social Attitudes, 1999–2007; Welsh Assembly Election Study, 1999; Wales Life and Times, 2001–7.

tions. Evidently, the SNP generally does better in devolved elections because it is more attractive on such occasions to those with a distinctively Scottish sense of national identity.

Much the same pattern in evident in Wales, though unfortunately here we do not have any data for the 2005 UK general election. Amongst those who said they were wholly or predominantly Welsh, support for Plaid Cymru was markedly higher in all three devolved elections than in the 2001 general election. The differences are mostly rather smaller amongst the remaining three groups. Plaid Cymru, too, seems to prosper relatively well in devolved elections amongst those with a distinctively Welsh sense of national identity.

Someone with a strong sense of national identity may well feel that their distinctive sense of nationhood should be recognised in the form of a nation state. Independence may also be thought to be in a country's material interest. Either way, it seems that in Scotland at least, people not only

Table 7.12 Constitutional preference and support for nationalist parties, 1999–2007

	Devolved election 1999 (%)	*UK election 2001 (%)*	*Devolved election 2003 (%)*	*UK election 2005 (%)*	*Devolved election 2007 (%)*
Scotland					
(Vote for SNP)					
Favour independence	62	35	58	33	78
Favour devolution	17	10	12	9	22
No parliament	5	3	4	3	6
Wales					
(Vote for Plaid Cymru)					
Favour independence	65	36	42	Na	38
Favour parliament	43	18	29	Na	28
Favour assembly	24	10	11	Na	11
No assembly	11	6	7	Na	14

Note: On support for the nationalist parties, see the notes to Table 7.11. In Wales, 'favour parliament' refers to those who would like the Welsh Assembly to have primary legislative and some taxation powers, while 'favour assembly' refers to those who would prefer only to have the limited legislative powers granted to the Welsh Assembly in 1999.
  Na=Not asked.
Sources: Scottish Social Attitudes, 1999–2007; Welsh Assembly Election Study, 1999; Wales Life and Times, 2001–7.

appear to use devolved elections to express a distinctive sense of national identity, but also to indicate their support for independence As can be seen in Table 7.12, support for the SNP amongst those who favour independence has consistently been markedly higher in the three devolved elections held to date, while the variation in support amongst the advocates of devolution has been more modest, and has been almost non-existent amongst those who do not want any kind of parliament at all.

In Wales, the evidence is somewhat less clear cut. In 1999, Plaid Cymru seems be have been successful in garnering additional support across the board, except, perhaps, amongst those who did not want any kind of assembly at all. Nevertheless, if we compare the 2003 and 2007 elections with what happened in 2001, the higher levels of support for Plaid in the two devolved elections seems to have been concentrated amongst those who either wanted Wales to be independent, or at least to enjoy a stronger form of devolution than it does now.

But what of more direct measures of the degree to which parties are

Table 7.13   Perceptions of the willingness of parties to look after
Scotland's interests, 1999-2007

	1999 (%)	2001 (%)	2003 (%)	2007 (%)
Scottish Labour Party looks after Scotland's interests:				
Very closely	7	13	8	7
Fairly closely	55	55	58	57
Not very/not at all closely	34	23	30	31
Scottish National Party looks after Scotland's interests:				
Very closely	23	22	21	23
Fairly closely	45	45	49	48
Not very/not at all closely	27	26	27	23

Source: Scottish Social Attitudes, 1999–2007.

thought to be willing and able to promote national interests? In Scotland,
at least, we have a reasonable time series available to us, although unfortunately it only covers one UK general election. And, as Table 7.13 shows,
the SNP has consistently been more likely than Labour to be regarded as a
party that looks after Scotland's interests 'very closely'. While between one
in five and one in four hold that opinion of the SNP, typically less than one
in ten do so of Labour.

But is it the case that such perceptions matter more in devolved elections than they do in a UK general election? The answer to this question,
suggested by Table 7.14, is that it can be the case, albeit perhaps to varying
degrees. Much of the advance in SNP support in 2007 seems have come in
particular from those who think the party looks after Scotland's interests
very closely. On the other hand, perceptions of the SNP on this dimension
seem not to have mattered more in the 2003 Scottish election than they
did in the 2001 UK-wide contest. This suggests that perceptions of who is
best able to look after Scotland's interests are particularly capable of being
mobilised in devolved elections, but that there is no guarantee that they
will be.

Conclusion

The advocates of devolution demonstrated considerable faith in what the
creation of devolved elections could achieve for the quality of democracy in
Scotland and Wales. They hoped such elections would make government in

Table 7.14 Support for SNP by perceptions of its willingness to look after Scotland's interests, 1999–2007

	Devolved election 1999 (%)	UK election 2001 (%)	Devolved election 2003 (%)	Devolved election 2007 (%)
Support for SNP among those who think the SNP looks after Scotland's interests:				
Very closely	46	35	39	61
Fairly closely	28	14	26	30
Not very/not at all closely	6	6	8	11

Note: On support for the nationalist parties, see the notes to Table 7.11.
Source: Scottish Social Attitudes, 1999–2007.

the two countries more accountable and more representative. But if those hopes were to be realised, voters in those two countries would have to behave in certain ways in devolved elections. First, they would have to form a judgement about the effectiveness of their devolved government and be willing to act on that judgement and, second, in deciding how to vote, they would have to take into account the policy proposals of the parties on devolved matters.

For the most part, however, our analysis has suggested that voters do not necessarily behave in that way in devolved elections. In Scotland, at least, there is little indication that the way in which people vote in devolved elections reflects their views about devolved policy issues. It seems that devolved elections do little to help ensure that Scottish ministers will pursue policies that are in tune with majority public opinion north of the border. Meanwhile, we have uncovered only limited evidence that voters' choices in devolved elections reflect their views about the performance of their devolved administration. The one election for which there is relatively strong evidence of this happening is Wales in 2007, though even then evaluations of the performance of the UK Government mattered too. And while voters do seem to take their evaluations of devolved leaders into account in devolved elections, they do so alongside their evaluations of the performance of the incumbent UK Prime Minister.

Yet devolved elections in the United Kingdom cannot be dismissed as useless 'second order' affairs. Rather, it seems that they provide an opportunity for the expression of national identity and, perhaps to a lesser degree, national interest. The Scottish Parliament and Welsh Assembly were, after all, created in part in recognition of the distinctive sense of national identity that exists in Scotland and Wales. And it seems as though voters in the two countries are inclined to believe that the membership of those bodies should reflect that distinctive national identity too. Devolved elections may achieve relatively little to advance the instrumental objectives of those who advocated devolution, but they do provide an opportunity for the symbolic expression of identity. Moreover, in so doing they have provided an environment in which nationalist parties find it easier to prosper. Whether the creation of that environment is consistent with hopes that devolution would strengthen the Union remains to be seen.

References

Anderson, C. (2006) 'Economic voting and multi-level governance: A comparative individual level analysis', *American Journal of Political Science*, 50:2

Anderson, C. (2007) 'The end of economic voting? Contingency dilemmas and the limits of democratic accountability', *Annual Review of Political Science*, 10

Bartels, L. (1996) 'Uninformed votes: Information effects in presidential elections', *American Journal of Political Science*, 40:1

Butler, D. and Stokes, D. (1974) *Political Choice in Britain*, (2nd edn), London: Macmillan

Delli Carpini, M. and Keeter, S. (1996) *What Americans Know about Politics and Why it Matters*, New Haven, CT: Yale University Press

Evans, G. and Andersen, R. (2006) 'The political conditioning of economic perceptions', *Journal of Politics*, 68:1

Gélineau, F. and Bélanger, É. (2005) 'Electoral accountability in a federal system: National and provincial economic voting in Canada', *Publius: The Journal of Federalism*, 35:3

Jeffery, C. and Hough, D. (2003) 'Regional elections in multi-level systems', *European Urban and Regional Studies*, 10:3

Kiewit, D. (1983) *Macroeconomics and MicroPolitics: The Electoral Effects of Economic Issues*, Chicago: Chicago University Press

Page, B. and Shapiro, R. (1992) *The Rational Public*, Chicago: Chicago University Press

Popkin, S. (1991) *The Reasoning Voter: Communication and Persuasion in Presidential Campaigns*, Chicago: Chicago University Press

Reif, K. (1984) 'National electoral cycles and European elections 1979 and 1984', *Electoral Studies*, 3:3

Reif, K. and Schmitt, H. (1980) 'Nine second-order national election results: A conceptual framework for the analysis of European election results', *European Journal of Political Research*, 8:1

Whitten, G. and Palmer, H. (1999) 'Cross-national analyses of economic voting', *Electoral Studies*, 18:1

8
Conclusion: has devolution worked?

John Curtice and Ben Seyd

Devolution to Scotland and Wales has not been without drama and crisis since its introduction. In Scotland, the initial First Minister, Donald Dewar, who as Secretary of State for Scotland had guided the Scottish devolution legislation through Westminster, died suddenly in October 2000. His successor, Henry McLeish, only lasted twelve months before being ousted in the wake of 'sleaze' allegations. The Scottish Parliament's new building cost ten times its original budget while its completion suffered significant delays. In Wales, Ron Davies, who as Secretary of State for Wales had been responsible for that country's devolution legislation and who had been expected to lead the new Assembly, saw his political career crumble following a 'moment of madness' on Clapham Common in October 1998. His successor as Labour leader in Wales and the principality's initial First Secretary, Alun Michael, was forced to resign within the first year of the Assembly's life. Wales's new assembly building, too, had a rather chequered history; the project was suspended for two years because of a dispute with the architect, while the building eventually cost five times its original budget.

These trials and tribulations did little to enhance the public reputation of the new institutions. But the doubts they raised about their effectiveness were as nothing compared with the developments that occurred in the wake of the third set of devolved elections in 2007. In Scotland, the Scottish National Party (SNP) emerged with the most seats – one more than Labour – and went on to form a single party minority administration. In Wales, after protracted negotiations that involved more than one attempt to form a new administration, the nationalist party, Plaid Cymru, formed a coalition administration with Labour. Far from cementing the position of Scotland and Wales within the Union, devolution had provided a platform for nationalist parties committed to either full independence (Scotland) or considerable autonomy (Wales) to acquire ministerial office for the first time. Nothing seemed a surer testament to the veracity of those who warned that devolution would result in the 'break-up' of Britain.

But events and dramas are a poor basis on which to judge the success or otherwise of new political institutions. For example, simplistic readings of election outcomes can prove a misleading guide to the attitudes of voters. We need to look behind the headlines to investigate perceptions of the day to day workings of the devolution settlement. Thus, our approach in answering the question, 'Has devolution worked?' has been to look at how politicians feel the new institutions have performed, at the way that interest groups have interacted with them, at what citizens think about devolution and at how voters have behaved in devolved elections. This strategy enables us to paint a richer, if more nuanced, picture.

In the Introduction to this book we identified three objectives the new institutions were designed to fulfil. First, it was anticipated that devolution would enable the policies pursued in Scotland and Wales to be tailored to those countries' needs and requirements, and so bring material benefit to their populations. Second, the Scottish Parliament and Welsh Assembly would provide a more representative and accountable form of government, and encourage people in Scotland and Wales to participate in the political process. Third, by demonstrating the Union's ability to recognise the distinctive national identities felt by many people in Scotland and Wales, devolution would strengthen public support for the United Kingdom. Our task in this final chapter is to draw together our evidence and indicate how successful devolution has been in meeting these objectives.

Of course, it can be argued that the eight years over which our research extends is too short a period on which to judge the success of devolution. But first impressions matter. If in their early years, the Scottish Parliament and Welsh Assembly were judged by the public to be damaging their interests, by interest groups to be not worth lobbying, and by politicians to be not worth retaining, there would be a serious question mark over their future. If, in contrast, the public reckoned the devolved institutions had brought them a clear benefit, interest groups swiftly opted to make them a key focus of their activity, and politicians of all parties concluded the current devolution settlement should be retained with little or no amendment, both the institutions and the Union would have developed a solid and durable reputation. In short, in identifying the successes and failures of devolution in its early years, we will acquire an important indication of its future prospects.

Functional decision making: the effectiveness of public policies

The first goal of devolution we identified was that, by taking greater cognisance of the needs and requirements of their particular part of the United Kingdom, the new institutions would produce more effective government. In part, this goal may be linked to the degree of public engagement in the policy making process; governments will have greater information about popular demands if the public and interest groups engage with the policy making process. In that respect at least, the greater involvement of a wider range of interest groups in decision making in Scotland might have laid some of the necessary foundations for more effective government.

Politicians themselves, however, seem to have their doubts about how effective the devolved institutions have been. Unsurprisingly, few opposition Members of the Scottish Parliament (MSPs) and Welsh Assembly Members (AMs) believe that the devolved institutions have met public expectations of what devolution would deliver in terms of policy outcomes. But in Scotland at least, even Labour MSPs seem to have lost some of their initial optimism. As revealed in Chapter 4, in 2000 six in ten Labour MSPs thought that devolution was delivering, but by 2004 this figure had fallen to less than one half. In Wales, however, the trend has been in the opposite direction. Indeed by 2004, Labour AMs were more likely than their counterparts in Scotland to claim their institution was delivering. Given the weaker powers enjoyed by the Welsh Assembly, this finding may be regarded as truly remarkable. However, as we noted in Chapter 4, the success or otherwise of devolution does not simply depend on the formal powers or competences commanded by new institutions, but also on the way they are used. It may be that the willingness of Rhodri Morgan's administration in Wales to highlight the differences between its approach and that of the UK Government, in contrast to Jack McConnell's reticence in Scotland, helps to account for this optimistic mood amongst Labour AMs.

But arguably the acid test of whether or not government is thought to be more effective is whether the public are convinced they are being better governed. Here, there seems to have been one important obstacle; during the early years of the Scottish Parliament and Welsh Assembly, relatively few people saw these bodies as being primarily responsible for the success or failure of government policy. As noted in Chapter 5, most citizens attributed outcomes in health, education and the standard of living to the UK Government in London, not to the devolved administrations in Edinburgh or Cardiff. However, this picture is gradually changing. Although more people still attribute responsibility for living standards in Scotland and

Wales to decisions taken in London, this is now less clearly the case for health and education.

However, if the public are gradually being convinced that the devolved institutions matter, this does not mean they increasingly think they are having a positive impact. At best, the proportion thinking that creating the devolved institutions has improved policy outcomes in Scotland and Wales has changed little since the early days of devolution. Moreover, that proportion is very much a minority and falls far short of the large majorities who, prior to 1999, had anticipated devolution having a positive impact. True, very few people believe that devolution has made matters worse, but it seems that the devolved institutions in Scotland and Wales still have much to do to convince their populations that they are capable of stimulating improvements in public services.

There is, then, only limited evidence that the devolved institutions are thought to be providing more effective government. Interest groups have become more heavily involved in the policy process, and the public may gradually have come to appreciate that the devolved institutions do wield influence. But most people have yet to be convinced that devolution has had a positive impact, and there are even some signs of doubt among the Labour politicians who were principally responsible for running the devolved institutions between 1999 and 2007.

Democratic decision making: accountability, representation and engagement

The second criterion against which we need to judge the success of devolution is whether it has resulted in more accountable, representative and participatory government. So far as producing more accountable government is concerned, we examined in Chapter 7 whether the way that people vote in devolved elections reflects judgements of the performance of their devolved administration. However, the analysis in that chapter suggests that, if anything, voters' choices in devolved elections are more likely to reflect judgements of the performance of central government than of the devolved administrations. True, evaluations of performance by the devolved administrations do apparently have some influence on the way people vote, most noticeably in the 2007 Welsh election. However, for the most part, these evaluations seem to have been a secondary consideration in voters' minds. Thus far, devolved elections have not ensured that mistakes made by those responsible for the governance of Scotland and Wales are duly punished at the ballot box.

Chapter 7 also addressed whether devolution has helped to ensure more representative government. It did so by examining how far voting in devolved elections reflects people's attitudes towards some of the key policy questions facing their devolved institutions. Our presumption is that the more that attitudes are reflected in how people vote, the more likely it is that decisions reached by the Scottish Parliament and Welsh Assembly will reflect popular opinion. However, the analysis in Chapter 7 suggests that the way people vote in devolved elections in Scotland bears little relation to their attitudes on such devolved issues as local taxation and the funding of universities and healthcare. In fact, voting decisions appear more strongly related to issues not falling within the competence of the Scottish Government, such as overseas armed conflict (the Iraq conflict) and domestic defence (the renewal of the Trident missile system). There is little evidence here to suggest that the introduction of devolved elections has helped ensure that policy decisions made for Scotland and Wales reflect public opinion in those two countries.

There is, however, a different sense in which devolution seems to have provided representation that was previously lacking. Devolved elections appear to be occasions at which many voters seek *symbolic* representation of their national identities and interests. Compared with UK general elections, national identity and perceptions of the parties' ability to stand up for their country's interests seem to be more closely linked to voting behaviour, a pattern from which the nationalist parties in Scotland and Wales derive particular advantage. So while devolved elections may not have functioned well as vehicles for securing narrow instrumental goals like policy representation or accountability, they do seem to provide an opportunity to pursue wider expressive qualities.

Moreover, when it comes to ensuring greater engagement with the political process, devolution has achieved some success. True, the limitations are clear. As reported in Chapter 5, only around one in three people in Scotland and Wales believe that devolution has increased ordinary people's say in how they are governed, while over one half feel that devolution has not made any difference at all. Turnout in devolved elections has been lower than in contemporaneous UK general elections, especially in Wales. Meanwhile, as we noted in Chapter 4, only around one half of Labour MSPs and AMs feel the Scottish Parliament and Welsh Assembly have managed to involve ordinary people in policy making, while the elected representatives of other parties are even more sceptical.

But devolution does seem to have ensured greater involvement by interest groups in the policy making process. Around three-quarters of Labour MSPs and AMs felt the Scottish Parliament and Welsh Assembly involved these organisations more closely in policy making, a view shared by approximately half of those belonging to other parties. Meanwhile, Chapter 3 demonstrated that policy makers in Scotland have engaged in substantial consultation with business, trade unions, voluntary groups and other representative associations. Devolution has served to increase the opportunities for lobbying organisations to engage with policy makers; this is particularly the case for groups (such as the voluntary sector) that were largely denied such access under the previous 'unitary' arrangements. True, this development may also reflect the transition in 1997 from a Conservative regime (sympathetic to business) to Labour-dominated regimes (sympathetic to trade unions and voluntary organisations). Yet the contrast between the level and pattern of engagement in Scotland with that in the North East of England suggests that devolution, too, has made a difference.

So while not fully meeting all the hopes that were originally expressed for it, devolution has had some effect on the nature of democracy in Scotland and Wales. The decentralisation of political authority has encouraged more groups to engage in the policy process, though this process is still not seen as being sufficiently open to ordinary people. Voters have used the additional elections that devolution has brought to secure symbolic representation of their identities and interests. However, it is not clear that these elections ensure that policy decisions reflect the preferences of voters or their judgement of the way the devolved administrations have performed. Still, we should bear in mind that while the gains to the democratic process may have been limited, there is little evidence of any significant losses.

The health of the Union

Finally, what does our evidence suggest that devolution has done to the health of the Union? Devolution was meant to help the Union accommodate nationalist sentiment that demanded institutional recognition of national identities in Scotland and Wales. As a result, commitment to the Union itself would be strengthened. If that is indeed what has happened, then we might anticipate fewer people now wanting Scotland and Wales to become independent, with more perhaps willing to acknowledge that they feel British. Meanwhile, these gains would have to have been achieved without undue resentment being created in England at the 'privileges' granted to its neighbours.

Let us begin with national identity. The evidence in Chapter 6 does not suggest there has been any revival of Britishness in either Scotland or Wales since 1999; in both cases readiness to acknowledge a British national identity continues to be markedly less prevalent than willingness to claim a Scottish or Welsh one. On the other hand, there is little sign either that adherence to a British national identity has significantly weakened since 1999. In Scotland, neither of the two measures of national identity we presented suggests any decline has occurred. In Wales, one measure suggests a small increase in the proportion who explicitly reflect a British identity, but the other measure fails to detect any consistent change. If devolution has not realised the hopes of its advocates by helping to strengthen British national identity, nor has it justified the concerns of those who feared devolution would undermine Britishness.

But if devolution does not seem to have instigated much change in people's feelings of national identity, what has it done for people's views about the merits of Scotland and Wales remaining part of the Union? Again, it seems to have had remarkably little impact either way. In Scotland, support for independence as measured by the Scottish Social Attitudes survey has fluctuated between a quarter and a third of the population; devolution has apparently neither killed nationalism stone dead nor persuaded people of the merits of full independence. Meanwhile in Wales, where support for independence has always been weaker, only around one in eight support independence, no different from the position a decade ago.

In addition, whatever disappointment people in Scotland and Wales may feel about its achievements, devolution itself remains relatively popular. Asked to select their preferred constitutional status for Scotland or Wales, the latest figures – for 2007 – show that around two-thirds of people in Scotland (62 per cent) and Wales (68 per cent) favour devolution over either a return to rule from London or else independence from England. Further, interest groups have accepted that devolution now constitutes the 'rules of the game'. Although, as discussed in Chapter 3, not all groups in Scotland initially supported the creation of a Scottish Parliament, few if any now favour a return to the centralised status quo ante. Among the political parties, not only have Labour and the Liberal Democrats maintained their support for devolution, but the Conservatives, who in the 1997 referendums urged people to vote against devolution on the grounds that it 'would create strains which could well pull apart the Union' (Conservative Party, 1997), have been won around too. As shown in Chapter 4, as early as 2000, half of Conservative MSPs agreed with the proposition that the Scottish Parliament, not Westminster, should have most influence over the way Scotland is run. By the time of the 2005 general election campaign, the Conservative Party was committing itself to 'making a success of devolution in Scotland' (Conservative Party, 2005: 21). And although the party's 2005 UK general election manifesto pledged to hold a referendum on the status of the Welsh Assembly, including the option of abolishing it (Conservative Party, 2005: 21), its 2007 manifesto for that year's Welsh Assembly election affirmed that the party 'is committed to devolution in Wales' (Welsh Conservatives, 2007: 3). In short, devolution seems to have become firmly embedded in the body politic during the course of its early years.

But that does not mean there are not pressures for change in the devolution settlement. In fact, one of the most striking themes emerging from the preceding chapters is the widespread desire for change. Among the public in Scotland and Wales, this manifests itself in support for the devolved tiers to be granted greater legislative and financial powers. As we noted above, although there has been a growing recognition of the influence of the devolved institutions, there is still a widespread perception among the public that the key policy decisions in Scotland and Wales are determined by Westminster. (Indeed, despite the greater powers of the devolved institutions in Scotland, this is just as true in Scotland as it is in Wales.) Most people in both countries disapprove of this state of affairs; in both cases, over seven in ten people would prefer the devolved bodies to be pre-eminent. There is also evidence of public support for boosting the formal powers available to the devolved bodies. As Chapter 6 noted, a clear majority of people in Scotland favour giving the Scottish Parliament more powers, while in Wales the single most popular constitutional option is to have a devolved assembly that, unlike the present body, has primary legislative and tax raising powers.[1] Moreover, in both countries, a majority of people believe that their devolved institutions should make most of the decisions about welfare benefits in their country, a proposal none of the unionist parties has endorsed.

Members of the Scottish Parliament do not fully share the concern of the Scottish public with Edinburgh's lack of influence relative to Westmin-

[1] Looking at the time series data reported in Chapter 6, it seems that people in Scotland have hankered for a more extensive form of devolution since the outset. Support for more powers for the Scottish Parliament, and for the devolved institutions to be the dominant influence in determining policy in Scotland, was just as high in 1999 as it was in 2007. But in Wales, support for extending devolution has only become apparent as people have experienced the Welsh Assembly in operation. Thus, only in 2007 did as many as seven in ten people in Wales believe that the Welsh Assembly, not Westminster, should determine policy decisions in the country, while the proportions favouring an Assembly with primary legislative and fiscal powers have steadily increased since 1997.

ster. Labour, Liberal Democrat and Conservative MSPs are more inclined to believe that their institution is relatively powerful. However, in Wales, elected representatives tend to share the public's perception that Westminster is dominant. Even so, while the public appears to favour a stronger Welsh Assembly with legislative and taxation powers, opinions among elected representatives are split. Conservative AMs do not want the Assembly to have primary legislative authority, while they are joined in their scepticism by Labour AMs when it comes to giving the Assembly fiscal powers. Nevertheless, despite these differences, we can see why, in practice, there has been sufficient public and political pressure in recent years to instigate moves to extend the powers of both the Welsh Assembly and the Scottish Parliament.[2]

But what about England? Devolution would hardly have strengthened the Union if it caused such resentment in England that people there began to question whether they would be better off without Scotland and Wales. And certainly the current settlement could not be regarded as stable if there were demand from England for significant change in its relationship with the rest of the United Kingdom. In practice, there seems little evidence of a growing wish to end the Union amongst people in England. Chapter 6 showed that, over the last decade, typically a little under one in five people in England have said that Scotland should become independent, while only around one in six have said the same about Wales. Neither figure has shown any sign of increasing. Asked in 2007 what would be better for England itself, only 16 per cent nominated separation from Scotland and Wales. While we also uncovered some reason to doubt the intensity of support for the Union in England, it certainly seems to be under little threat from public opinion there.

Nonetheless, the example of Scotland and Wales could well have persuaded people in England that they should embrace devolution for themselves. Chapter 6 showed, however, that the demand for devolution in

---

2 The Government of Wales Act 2006 allows the UK Parliament to grant the Welsh Assembly primary legislative power for a defined purpose, and paves the way for a referendum on giving the Assembly primary legislative powers in all the areas for which it is responsible. A Convention has been established under the chairmanship of Sir Emyr Jones Parry to assess public opinion on the issue and advise ministers whether that referendum should be held. In Scotland, a Commission on devolution was jointly established by the Conservatives, Labour and the Liberal Democrats (at both UK and Scottish levels) with the formal backing of the UK Government and the Scottish Parliament. Chaired by Sir Kenneth Calman, its remit invited it in particular to consider whether the Scottish Parliament should have responsibility for raising some of the money it spends.

England – either in the form of an English Parliament or regional assemblies – remains limited, with a majority of the population still content to be governed 'as now' by Westminster. Among interest groups, the case study of the North East in Chapter 3 highlighted the absence of a concerted drive for political decentralisation. While some groups – for example trade unions and the voluntary sector – favour the establishment of an elected regional assembly, it is apparent that others – notably business and, indeed, some local Labour officials – remained opposed.

Of course in rejecting devolution for themselves, people in England might also take a dim view of the devolution of authority granted to Scotland and Wales. Yet there is little sign of this either. The most popular view in England about how Scotland and Wales should be governed has consistently been that they should have some form of devolution, albeit there was perhaps a slight waning of this view by the time of our most recent survey in 2007. Yet this does not necessarily mean that people in England are entirely content with the current constitutional arrangements. They have long had potential reason to be unhappy with the distribution of public expenditure across the United Kingdom, with Scotland and Wales enjoying higher public spending per head well before the introduction of devolution. And even if people in England do not want devolution for themselves, they might still ask whether Scottish and Welsh MPs should have the right to vote when the House of Commons is dealing with purely English legislation.

Our evidence has, however, suggested that only a minority of people in England feel that Scotland gets more than its fair share of public spending. True, this minority has grown from one in four in the early years of devolution to one in three now. Moreover, there is ready acceptance of the idea that services delivered in Scotland should be paid for by taxes raised in Scotland. Yet as we have already noted, people in Scotland would also like their parliament to have greater responsibility for fiscal matters, so this is an adjustment to the current settlement that might find support on both sides of the border. The fact that Scottish MPs can vote on English laws seems anomalous to a clear majority of people in England. Yet although any change to the current position is opposed by the Labour Party in particular, our evidence suggests that here, too, the devolution settlement could be amended without rousing the ire of most people in Scotland.

Overall, then, throughout Great Britain, devolution seems neither to have strengthened nor to have weakened commitment to the maintenance of the Union. In this respect, neither the hopes of devolution's advocates, nor the fears of its opponents, have been realised. How far the current settlement provides a permanent basis for the governance of the Union is, however, less certain. In both Scotland and Wales, there are clear pressures amongst both politicians and the public to strengthen the powers of the devolved institutions. And although England may still not want devolution for itself, there is a degree of discontent with some of the apparent anomalies created by the current asymmetric settlement. However, in satisfying the demand in Scotland and Wales for more devolved powers it might also be possible to address some of England's concerns, not least with the way the various parts of the United Kingdom are financed.

Has devolution worked?

In the Introduction to this book, we noted that Britain was far from unique in decentralising power to smaller units. Globalisation has helped to weaken the role of the state, while enhancing the potential role of regional tiers of government. At the same time, globalisation is often seen to threaten distinctive national cultures, including those of stateless nations. Giving greater political autonomy to such nations helps to ensure that the functional role of sub-state government is more effective and more clearly subjected to proper democratic control, while recognising and respecting those nations' distinctive identities and cultures. Does Britain's experience so far suggest that devolution can be an effective response to these pressures?

It certainly seems that devolution, even the heavily asymmetric variety introduced in Britain, can acquire legitimacy. There now seems to be a consensus in favour of the devolved institutions amongst the general public, interest groups and political representatives in Scotland and Wales. Given the Conservative Party's initial opposition to devolution, the scepticism among some interest groups and the lukewarm popular endorsement of the Welsh Assembly in the 1997 referendum, this is no mean feat. In addition, it appears that people in England do not seriously question the right of those in Scotland and Wales to a measure of self-rule, while people in Scotland and Wales are no more enamoured of independence now than they were a decade ago.

Yet there are doubts about what devolution has achieved in practice. The majority of citizens and elected representatives do not believe devolution has improved policy outcomes in Scotland or Wales. Equally, they are not convinced that devolution has met all their hopes for better democratic control and participation. The new institutions are not thought to have secured sufficient public participation in the decision making process, while the way in which people have voted in devolved elections does not ensure that those in power are representative of, or accountable to, the general public. Perhaps the lesson is that devolution is valued not for what it achieves but for what it represents; recognition by the British state of the distinctive national identities of its stateless nations. If so, the ongoing balancing act for devolution will be to continue to deliver that recognition, without undermining support for the British state itself.

References

Conservative Party (1997) *You Can Only be Sure with the Conservatives*, Conservative Party General Election Manifesto 1997, available at www.psr.keele.ac.uk/area/uk/man/con97.htm (accessed 20 October 2008)

Conservative Party (2005) *It's Time for Action*, Conservative Party General Election Manifesto 2005, available at www.conservatives.com (accessed 20 October 2008)

Welsh Conservatives (2007) *Vote Welsh Conservative for a Change*, Conservative Party Welsh Assembly Election Manifesto 2007, Cardiff: Welsh Conservative Party

Appendix: details of public opinion surveys

The public opinion data reported in this volume derive from surveys of the population conducted in Scotland and Wales, and across Britain. This appendix provides brief details of these surveys, along with supporting references and weblinks which can be consulted if further details are required. The main surveys examining public attitudes to devolution, on which Chapters 5, 6 and 7 draw, are set out in Table A.1.

Scotland

Data on public reactions to devolution in Scotland since the establishment of the Scottish Parliament have been drawn from the Scottish Social

Table A.1 Main public opinion surveys on devolution, 1970–2007

Year	Scotland	Wales	England
2007	Scottish Social Attitudes	Wales Life and Times	British Social Attitudes
2006	Scottish Social Attitudes		British Social Attitudes
2005	Scottish Social Attitudes		British Social Attitudes
2004	Scottish Social Attitudes		British Social Attitudes
2003	Scottish Social Attitudes	Wales Life and Times	British Social Attitudes
2002	Scottish Social Attitudes		British Social Attitudes
2001	Scottish Social Attitudes	Wales Life and Times	British Social Attitudes
2000	Scottish Social Attitudes		British Social Attitudes
1999	Scottish Social Attitudes	Welsh Assembly Election Study	British Social Attitudes
1997	Scottish Referendum Study	Welsh Referendum Study	
	Scottish Election Study	British Election Study	British Election Study
1992	Scottish Election Study	British Election Study	British Election Study
1979	Scottish Election Study	Welsh Election Study	
1974	British Election Study (October): Scottish Sample		
1970	Kilbrandon Commission	Kilbrandon Commission	Kilbrandon Commission

Attitudes Survey. The series began in 1999, and has run each year since then, with the most recent data collected in 2007. Scottish Social Attitudes is a sister survey to the long-standing British Social Attitudes Survey (see below), and is designed to support the development of public policy and the academic study of public opinion north of the border. It consists of a face to face interview, conducted in the respondent's home, along with a self-completion supplement. Each survey is based on a multi-stage strati-fied random sample of adults living in private households (aged 18 years and above) throughout Scotland (including north of the Great Glen/Cale-donian Canal). Addresses at which interviews are conducted are drawn from the Postcode Address File. Fieldwork is conducted by the Scottish Centre for Social Research (ScotCen), part of the National Centre for Social Research (NatCen). The data are weighted to take account of known unequal probabilities of being selected for interview, and in more recent years are further weighted so that the data match the known age and sex profile of the adult Scottish population. Funding for the Scottish Social Attitudes surveys was provided by a variety of bodies, notably the Economic and Social Research Council, the Scottish Government (formerly Executive) and charitable bodies such as the Nuffield Foundation and the Leverhulme Trust.

Brief technical details of each of the Scottish Social Attitudes surveys used in this volume are contained in Table A.2. Further information on the surveys – along with the data – can be obtained from the Economic and Social Data Service's Scottish Social Attitudes Survey website: www.esds .ac.uk/government/ssa/.

Table A.2   Details of Scottish Social Attitude surveys since 1999

Year	*Fieldwork*	*Sample size*	*Response rate*[a] (%)
1999	May–Aug 1999	1,482	59
2000	June–Nov 2000	1,663	65
2001	June–Sept 2001	1,605	60
2002	June–Sept 2002	1,665	62
2003	May–Nov 2003	1,508	57
2004	July–Nov 2004	1,637	61
2005	Aug–Dec 2005	1,549	56
2006	Aug 2006–Jan 2007	1,594	58
2007	May–Nov 2007	1,508	56

Note: [a] For main questionnaire, not self-completion questionnaire.

Data on attitudes to devolution among people in Scotland prior to 1999 were obtained from a number of surveys, notably:

Scottish Referendum Study 1997

This survey – along with the Welsh Referendum Study 1997 (see below) – was designed to study attitudes to devolution and voting behaviour on the occasion of the referendum on the Scottish Parliament in September 1997. Interviews were conducted with a multi-stage stratified random sample of adults aged 18 years and above resident in Scotland; addresses at which interviews were conducted were drawn from the Postcode Address File. The survey comprised both a face to face interview and a self-completion questionnaire. Fieldwork was conducted by Social and Community Planning Research (now known as the National Centre for Social Research) and undertaken in September and October 1997. A total of 676 interviews were obtained, representing a response rate of 68 per cent. Funding was provided by the Economic and Social Research Council. Further details of the survey are reported in Thomson, 1999.

Scottish Election Studies

Surveys of the Scottish population were conducted alongside the British Election Study immediately after general elections in October 1974, 1979, 1992 and 1997. The purpose of these studies was to allow for more detailed examination of social and political attitudes among people in Scotland than was possible through the British Election Study alone. The studies both interviewed booster samples of respondents living in Scotland and administered questions additional to those included on the British Election Study. For each survey, a multi-stage stratified random sample was used, based on the Electoral Register (in 1974, 1979 and 1992) or the Postcode Address File (in 1997). In each case, funding was provided by the Economic and Social Research Council. Brief technical details of each of these surveys are contained in Table A.3.

Wales

Data on public reactions to devolution in Wales have been drawn from two surveys. The first is the Welsh Assembly Election Study, conducted in 1999. The second is the Wales Life and Times Survey, conducted in 2001, 2003 and 2007. All of these surveys consist of a face to face interview,

Table A.3   Details of Scottish attitudinal surveys prior to 1999

Year	Title	Fieldwork	Sample size	Response rate (%)
1974	British Election Study: Scottish Cross-Section Sample	Oct 1974–Jan 1975	1,170	76
1979	Scottish Election Study	May–Oct 1979	729	61
1992	General Election in Scotland	Apr–Aug 1992	957	74
1997	Scottish Election Survey	May–Aug 1997	882	62

conducted in the respondent's home (but by telephone if the respondent opts to be surveyed in Welsh), along with a self-completion supplement. Each survey is based on a multi-stage stratified random sample of adults living in private households (aged 18 years and above) throughout Wales. Addresses at which interviews are conducted are drawn from the Postcode Address File. Fieldwork was conducted by the National Centre for Social Research (NatCen). The data are weighted to take account of known unequal probabilities of being selected for interview, and in 2007 are further weighted so that the data match the known age and sex profile of the adult population in Wales. The surveys were funded by the Economic and Social Research Council. Brief technical details of each of these surveys are contained in Table A.4.

Table A.4   Details of Welsh attitudinal surveys since 1999

Year	Title	Fieldwork	Sample size	Response rate[a] (%)
1999	Welsh Assembly Election Study	May–June 1999	522[b]	67
2001	Wales Life and Times Survey	June–Sept 2001	1,085	69
2003	Wales Life and Times Survey	May–July 2003	988	63
2007	Wales Life and Times Survey	May–Aug 2007	884	54

Notes: [a]For main questionnaire, not self-completion questionnaire.

[b]This represents respondents to face to face interviews. A further 729 interviews were conducted by telephone (without the self-completion supplement); this represented a response rate of 35 per cent. The analyses in this book are based on the combined samples.

Data on attitudes to devolution among people in Wales prior to 1999 were obtained from two surveys:

Welsh Referendum Study 1997

This survey – along with the Scottish Referendum Study 1997 (see above) – was designed to study attitudes to devolution and voting behaviour on the occasion of the referendum on the Welsh Assembly in September 1997. Interviews were conducted with a multi-stage stratified random sample of adults aged 18 years and above resident in Wales; addresses at which interviews were conducted were drawn from the Postcode Address File. The survey comprised both a face to face interview and a self-completion questionnaire. Fieldwork was conducted by Social and Community Planning Research (now known as the National Centre for Social Research) and undertaken in September and October 1997. A total of 686 interviews were obtained, representing a response rate of 73 per cent. Funding was provided by the Economic and Social Research Council. Further details of this survey are reported in Thomson, 1999.

Welsh Election Study 1979

This survey of the Welsh population was conducted alongside the British Election Study after the general election in 1979. The purpose of this study was to allow for more detailed examination of social and political attitudes among people in Wales than was possible through the British Election Study alone. The study both interviewed a booster sample of respondents living in Wales and administered questions additional to those included on the British Election Study. The survey was based on a single-stage stratified random sample drawn from the Electoral Register. Fieldwork was conducted by Gallup, and carried out between May and September 1979. A total of 858 interviews were obtained, representing a response rate of 60 per cent. The study was funded by the Economic and Social Research Council.

England

Data on public attitudes and identities among people in England – drawn on in Chapter 6 – are derived from two sources:

British Social Attitudes

Attitudes since 1999 are derived from the British Social Attitudes Survey. Begun in 1983, the British Social Attitudes Survey is designed to support the development of public policy and the academic study of public opinion. It consists of a face to face interview, conducted in the respondent's home, along with a self-completion supplement. Each survey is based on a multi-stage stratified random sample of adults living in private households (aged 18 years and above) throughout Britain (south of the Great Glen/Caledonian Canal). Addresses at which interviews are conducted are drawn from the Postcode Address File. Fieldwork is conducted by the National Centre for Social Research (NatCen). The data are weighted to take account of known unequal probabilities of being selected for interview, and in more recent years are further weighted so that the data match the known age and sex profile of the adult population. The survey has a modular structure, which means that not all questions are asked of all respondents. In this book, the answers of those living in Scotland or Wales are excluded from the analysis. British Social Attitudes is core funded by the Gatsby Charitable Foundation while funding for the questions used in this book came mostly from the Leverhulme Trust and the Economic and Social Research Council.

Further details about the British Social Attitudes Survey can be found in Park *et al.* (2009) and its predecessor volumes. Further information about the surveys – along with the data – can also be obtained from the Economic and Social Data Service's British Social Attitudes Survey website: www.esds.ac.uk/government/bsa/.

British Election Study, 1992 and 1997

Attitudes to devolution and national identity among people in England prior to 1999 are derived from the British Election Study. The British Election Study has been conducted after all general elections in Britain since 1964. The 1992 and 1997 cross-sectional surveys consist of a face to face interview, along with a self-completion supplement. Both surveys are based on a multi-stage stratified random sample of adults living in private households (aged 18 years and above) throughout Britain (south of the Great Glen/Caledonian Canal). In 1992, the sample of respondents was drawn from the Electoral Register, and in 1997, the sample of addresses at which interviews were conducted was obtained from the Postcode Address File. The data are weighted to take account of known unequal probabilities of being selected for interview. Fieldwork was conducted by Social and Community Planning Research (now known as the National Centre for

Social Research). In this book, the answers of those living in Scotland or Wales are excluded from the analysis. Funding for the surveys came from the Economic and Social Research Council and the Sainsbury Family Charitable Trusts. Further details of these two studies are to be found in Taylor *et al.* (1994) and Taylor and Thomson (1999).

Kilbrandon Commission

As part of its investigation into devolution the Royal Commission on the Constitution (chaired by Lord Kilbrandon) commissioned a survey on attitudes to devolution and the governance of the United Kingdom. It was undertaken on the Commission's behalf in June 1970 by Social and Community Planning Research (now known as the National Centre for Social Research). The survey interviewed face to face a sample of 4,894 people designed to be representative of the adult population within each economic planning region in Great Britain. It consisted of a multi-stage random probability sample drawn from the Electoral Register. In England, 3,276 interviews were conducted, while 892 were completed in Scotland and 726 in Wales. We are grateful to the UK Data Archive for supplying these data; responsibility for their interpretation lies solely with the editors. Further details of this survey can be found in Social and Community Planning Research (1973).

References

Park, A. *et al.* eds (2009) *British Social Attitudes: The 25th Report*, London: Sage

Social and Community Planning Research (1973) *Devolution and Other Aspects of Government: An Attitudes Survey*, London: HMSO

Taylor, B., L. Brook and G. Prior (1994) 'Appendix: The 1992 cross-section and panel surveys', in A. Heath, R. Jowell and J. Curtice with B. Taylor, eds, *Labour's Last Chance? The 1992 Election and Beyond*, Aldershot: Dartmouth

Taylor, B. and K. Thomson (1999) 'Technical appendix', in G. Evans and P. Norris, eds, *Critical Elections: Voters and Parties in Long-Term Perspective*, London: Sage

Thomson, K. (1999) 'Technical details of the survey', in B. Taylor and K. Thomson, eds, *Scotland and Wales: Nations Again?* Cardiff: University of Wales Press

Index

Note: 'n.' after a page reference indicates the number of a note on that page.